T0212894

The Fraunhofer IESE Series on Software and Systems Engineering

Series Editor

Dieter Rombach
Peter Liggesmeyer

Editorial Board

W. Rance Cleaveland II
Reinhold E. Achatz
Helmut Krcmar

For further volumes:
http://www.springer.com/series/8755

Victor Basili • Adam Trendowicz •
Martin Kowalczyk • Jens Heidrich •
Carolyn Seaman • Jürgen Münch •
Dieter Rombach

Aligning Organizations Through Measurement

The GQM⁺Strategies Approach

Victor Basili
Department of Computer Science
University of Maryland
College Park
Maryland
USA

Adam Trendowicz
Jens Heidrich
Dieter Rombach
Fraunhofer Institute for Experimental
     Software Engineering
Kaiserslautern
Germany

Martin Kowalczyk
Department of Information Systems
Technical University of Darmstadt
Darmstadt
Germany

Carolyn Seaman
Department of Information Systems
University of Maryland Baltimore County
Baltimore
USA

Jürgen Münch
Department of Computer Science
University of Helsinki
Helsinki
Finland

ISSN 2193-8199   ISSN 2193-8202 (electronic)
ISBN 978-3-319-38028-5   ISBN 978-3-319-05047-8 (eBook)
DOI 10.1007/978-3-319-05047-8
Springer Cham Heidelberg New York Dordrecht London

Printed on acid-free paper

Springer is part of Springer Science+Business Media (www.springer.com)

About this Series

Whereas software engineering has been a growing area in the field of computer science for many years, systems engineering has its roots in traditional engineering. On the one hand, we still see many challenges in both disciplines. On the other hand, we can observe a trend to build systems that combine software, microelectronic components, and mechanical parts. The integration of information systems and embedded systems leads to so-called cyber-physical systems.

Software and systems engineering comprise many aspects and views. From a technical standpoint, they are concerned with individual techniques, methods, and tools, as well as with integrated development processes, architectural issues, quality management and improvement, and certification. In addition, they are also concerned with organizational, business, and human views. Software and systems engineering treat development activities as steps in a continuous evolution over time and space.

Software and systems are developed by humans, so the effects of applying techniques, methods, and tools cannot be determined independent of context. A thorough understanding of their effects in different organizational and technical contexts is essential if these effects are to be predictable and repeatable under varying conditions. Such process-product effects are best determined empirically. Empirical engineering develops the basic methodology for conducting empirical studies, and uses it to advance the understanding for the effects of various engineering approaches.

The series presents engineering-style methods and techniques that foster the development of systems that are reliable in every aspect. All the books in the series emphasize the quick delivery of state-of-the-art results and empirical proof from academic research to industrial practitioners and students. Their presentation style is designed to enable the reader to quickly grasp both the essentials of a methodology and how to apply it successfully.

I do not believe you can do today's job with yesterday's methods and be in business tomorrow.

—Nelson Jackson

Foreword

A highly recommended practice for controlling software and other projects is the Earned Value Management System (EVMS). The EVMS approach involves developing a complete set of budgets and schedules for a project's tasks. As the project proceeds, the completion of each task adds its allocated budget to the project's accumulated earned value, even though the actual expenditures on the task were higher or lower. At any time, one can compare the accumulated earned value with its scheduled earned value and with its actual expenditures at that point in time and determine whether the project is underrunning or overrunning its planned schedule or budget.

Unfortunately, however, the "earned value" method says nothing about the actual contribution to the business, mission, or multistakeholder values that the system being developed is intended to earn. If the system definition is off target with respect to its ability to earn those values, or is not modified to reflect changes in those values, a project perfectly accumulating its "earned value" will find that it has likely achieved the on-budget, on-schedule delivery of a useless or obsolete system.

The Goal-Question-Metric plus Strategies (GQM$^+$Strategies) approach presented in this book enables organizations to avoid such unfortunate outcomes. It extends the widely used GQM approach to include a project's strategies to achieve its goals; connects the questions and metrics to the strategies and goals via a GQM$^+$Strategies grid; and provides guidance on evolving the grid to accommodate changes in the goals, the environment, and the key technologies.

In doing so, it capitalizes on the decades of experience in applying GQM artifacts and processes across a wide variety of organizations and enterprise sectors. It is being presented in this book after several years of lessons learned from pilot applications of its evolving nature and from workshop interactions with the empirical methods community.

Based on these foundations and this experience, the book provides an accessible and logical pathway to understanding and applying the GQM$^+$Strategies approach. It starts off by providing clear definitions that can be used to represent organizational goals and define a GQM$^+$Strategies grid that links the goals to the strategies, questions, and metrics. It uses the GQM-adjunct, plan-do-check-act, spiral-type Quality Improvement Paradigm to establish an iterative Develop–Implement–Learn cycle aimed at converging on an initial GQM$^+$Strategies grid and evolving it based on experience.

The next seven chapters cover the initialization phase (How do projects get started), the two Develop phases (Characterize Environment; Define Goals, Strategies, and Measurement), the two Implement phases (Plan Grid Implementation; Execute Plans), and the two Learn phases (Analyze Outcomes; Package Improvements). The chapters use a common-thread example from the financial services sector and include numerous templates and subprocesses. These also draw on external best practices, for example, the Strengths-Weaknesses-Opportunities-Threats (SWOT) method and the Porter's Five Forces method for the Define Goals and Strategies activity.

Part II of the book provides examples of GQM$^+$Strategies usage. It begins with a discussion of the major challenges in applying GQM$^+$Strategies in practice: (1) aligning goals and strategies; (2) establishing mechanisms for measurement-based decision-making; and (3) communicating goals, strategies, and measurement data for evaluation and consistent decision-making across the success-critical implementation groups. It then summarizes GQM$^+$Strategies usage to date and lessons learned across applications in the telecom, automotive, insurance, space agency, banking, energy, and embedded systems research sectors. These show the versatility of the GQM$^+$Strategies approach and provide specifics of use for organizations in similar sectors.

A particularly attractive aspect of the GQM$^+$Strategies movement is shown at the end of the book, in which it applies its methods to itself. One example is the SWOT-type analysis of future trends offering opportunities to improve GQM$^+$Strategies and the approach for exploring value-based approaches to strategies, questions, and metrics. Many of the current GQM$^+$Strategies metrics are value-neutral, in terms of the assumption—when counting and managing numbers and percentages of defects—that all defects are equally important. Our research in value-based inspections and testing indicates that prioritizing these activities by business value and criticality will often double the cost-effectiveness of these practices, based on the frequently encountered Pareto distribution (meaning that 20 % of the defects account for 80 % of the business value).

Another good example of GQM$^+$Strategies applying its methods to itself is the inclusion of an Appendix, which provides a GQM$^+$Strategies Evaluation Questionnaire asking users of the method to evaluate how well it satisfies its own goals and strategies and building in a commitment to act on the evaluations. Given the challenges of the rapid pace of change in technology, competition in products and services, and workforce skills (in 2012, over 20 countries had over 83 % of their population using the Internet, as compared to 1 in 2005), this adds confidence that GQM$^+$Strategies will continue to evolve to meet the challenges.

As a bottom line, I would subscribe to GQM$^+$Strategies' self-assessment that its strongest contributions to current enterprises are its provision of more consistent alignment of an enterprise's goals with its management metrics and its use of feasibility evidence metrics rather than the mere existence of artifacts and assertions as a basis of decision-making in a project. Beyond this, though, I believe that GQM$^+$Strategies' consistent commitment to self-improvement is the strongest recommendation for using GQM$^+$Strategies to manage current and future initiatives.

Los Angeles, CA   Barry Boehm

Quotes from Industry

"With GQM⁺Strategies, we were able to make the contribution of the information management strategy to the business goals explicit."

Dr. Alexis Ocampo
Group Leader Enterprise Architecture
ECOPETROL, Columbia

"GQM⁺Strategies supported us and multiple other Japanese organizations in aligning IT- and software-related activities to the strategic needs of our business."

Katsutoshi Shintani
Former Senior Adviser, Software Engineering Center
Information-technology Promotion Agency, Japan

"The experience of using the GQM⁺Strategies approach at JAXA shows that the approach helps to clarify the relationship between activities of different organizational units on different levels of the organization, as well as to explicitly show the contributions of those activities to the attainment of top-level business goals."

Masafumi Katahira, Yuko Miyamoto, Tatsuya Kaneko
Japan Aerospace Exploration Agency (JAXA)

"The collaboration helped us to formulate action plans that align with both our business objectives and industry best practices. A critical ingredient for success was Fraunhofer IESE's ability to quickly grasp our business mode and challenges, establish credibility with our internal teams, and provide concrete recommendations and results."

Jean-Pierre Dacher
COO and Head of Software Engineering
Murex S.A.S., France

Preface

Building the right products and services as well as building products and services right is the key to the success of most organizations. This requires that an organization is able to establish well-suited goals and strategies, connect and communicate them to assure that all parts of the organization are working in the same direction, recognize when goals or strategies need to be changed, and understand the effects of those changes. Aligning and integrating goals and strategies in an organization helps direct all resources, competencies, and activities towards value creation.

Aligning an organization's goals and strategies requires specifying the connections between them so that the links are explicit and allow for analytic reasoning about what is successful and where change is necessary. Applying measurement principles can support this analytic reasoning. In particular, goal-oriented measurement helps organizations analyze if and where they should preserve or change their goals or strategies. This book presents innovative steps on how to align organizations to achieve sustainable success by applying principles from goal-oriented measurement.

Why a Book on Aligning Organizations Through Measurement?

There is a tremendous need to better align organizations so that everyone is pulling in the same direction. If an organization is unable to integrate business-critical competencies such as system and software development, IT, product innovation, or customer advocacy into its overall goals and strategies and use them to shape its business strategies, it is risking its competitive advantage and market position. At the same time, it is necessary to translate a company's vision into a hierarchy of operational and actionable goals and strategies to achieve sustainable success for this organization. This book provides comprehensive information on how to do this alignment, how to control for the success of goals and strategies and recognize potential failures through measurement, and how to close alignment gaps.

Although there are many books on performance management frameworks and strategy-driven organizations, a method that aligns goals and strategies across different units of an organization in a seamless, rationale-based, and measurable way does not exist yet. This book gives structure and clarity to what is typically informal and fuzzy. It presents the GQM$^+$Strategies approach, which provides concepts and actionable steps for creating the link between goals and strategies across different units of an organization and allows for measurement-based decision-making.

Who Should Read This Book?

This book is aimed at organizational leaders, managers, decision-makers, and other professionals interested in aligning their organization's goals and strategies and establishing an efficient strategic measurement program. Practitioners should find the book useful for improving the understanding of their role in supporting the top-level goals of the organization and for getting advice on how to control the successful implementation of business strategies. The book enables all members in the organizational hierarchy to integrate all kinds of goals, strategies, and activities in an organization in a way that is clearly motivated by rationales and directed towards organizational success. Besides enterprise managers and their staff, the book is especially relevant for project and quality managers, members of improvement groups, measurement experts, system engineers and developers, and consultants. The book is also interesting for academic faculty researchers looking for mechanisms to integrate their research results into organizational environments.

What Are the Benefits for the Reader?

Readers will gain the knowledge and skills needed for aligning an organization through measurement. This will enable them to consistently align their organizational goals and strategies across different units, make informed decisions based on measurement, transparently communicate goals and strategies within the organization, and objectively monitor goal attainment and the success/failure of defined strategies.

- Enterprise managers and their staff will be supported in steering the organizations based on an aligned set of goals and strategies and the required data for decision-making.
- Project and quality managers in an organization will be supported in demonstrating the value of their activities in terms of the larger organizational goals and strategies.
- Members of improvement groups will be supported in objectively evaluating the impact and success of improvement programs.
- Measurement experts will be supported in setting up a strategic measurement program in which all collected data has a clear linkage to organizational goals and strategies.
- Systems engineers and developers will gain greater insight into the goals and strategies of the organization and the purpose for which the data collected from the development process is actually needed.

- Consultants will be supported with a structured model and process regarding how to set up strategic measurement programs.
- Researchers will be supported with a collection of best practices in setting up a strategic measurement program incorporated into the GQM$^+$Strategies approach.

How Is the Book Organized?

After giving a general motivation for the issue of aligning organizations through measurement, the GQM$^+$Strategies approach is described in a nutshell, with a focus on the basic model that is created and the process for creating and using this model. Afterwards, the recommended steps of all six phases of the process are described in detail with the help of a comprehensive application example. Finally, industrial challenges and application cases of the method are presented, and the relation to other approaches, such as Balanced Scorecard, is described. The book concludes with supplementary material, such as checklists and guidelines, to support the application of the method.

Who Are the Authors?

The foci of this book were selected based on the comprehensive experience of the authors. The authors have defined and established many organizational measurement programs. They have supported many organizations in aligning goals and strategies and have been involved in a multitude of international industrial improvement programs. The coauthors include the inventors of the GQM$^+$Strategies.

We wish you an interesting reading experience—hoping it will give you insights and support you in using measurement-based alignment to achieve sustainable organizational success.

College Park, MD	Victor Basili
Kaiserslautern, Germany	Adam Trendowicz
Darmstadt, Germany	Martin Kowalczyk
Kaiserslautern, Germany	Jens Heidrich
Baltimore, MD	Carolyn Seaman
Helsinki, Finland	Jürgen Münch
Kaiserslautern, Germany	Dieter Rombach

Disclaimer

Any of the trademarks, service marks, collective marks, registered names, or similar rights that are used or cited in this book are the property of their respective owners. Their use here does not imply that they can be used for any purpose other than for the informational use as contemplated in this book.

The following table summarizes the trademarks used in this book. Rather than indicating every occurrence of a trademarked name as such, this report uses the names only in an editorial fashion and to the benefit of the trademark owner, with no intention of infringement of the trademark.

Trademark	Subject of trademark	Trademark owner
CMMI®	Capability Maturity Model Integrated	Software Engineering Institute (SEI)
CoBIT®	Control Objectives for Information and Related Technology	Information Systems Audit and Control Association and the IT Governance Institute (ISACA/ITGI)
ITIL®	Information Technology Infrastructure Library	Office of Government Commerce (OGC)
MS Office®	MS Word®, MS Excel®, and MS PowerPoint®	Microsoft® Corporation
PMBOOK®	Project Management Body of Knowledge Guide	Project Management Institute (PMI)
PRINCE2™	Projects in Controlled Environments 2	Office of Government Commerce (OGC)

GQM⁺Strategies is registered trademark no. 302008021763 at the German Patent and Trade Mark Office; international registration number IR992843.

Acknowledgments

We would like to express our gratitude to the many people who contributed to this book: to all those who provided support, talked things over, read, wrote, offered comments, allowed us to quote their remarks, and assisted in editing, proofreading, and design.

First, we would like to express our great appreciation to Mikael Lindvall and Myrna Regardie, who codeveloped the GQM⁺Strategies approach from its very beginning. We would also like to thank Vladimir Mandić, Sylwia Kopczyńska, Giovanni Cantone, Madeline Diep, Teresa Baldassarre, Barbara Russo, Forrest Shull, Michael Kläs, Barry Boehm, and Markku Oivo for their recent contributions to the GQM⁺Strategies approach.

In addition, we would like to particularly thank the providers of the three industrial applications highlighted in this book for their continuous support of the approach, its evolution, and its promotion: (1) the Information-technology Promotion Agency, Japan (IPA), the Software Reliability Enhancement Center (SEC), and its major contact person over the years, Katsutoshi Shintani, (2) the Japan Aerospace Exploration Agency (JAXA), JAXA Engineering Digital Innovation Center (JEDI), and its major contact person, Masafumi Katahira, and (3) ECOPETROL S.A., Colombia and its major contact person, Alexis Ocampo. Our special thanks also go to Yasuhiro Kikushima, Norifumi Nomura, and Hisayoshi Adachi for promoting the GQM⁺Strategies approach in Japan and for their valuable contributions to evolving the approach.

Finally, we would like to thank Katsutoshi Shintani and Vladimir Mandić for their valuable review comments and Sonnhild Namingha for proofreading the book.

Acronyms

BI	Business Intelligence
BMM	Business Motivation Model
BPM	Business Process Management
BSC	Balanced Scorecards
CBR	Checklist-Based Reading
CEO	Chief Executive Officer
CESE	Fraunhofer Center for Experimental Software Engineering
CIO	Chief Information Officer
CMMI	Capability Maturity Model Integrated
CRM	Customer Relationships Management
EF	Experience Factory
ERP	Enterprise Resource Planning
ETL	Extract-Transform-Load
EVMS	Earned Value Management System
GQM	Goal-Question-Metric
IESE	Fraunhofer Institute for Experimental Software Engineering
IPA	Information-technology Promotion Agency, Japan
IPA/SEC	IPA Software Engineering Center (since 2013 "Software Reliability Enhancement Center")
IS	Information System
IT	Information Technology
JAXA	Japanese Aerospace Exploration Agency
JEDI	JAXA's Engineering Digital Innovation Center
KPI	Key Performance Indicator
LOC	Lines of Code
ODC	Orthogonal Defect Classification
OMG	Object Management Group
OLAP	Online Analytical Processing
OPF	Organizational Process Focus
OPM	Organizational Performance Management
OPP	Organizational Process Performance
PBR	Perspective-Based Reading
PDCA	Plan-Do-Check-Act
PMO	Project Management Office

PSM	Practical Software Measurement
QA	Quality Assurance
QIP	Quality Improvement Paradigm
ROI	Return on Investment
RUP	Rational Unified Process
SAF	Strategic Alignment Framework
SCM	Supply Chain Management
SPI	Software Process Improvement
SPICE	Software Process Improvement and Capability Determination
SW	Software
SWOT	Strengths-Weaknesses-Opportunities-Threats
TDD	Test-Driven Development
VBSE	Value-Based Software Engineering
V&V	Verification and Validation
XP	Extreme Programming

Contents

Introduction

This chapter summarizes the origins and benefits of the GQM⁺Strategies approach. We discuss the challenges business organizations face with regard to alignment and briefly explain how GQM⁺Strategies helps to address these challenges by describing the fundamentals of the approach as well as its core components. Furthermore, we provide insights into how GQM⁺Strategies evolved from and uses the Goal–Question–Metrics (GQM) approach, which is a well-known measurement approach in the software development domain, and we discuss the benefits of this evolution.

1.1 Issues

In today's competitive markets, organizational survival and growth requires effective means of aligning the large variety of organizational goals and strategies in order to achieve business objectives. Effective alignment helps all parts of the organization move in the same direction, promising numerous benefits such as the effective use of resources and rapid and focused improvement.

However, the reality with respect to organizational alignment in many organizations is grim. Symptoms reflecting bad organizational alignment include: strategies across different units of an organization are not linked to each other; goals are imposed from different directions without clear priorities; activities are optimized locally; reorganizations create a great deal of inefficiency; long-term goals and strategies are not systematically followed, traced, evaluated, and updated.

For business-critical competencies, organizational alignment is necessary in particular. But even here, it is often missing. For instance, in software-dependent organizations, we can often observe that it is not clear how software can be used in intelligent ways to differentiate products and services from those of competitors. Software is seen as a pure cost driver that is easy to outsource, and as a consequence, core software competencies for business success are often outsourced. Software and system engineers are frequently faced with apparently unrealistic goals. It is often hard to demonstrate how improvement programs generate business

V. Basili et al., *Aligning Organizations Through Measurement*, The Fraunhofer IESE Series on Software and Systems Engineering, DOI 10.1007/978-3-319-05047-8_1,
© Springer International Publishing Switzerland 2014

value. Software units are not able to explicitly demonstrate their contributions to higher-level goals and business success.

Having observed and been involved in alignment activities in small, medium-sized, and large organizations, we recognized that successful organizational alignment does not happen by accident and does not result automatically from simply having the right leaders and management frameworks in place. We learned that successful organizational alignment can be achieved by applying a set of basic principles to explicitly link goals and strategies throughout the organization and by following steps to systematically integrate them into the larger business context. We have also seen that using measurement as a mechanism for quantifying goals and strategies across different units significantly helps to align an organization.

Organizations that know how to align their innovative capabilities and relevant competencies towards important and new business opportunities will have a strategic advantage. Companies that understand and can trace the implications of changes in modern dynamic business and technology environments will be able to react fast to such changes.

1.2   Approach

GQM$^+$Strategies is an approach for aligning organizations through measurement. It enables an organization to consistently align goals and strategies across different units, make informed decisions based on measurement, transparently communicate goals and strategies within the organization, and objectively monitor goal attainment and the success/failure of defined strategies.

The approach has two core components: a model and a process. The model (called the *grid*) documents the goals and strategies the organization wants to focus on, the rationales for linking those goals and strategies across different units, a measurement model for evaluating goal attainment, and guidelines for interpreting the measurement data for decision-making. The second component is a comprehensive process for creating the model, implementing its strategies, collecting and analyzing the data collected, and initiating improvement actions.

The model/grid represents a tremendous value for the organization as it communicates the alignment of all goals and strategies and the relationships among all elements within the organization. The process of creating the grid is an intense learning opportunity as it forces the organization to identify and formalize its operational goals and strategies and their interconnections at all levels of the organization. The need for organizational alignment is of critical importance in all types of organizations and industrial sectors. Therefore, we defined the approach in such a way that it is independent of any specific organizational type or industrial sector and can be widely applied.

1.3   Background

For many years, we have helped companies analyze corporate data and implement measurement programs. A common problem we frequently encountered was that the information needs of an organization were often fuzzy and ill-specified. When the information needs were clear, the data available in the organization were not sufficient to satisfy the information needs. This revealed the more fundamental problem that the organizational goals and strategies, their interconnections, and the required level of goal fulfillment were undefined or nebulous. The negative consequences of this situation were that these organizations suffered due to the lack of organizational alignment needed for value creation.

However, there are promising approaches that support the identification of information needs in an organization and the alignment of organizational goals; we found goal-oriented approaches very helpful in addressing many of the challenges. Goal-oriented approaches use goals to systematically identify the information needs of an organization and determine the necessary data that needs to be collected for fulfilling these information needs.

One example of such a goal-oriented approach that we used is the Goal–Question–Metric (GQM) approach proposed by Basili and Weiss (1984). The approach provides a method for defining goals and for systematically refining these goals into measures that specify the data to be collected. This approach supports the analysis and interpretation of the resulting data in the context of the original goals. The GQM approach is a quasistandard for goal-oriented measurement in general, specifically in the area of software development. Although the GQM approach has been applied successfully for decades in many industrial sectors and public organizations, it does not provide explicit support for integrating its measurement of goals with elements of the larger organization, such as higher-level business goals, strategies, or relationships between goals.

Based on more than 30 years of experience with applying and evolving GQM, we derived the GQM$^+$Strategies approach, which extends GQM by adding the capability to create measurement programs that ensure the alignment of an organization's goals, strategies, and data. GQM was first developed to align an organization's information needs (goals) to the data that needs to be collected and does, in turn, provide a mechanism for interpreting that data with respect to those goals. Its premise was that measurement was a good mechanism for gathering information. GQM addressed the problem of understanding what data to collect based upon what the organization or the project wanted to know (goals) and use those goals to generate the questions that provide data to satisfy those goals. Top-down, it provided a mechanism for deciding what data was needed by the organization to understand the goal and evaluate goal attainment. At the same time, bottom-up, it provided a structure that allowed the organization to interpret the data appropriately (Basili and Weiss 1984). The approach evolved technically over time, based upon use, allowing us to identify new problems to be solved. For example, goal templates were developed to aid an organization in defining its goals and recognizing the context variables that bounded the ability to generalize the results

(Basili and Rombach 1988); abstraction sheets were developed to aid an organization in identifying the relevant baselines and potential variation factors (Gresse et al. 1995; Briand et al. 1996).

GQM+Strategies (Basili et al. 2010) was a major evolution of the idea of goal-oriented measurement. It aimed at the comprehensive alignment of organizational goals and strategies across different units of an organization (e.g., from a business unit to an IT group or to concrete projects within the IT group) and integrated GQM measurement capabilities to interpret data throughout the graph of goals and strategies in order to evaluate goal attainment and the success/failure of strategies. Furthermore, GQM+Strategies focuses on providing concrete rationales as to why goals and strategies across different units are linked with each other. These rationales constitute valuable input when interpreting the data for decision-making. The whole model provides a blueprint for interpreting the data across the different units involved. Most importantly, the effects of any changes can be understood and traced in the context of the entire goal set.

As with GQM, the GQM+Strategies approach has evolved in an iterative way by applying it in projects in many types of organizations. The approach benefited from the lessons learned from these applications and has been modified accordingly. A research consortium has been built that systematically collects the experiences from applications, coordinates research efforts, and continues to refine the approach systematically.

After initial pilot applications, the approach has been adopted by several organizations in different industrial sectors such as telecommunications, critical systems, automotive, aerospace, and service sectors. It has been used for a variety of purposes, e.g., for driving strategic improvement programs, for modernizing an existing product suite, for increasing the visibility at all organizational units of how strategic decisions impact operations, for aligning strategies and goals for new business domains, for aligning project objectives with business objectives, and for selecting the right strategy from a set of potential strategies for creating a new suborganization.

Although we initially focused on software-dependent organizations, the GQM+Strategies blossomed into other sectors. Companies such as insurance companies, government organizations (Trendowicz et al. 2011), or military organizations (Sarcia 2010) have used the approach to define their strategies and align their organizations. In addition, new application domains such as aligning and optimizing training efforts with corporate goals were pursued. In parallel, researchers evaluated the approach or discovered the approach as a relevant topic, e.g., for analyzing value alignment (Mandić et al. 2010a) or for identifying strategy and measurement patterns.

1.4 Benefits

To demonstrate the practical benefits, let us take a look at a story from a supplier for critical embedded systems. A software development unit of a company with around 80 engineers locally and more than 150 engineers abroad was facing cost cuts due to an economic crisis. In addition to that, the collaboration between the local and the foreign development sites and other organizations such as third-tier suppliers was inefficient and lacking in trust. Although the unit was aware of significant contributions to the company's goals, this was not visible and obvious to others. There was an urgent need to demonstrate these contributions to higher-level business goals in order to avoid budget cuts and demonstrate their consequences. Furthermore, it was not clear how to prioritize areas for optimization and how to improve the interfaces to the sites abroad and to other organizations.

The tasks this software development unit was facing were immense: It had to align its activities within the unit and connect them to the larger business context as well as to the third-tier suppliers. To do this, the unit needed to find ways to identify what business value meant for the unit itself and for the organization as a whole, and it needed to understand how its own contributions were connected to higher-level goals and business values. It also needed to communicate its goals and needs to the third-tier organizations. Finally, there was time pressure due to economic constraints.

This company unit decided to define agreements on measurable objectives in the context of a large-scale process improvement program as part of the decision analysis and resolution process. The unit created a GQM⁺Strategies model of internal goals inside their unit and interface goals to sites abroad and external organizations. The rationales for having each goal were attached to the goal descriptions. As part of the process, the unit assigned statuses to the goals, such as "inactive," "proposed," and "accepted." It made the decision to stop refining goals at the group level to avoid the impression that individual performance was being assessed. Different rules were defined to break goals down to lower levels, i. e., by refinement, inheritance, or delegation. In addition, the unit elicited the higher-level business goals and the larger business context. Furthermore, they defined measurable criteria for goal fulfillment. They specified different degrees of fulfill-ment, e.g., fulfillment of the minimum requirements, expected fulfillment, or bonus fulfillment. Afterwards, they described the links between all these goals.

After some time, the first positive effects could be observed:

- Improved alignment: The explicit description of the goals, strategies, context, and measures helped the unit to better understand the relationships among different activities. The contributions of the business unit to the business value could be shown explicitly, the motivation of the employees increased because they were now pulling together and coordinating their efforts, and the unit had a clear orientation regarding where to improve.

- Improved communication: By being more open and transparent to external organizations and sites abroad, the unit communicated more openly and received more trust.
- Improved decision-making: The goals helped the unit to better negotiate target values. The results of budget cuts could be demonstrated, and decisions could be made based on data instead of on gut feelings.

1.5   Structure

This book is organized into three major parts. Part I of the book provides a full-featured introduction to the GQM+Strategies approach:

- Chapter 2 describes the approach in a nutshell, focusing on the basic model that is created and the process for creating and using this model.
- Chapters 3–9 describe the recommended steps of all phases of the process in detail with the help of a comprehensive application example. The first stage deals with the development of a model for aligning goals and strategies through measurement. The key benefit of having such a model is the ability to reach a consensus of goals and strategies and communicate that consensus to the entire organization (Chaps. 3–5). The second stage involves the execution of the strategies and measurements defined by the grid, allowing us to check the attainment of the goals, the effectiveness of the strategies, etc. (Chaps. 6 and 7). The third stage involves learning from what has been done by analyzing the results and improving the process for generating further goals and strategies (Chaps. 8 and 9).

In Part II of the book, we discuss GQM$^+$Strategies from the perspective of its application in daily practice:

- Chapter 10 discusses general industrial challenges and presents three concrete industrial applications of GQM$^+$Strategies.
- Chapter 11 presents how GQM$^+$Strategies relates to other approaches.
- Chapter 12 summarizes current achievements and looks at future developments regarding the approach.

In the appendices of the book, we provide additional tools for supporting the successful application of GQM$^+$Strategies:

- Appendix A specifies a checklist for guiding the application of GQM$^+$Strategies.
- Appendix B provides a questionnaire for assessing the GQM$^+$Strategies approach.

Part I
The GQM⁺Strategies Approach

In the first part of the book, we present the details of the GQM⁺Strategies approach. The following chapters present the basic concepts, techniques, and activities of the method. In particular:

- Chapter 2 provides an overview of the 7-phase GQM⁺Strategies process as well as the basic concepts and terminology used in the approach.
- Chapter 3 explains the activities that are necessary for initiating the application of GQM⁺Strategies in an organization. Among others topics, we discuss how to motivate stakeholders, how to get their commitment, and how to plan the application.
- Chapter 4 explains how to characterize the environment in which GQM⁺Strategies is to be applied. In particular, we discuss how to identify the characteristics of the application context and the assumptions that may influence the feasibility of applying GQM⁺Strategies, and how the context and the assumptions help to determine the appropriate goals, strategies, and measurement mechanisms in the subsequent application phases.
- Chapter 5 presents a procedure for defining organizational goals and strategies and for specifying the metrics for the quantitative evaluation of the success (or failure) of these goals and strategies. We discuss how to develop the goal–strategy model, i.e., the GQM⁺Strategies grid, either from scratch or using assets (e.g., goals, strategies, and metrics) that already exist in the organization.
- Chapter 6 shows how to instantiate the GQM⁺Strategies grid and plan its deployment in the organization. We show how to instantiate the strategies using the appropriate business processes and measurement mechanisms to satisfy the goals defined in the grid. This involves the planning of projects to deploy the strategies.
- Chapter 7 explains how to deploy and apply organizational strategies according to the plans developed in the previous step, and how to analyze their performance based on the defined measurement mechanisms. Moreover, we discuss the issue of adjusting the grid and its deployment based upon what is being learned from its deployment and application.

- Chapter 8 explains how to analyze, visualize, and interpret the measurement data and other forms of information collected during the implementation of organizational strategies and how to identify improvement potentials regarding the GQM⁺Strategies gird and its deployment.
- Chapter 9 explains how to package, store, and communicate the knowledge and experiences gained during the previous phases of the GQM⁺Strategies process in order to improve the GQM⁺Strategies grid, its operationalization, deployment, and application in the context of a specific organization.

GQM⁺Strategies in a Nutshell

2

Data is like garbage. You had better know what you are
going to do with it before you collect it.

– Unknown author

This chapter introduces the GQM⁺Strategies approach for aligning organizational goals and strategies through measurement. We first explain the basic idea of combining alignment and measurement within GQM⁺Strategies, which provides an integrated method for explicitly defining organizational goals and controls for the execution of those plans. Next, we describe in detail the core components of GQM⁺Strategies. This includes a specification of the GQM⁺Strategies model as well as the description of the GQM⁺Strategies process for defining, controlling, and continuously improving organizational goals and strategies.

2.1   The Basic Idea

GQM⁺Strategies is an approach for aligning the goals and strategies of an organization across different units through measurement. Goals are future states the organization wants to achieve (e.g., in terms of its business). Strategies are any actions defined for obtaining these goals. The major outcome of the approach is a strategic measurement program allowing for data-based decisions to be made in an organization. Goals and strategies across all units are linked to each other, and measurement data is collected in order to systematically evaluate goal attainment and the success/failure of the strategies.

Consistent with common practices in organizational management, the approach considers two major perspectives: Organizational Planning and Control. The *Organizational Planning* perspective specifies the goals (*G*) of an organization and thus what the organization strives to achieve. Additionally, this perspective also defines the means by which the desired goals are expected to be achieved, by specifying explicit strategies (*S*) that prescribe the course of action to be taken. Applying GQM⁺Strategies supports an iterative definition and alignment of goals and

V. Basili et al., *Aligning Organizations Through Measurement*, The Fraunhofer IESE Series   9
on Software and Systems Engineering, DOI 10.1007/978-3-319-05047-8_2,

strategies across all organizational units within the application scope (see left side of Fig. 2.1).

Organizational goals should be defined to be measurable and achievable. Example goals might be to improve customer satisfaction, increase the market share, or reduce production costs. *Strategies* are defined and selected with the purpose of achieving the defined goals. Goals and strategies are typically defined in the context of a specific organization, where the number of potential options is limited by organization-specific capabilities or constraints. In order to account for those constraints, *context factors* and *assumptions* are specified during the definition of goals and strategies. Context factors and assumptions provide a rationale for selecting and linking a particular set of goals and strategies in the context of a specific organization and its organizational environment. Information about context factors and assumptions is attached to the goals and strategies at each level.

Based on an initial set of goals and strategies, further lower-level goals are defined. The process of defining goals, selecting strategies to accomplish those goals, and generating new goals to embody those strategies continues as long as new lower-level goals and strategies are required to adequately address the defined organizational scope. Applying the approach delivers a hierarchical model of goals and strategies, which often resembles the structure of the organization. Note that the scope is not limited to a single organization, but may encompass a network of organizations that share common top-level goals and want to achieve alignment with respect to lower-level goals and strategies.

Although a top-down process of defining goals and strategies might be obvious, the GQM$^+$Strategies process does not require any top-down refinement. In some cases, it might be more suitable to start with lower-level goals or strategies and integrate those bottom-level organizational goals and strategies with the higher-level context of the organization. The *Control* perspective specifies suitable controls for evaluating the success of the organizational goals from the Organizational Planning perspective. This is achieved by defining measurement models using the GQM approach. In this context, each organizational goal is associated with a measurement goal (*MG*), with questions (*Q*) and metrics (*M*) that help to obtain objective information about the success of goal attainment (see right side of Fig. 2.1).

For each of the defined measurement goals, *interpretation models* are specified, which support the evaluation of the goal attainment and strategy success with respect to the defined set context factors and assumptions.

Thus, the entire hierarchical model, which we call a *grid*, provides not only a mechanism for planning organizational goals and strategies, but also for defining a measurement model that is consistent and relevant to the organizational planning perspective. Through this well-designed integration of both perspectives, GQM$^+$Strategies (1) improves organizational effectiveness by getting the entire organization to work in the same strategic direction (means for *alignment*), while (2) optimizing efficiency through continuous monitoring of the attainment of goals and strategies, which allows for immediately initiating countermeasures when attainment of a goal is threatened (means for *decision-making*). Furthermore,

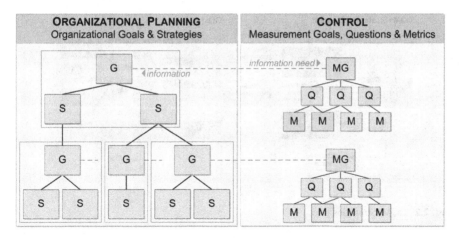

Fig. 2.1 GQM⁺Strategies: organizational planning and control perspectives

(3) the whole structure provides a means for transparently communicating goals, strategies, and the required data to the organization (means for *communication*).

2.2 GQM⁺Strategies Model

The first outcome of GQM⁺Strategies is a model of organizational goals, strategies, and associated measurement models. Figure 2.2 specifies the basic elements of a GQM⁺Strategies grid, which are grouped into two submodels: GQM⁺Strategies Element and GQM Graph.

The **GQM⁺Strategies Element** specifies organizational goals and strategies, context factors, assumptions, and their mutual relationships. An organizational goal can be linked to one or more strategies that aim at achieving this organizational goal. Conversely, a strategy can be linked to one or more organizational goals. Context factors and assumptions can be associated with organizational goals, strategies, or links between organizational goals and strategies. These associations indicate how context factors and assumptions influence the setting of organizational goals with respect to the selection of strategies or the refinement of organizational goals and strategies. A GQM⁺Strategies Element can be refined by further GQM⁺Strategies Elements. This represents the refinement of strategies by new organizational goals on a lower level of an organization. In GQM⁺Strategies, an **organizational goal** refers to an anticipated state in the future that an organization wants to achieve. The goal specifies "What is to be achieved?" and is systematically documented by means of a structured goal template. The template includes, for example, such aspects as the *object* and its exact characteristic (*focus*) that are subject to achievement, the desired *magnitude* of the improvement, the *time frame* for achieving the goal, the *organizational scope* of the goal including the individual primarily responsible for achieving the goal, the *constraints* that may limit

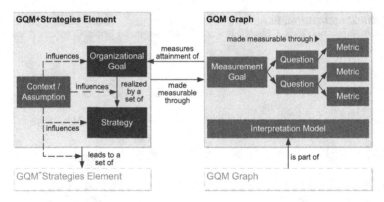

Fig. 2.2 GQM⁺Strategies grid

Table 2.1 Basic aspects of an organizational goal

Organizational goal	
Object	What is the object under consideration? Object refers to artifacts, processes, or personnel addressed by the goal. <u>Examples</u>: customers, software product, IT infrastructure, etc.
Focus	What characteristic of the object is considered? Focus refers to the object's attribute for which a certain state is going to be achieved. <u>Examples</u>: satisfaction, quality, performance, effectiveness, etc.
Magnitude	What is the quantity (measure) of the goal to be achieved? <u>Examples</u>: percentage of change relative to current state (50 %), absolute value (20), etc.
Time Frame	When should the goal be achieved? <u>Examples</u>: 6 months, next fiscal year, etc.
Organizational Scope	Who or what organizations are responsible for goal attainment? <u>Examples</u>: project manager, a particular set of projects, company, business unit, division, department, etc.
Constraints	What are relevant constraints that may prevent attainment of the goal? <u>Examples</u>: market situation, legal regulations, obligatory standards, available resources, etc.
Relationships	What are other goals the goal is related to? Goals can be related due to a strategy that leads to both goals: Goals are in agreement given a certain strategy if the strategy supports attainment of both goals. Goals are conflicting given a certain strategy if the strategy supports attainment of one goal while having a negative impact on the other goal. <u>Example</u>: Introducing a new testing approach in order to achieve a higher software quality goal will require additional investments and thus contradict a cost reduction goal

attainment of the goal, and *relationships* to other goals (in particular, conflicting goals). Table 2.1 specifies the aspects of an organizational goal in more detail.

For each goal, the planned procedure for achieving the goal is specified through one or more associated strategies. Hence, a **strategy** refers to a planned approach for achieving an organizational goal. It answers the question of "How is the goal to be achieved?" and defines rather general "means" for achieving the "end" (i.e., attaining the goal). Before implementing a GQM⁺Strategies grid in an organization, strategies are operationalized through operative activities and procedures (i.e., business or development processes). Strategies may further be linked to subgoals on lower levels that must be achieved for that strategy to be considered successful.

GQM⁺Strategies enforces the explicit documentation of the rationale for specific goals, strategies, and their mutual relationships. Rationale refers to information about the actual or presumed characteristics of the organization's environment that affected a decision about particular goals and strategies. In practice, the rationale encompasses the strengths and opportunities we want to utilize as well as weaknesses and risks we want to avoid when defining particular goals and strategies. In GQM⁺Strategies, we distinguish between two types of rationale: context and assumption. **Context** refers to an actual environmental characteristic. An assumption refers to a presumed, yet uncertain, aspect of the environment. It is a placeholder for something that needs to be evaluated through measurement. For example, we may base an organizational improvement goal on assumed, yet not quantitatively measured baselines. In the course of an application of GQM⁺Strategies, we should employ measurement to develop actual baselines and to re-evaluate our goals (i.e., attainment of the defined organizational improvement goal).

The **GQM Graph** specifies a measurement and evaluation framework. It uses the classical GQM approach to specify what data needs to be collected and how that data should be interpreted in order to make informed decisions about the success of strategies and the attainment of the organizational goals defined in the GQM⁺Strategies element. Each GQM graph consists of a measurement goal, questions, metrics, and an interpretation model.

A **measurement goal** describes what knowledge needs to be gained from the measurement activity in order to make a decision about the success or failure of an associated goal and/or strategy. For example, let us consider an organizational goal of improving development productivity by 10 %. We base this goal on the observation (context) that too much effort is being spent on software development activities and on the presumption (assumption) that this large effort is caused by low productivity of the software team. In order to make an informed decision on the attainment of the organizational goal, we would need knowledge about two aspects: the current (baseline) productivity and the productivity following the implementation of the strategies associated with the goal. Consequently, we would need to define two measurement goals, that is, objectives of measurement: characterize the development productivity of the software team to date, and evaluate the improvement in the team's productivity after implementation of the appropriate improvement strategies.

The measurement goal is systematically documented using the GQM goal template. The template specifies the measured *object* and its *attributes*, the *purpose* of measurement, the *viewpoint* that the measurement represents, and the *context* in which the measurement takes place. For example, the measurement goal regarding the characterization of baseline development productivity would be documented as follows: Analyze past software projects with respect to development productivity for the purpose of characterizing them to create a baseline from the viewpoint of the organization in the context of the software organization. If such historical data does not exist, we might start with a presumed baseline based upon expert opinion. This presumed baseline value is an assumption that must be checked as a real baseline value is established over time.

Measurement goals are defined in an operational, traceable way by refining them into a set of quantifiable questions. **Questions** are used as guidelines for extracting the appropriate information to fulfill the information need defined by the measurement goal. Questions specify **metrics** that define what quantitative data needs to be collected in order to answer the questions. Finally, interpretation models describe how the data items associated with different metrics are related and combined (interpreted) to answer the questions and satisfy the measurement goal (i.e., fulfill the information need). Continuing the example of measuring baseline productivity, example questions might be: What is the size of the delivered software products? How much effort has the team spent on delivering these products? What was the experience of the team members in the application domain? How large was the team? Note that these questions actually ask about basic development productivity (i.e., how much effort has been spent on delivering a product of a certain size) and potential factors that may influence productivity (e.g., experience and skills of the development team). Example metrics derived from these questions may be development effort in person-days, functional size of the delivered software product, years of experience in the application domain, and team size in terms of number of team members.

Typically, one GQM graph should be defined for each organizational goal in order to quantitatively evaluate its attainment. Each organizational goal in the GQM⁺Strategies element may have several associated measurement goals, each of which is the basis for an entire GQM graph. However, it is expected that different GQM structures will share several questions and metrics. Interpretation models may combine data from different GQM structures, thus optimizing the metrics collection process.

Table 2.2 briefly explains the meaning of all key elements of GQM⁺Strategies that we have discussed in the paragraphs above.

As already stated, defining the grid is a major contribution in its own right. If an organization stops here, they have provided an alignment of the perspective goals, strategies, and measures that align the organization's approach for achieving its high-level goals. The grid serves as a means of communication to all units in the organization of what is needed and required of them. Even if they never collect a single piece of data, they have laid out a plan for all to see.

2.3   GQM⁺Strategies Process

One may think of different ways for constructing such a model as presented in the previous sections. Depending on how deeply an organization wants to implement the GQM⁺Strategies model into their way of thinking, different activities should be performed. The process presented in this section basically describes a full-featured

Table 2.2   Key elements of a GQM⁺Strategies grid

Organizational Goal	An anticipated state in the future that an organization wants to achieve. It answers the question: "What is to be achieved?" The goal is formalized by using the organizational goal template and quantified by using GQM
Strategy	A planned procedure for achieving an organizational goal. It answers the question: "How is the goal to be achieved?" Strategy refers to the "means" for getting to the "end" (i.e., goal) and can be refined by a set of concrete activities (i.e., business or development processes)
Context Factor	A factual characteristic of an organization or its environment that affects the models and data used
Assumption	A presumed (expected, yet uncertain) characteristic of an organization, its environment, or the availability of data that affects the kind of models and data used
Measurement Goal	An objective of measurement derived from a particular information need. Information need refers to the information that the organization needs in order to make a certain decision (e.g., if an organizational goal is achieved). The measurement goal is formalized using the GQM goal template
GQM Graph	A hierarchy of measurement goals, questions, metrics, and interpretation models provided as the result of applying the GQM method. Questions are derived from measurement goals and lead to metrics

set of activities for constructing the GQM⁺Strategies model and actively using the model for driving continuous improvement programs in an organization. In practice, the process presented here and detailed in the upcoming chapters of this book should be tailored to the specific needs of an organization, which means that dedicated activities are skipped or merged with already existing procedures in place in the organization. However, in order to give the reader a complete picture of how the approach can be fully implemented in an organization, the following reference process is defined.

The reference process consists of six repeatable phases plus one phase for initializing the overall improvement program and the process of creating a strategic measurement program for an organization. The six phases are organized as a continuous improvement cycle (see Fig. 2.3) and are based upon the Quality Improvement Paradigm (QIP) as proposed by Basili and others (Basili 1985; Basili et al. 1994a; Basili and Caldiera 1995; Basili and Green 1994). The cycle will be repeated with a certain frequency. The frequency of running through the whole cycle largely depends on the speed with which the organization wants to evolve and continuously improve. It also depends on the size of the grid that is modeled and on whether this grid captures the entire organization or only different parts thereof.

Phase 0 describes the initialization phase and ensures that the infrastructure and the resources necessary for the application of GQM⁺Strategies are available and that initial planning for the subsequent process phases is performed. The six-phase improvement cycle involves three major stages, each consisting of two phases:

- Develop: The first stage is the development of a hierarchical grid/model that aligns the goals, strategies, and required measurement data. The key benefit of

Fig. 2.3 Basic GQM⁺Strategies process

the grid is the ability to reach a consensus between goals and strategies and communicate this consensus to the entire organization. In Phase 1, the current organizational situation for which the grid is to be constructed is characterized. In Phase 2, the grid is defined as a model of organizational goals and strategies, the linkages between them, the rationales (context factors and assumptions), and the required measurement data.

- Implement: The second stage involves the execution of the strategies and measurements defined by the grid, which allows checking the attainment of the goals, the effectiveness of the strategies, etc. In Phase 3, the plans for executing the grid strategies and collecting the appropriate data are specified. In Phase 4, those plans are executed and analyzed in terms of whether the strategies are working and the goals are being achieved. If not, the leader of a corresponding improvement project can make the necessary local adjustments to the grid in real time. If a certain milestone is achieved or a defined trigger occurs (e.g., a goal cannot be achieved without serious global adjustments that go beyond the scope and resources of the project), we move to Phase 5.
- Learn: The third stage involves learning from what has been done by analyzing the results and improving the process for generating further goals and strategies. In Phase 5, we analyze the attainment of goals and try to investigate root causes for the success/failure of the strategies. In Phase 6, we record what we have learned in the previous phases and request improvement actions if the actual results differ from the planned ones. Example findings may be that our assumptions were wrong or that we did not consider relevant context characteristics—as a consequence of which we selected the wrong strategies

and the associated goals were not achieved. Requested improvements may include revising context characteristics and assumptions, adjusting the structure of goals and strategies, or redefining how measurements are made or interpreted.

Note that the six phases of the GQM⁺Strategies improvement cycle correspond closely to the popular Plan-Do-Check-Act (PDCA) improvement approach proposed by Shewhart (1939) and widely promoted by Deming (1986).

In the following seven chapters (initialization phase plus six QIP phases), we will present the GQM⁺Strategies process in more detail. For each phase of the process, we will describe the activities involved and the results that are delivered. Moreover, we will illustrate the process phases with an example that continues across all process phases; the description of each phase ends with its illustration using the example.

In this phase, we ensure the conditions for the successful application of GQM⁺Strategies by securing the commitment and resources for using the method. Furthermore, responsibilities are defined and training is provided for all people involved. Table 3.1 summarizes the objectives, inputs, basic activities, and outcomes of this phase. In the following sections, we will describe the individual activities of this phase in more detail.

3.1 Get Commitment

As with any other initiative within a software organization, successful application of GQM⁺Strategies requires appropriate planning and assignment of resources. For this purpose, a GQM⁺Strategies expert who is responsible for initiating and coordinating the method application must get the commitment of management

Table 3.1 Overview of the "Initialize" phase

Initialize application of the GQM⁺Strategies approach	
Objective	Setup of conditions for the successful application of GQM⁺Strategies by securing the commitment of management and the appropriate resources for using the method. Furthermore, responsibilities are defined, the application process is planned, and appropriate training is provided for all people involved
Inputs	• Overview and motivation talk (presentation slides) • Tutorial on the GQM⁺Strategies approach (presentation slides)
Activities	1. Get commitment 2. Specify scope 3. Plan the GQM⁺Strategies application process 4. Train people
Outcomes	• Commitment of management to apply GQM⁺Strategies, i.e., regarding the resources and infrastructure required for the method's application • Initial scope and plan for applying GQM⁺Strategies • Trained staff that will be involved in the GQM⁺Strategies application

V. Basili et al., *Aligning Organizations Through Measurement*, The Fraunhofer IESE Series   19
on Software and Systems Engineering, DOI 10.1007/978-3-319-05047-8_3,
© Springer International Publishing Switzerland 2014

and obtain sponsorship. In the first applications of GQM$^+$Strategies, the expert might be coached by an external consultant in GQM$^+$Strategies.

Typically, the GQM$^+$Strategies expert will give a presentation or talk to motivate the use of GQM$^+$Strategies. Besides a brief introduction of the method's principles and general benefits, the talk should focus on the challenges of the specific organization and the way they can be addressed with GQM$^+$Strategies. Therefore, in preparation for the talk, the expert identifies baseline problems within the organization, defines the purpose of the GQM$^+$Strategies application, determines the approximate scope of the GQM$^+$Strategies application, and plans for the necessary resources. Typically, the coordinator is supported by external GQM$^+$Strategies experts, particularly when the method is applied in the organization for the first time.

3.2   Specify Scope

In this step, the GQM$^+$Strategies expert defines the exact organizational scope to be addressed by the initial initiative. The scope refers to those parts of the organization that will apply GQM$^+$Strategies for defining, aligning, and measuring their goals and strategies. In other words, the organizational scope specifies those organizational units that are to be encompassed by the GQM$^+$Strategies grid. The coordinator can document the organizational scope in the form of an organizational chart (i.e., the specification of organizational units and their interdependencies). The scope of GQM$^+$Strategies can be adjusted in the later phases of the method's application.

3.3   Plan GQM$^+$Strategies Application Process

After obtaining management commitment and the resources needed for the application of GQM$^+$Strategies, the internal coordinator and the expert prepare a detailed application plan, which includes staffing and scheduling activities, analyzing risks, preparing the infrastructure, and calculating the budget.

3.4   Train People

The GQM$^+$ Strategies expert trains the personnel who will be actively involved in the method's application. All personnel involved should be familiar with the basic concepts of GQM$^+$Strategies, including strategic alignment and goal-oriented measurement. The exact content of the detailed training depends on the specific activities that each person will perform. For example, the personnel responsible for implementing the measurement program should obtain in-depth training on goal-oriented measurement, data collection, analysis, and visualization. The person responsible for rolling out and maintaining GQM$^+$Strategies and the associated assets (e.g., grids) in the organization requires comprehensive training on the entire method. Besides the detailed methodology, a comprehensive tutorial includes guidelines on how to train for GQM⁺Strategies.

3.5 Example

In the following paragraphs, we will illustrate the phases of GQM⁺Strategies with a continuous example of a fictitious Company X that provides banking and insurance services to enterprise and private customers on the European market. The company wants to establish a system of key performance indicators (KPIs) for the purpose of quantitatively understanding how well they are performing with respect to their goals and strategies and for evaluating their organizational success (or failure).

3.5.1 Get Commitment

Mr. Watson is the project and quality manager at the Software Development group at Company X. He has recently participated in a seminar where he learned about goal-oriented measurement and the GQM⁺Strategies approach. In a discussion with Mr. Smith, Head of Software Development group, he shared his idea of using GQM⁺Strategies for aligning the software development strategies with the business goals of Company X and for building up a corresponding KPI system. Smith supported Watson's idea and encouraged him to present it to the management board of Company X. Watson prepared and gave a motivational talk to the company's management board in April 2011. At its next meeting in June 2011, the board decided to apply GQM⁺Strategies to align Company X's goals and strategies and to establish a corresponding measurement program.

Company X has a lot of customers in the banking area, but only few in the insurance area. Therefore, the initial scope for evaluating the success and failure of their organizational strategies was focused on the insurance area. The current situation is that improvement activities undertaken in the past did not lead to more customers in the insurance area. The objective of using GQM⁺Strategies would then be to (1) identify alternative strategies for expanding insurance services, (2) quantitatively evaluate the success of these strategies, and (3) identify the root causes of and potential improvements for failed strategies.

3.5.2 Specify Scope

The original motivation for applying GQM⁺Strategies was to quantitatively plan and manage the expansion of the insurance services of Company X. The management of Company X expected the method to help identify strategies for expanding insurance services and for quantitatively managing the success of these strategies. At first, the management of Company X decided to focus strategic planning on

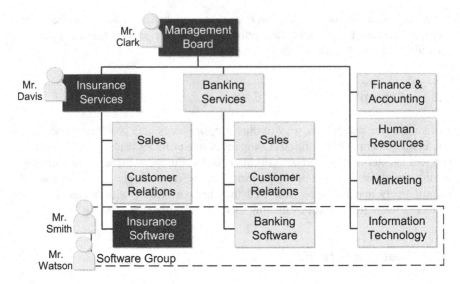

Fig. 3.1 Example: organizational chart of Company X

insurance services and their support through software development. As a consequence, two business units were involved in the application of GQM$^+$Strategies: Insurance Services and Software Development. Figure 3.1 illustrates the position of these business units within the organizational chart of Company X.

3.5.3 Plan GQM$^+$Strategies Application Process

After the board decided to apply the GQM$^+$Strategies, Watson prepared the initial scope and budget required for the method's application. At its next meeting in September 2011, the board authorized the initial scope and budget for applying GQM$^+$Strategies. Afterwards, Watson, as coordinator of the initiative, planned the implementation of the GQM$^+$Strategies process. First he clarified the responsibilities within the initiative. Table 3.2 summarizes the role assignments.

Next, Watson plans a rough schedule for the GQM$^+$Strategies application. The first cycle spans 9 months and includes the following milestones:

- Initialization phase completed (November 2011): Characterizing the environment (phase 0 as described in this chapter) has been finished.
- Development stage completed (December 2011): Characterizing the environment (phase 1 as described in Chap. 4) and defining goals, strategies, and measurement (phase 2 as described in Chap. 5) have been finished.
- Execution stage completed (June 2012): Planning the grid implementation (phase 3 as described in Chap. 6) and executing the plans (phase 4 as described in Chap. 7) have been finished.

Table 3.2 Example: roles in the GQM⁺Strategies application in Company X

Person	Position in Company X	Role in GQM⁺Strategies
Mr. Clark	Chief Executive Officer	Main stakeholder of measurement initiative who sponsors the GQM⁺Strategies initiative
Mr. Davis	Division Manager of Insurance Services business unit	Responsible for insurance-related strategies of Company X
Mr. Smith	Head of Software Development group	Responsible for in-house software development and IT support of business units; included because Company X's business is largely IT-driven
Mr. Watson	Project and quality manager at Software Development group	GQM⁺Strategies expert, coordinator of the method application at Company X

- Learning stage completed (July 2012): Analyzing the outcomes (phase 5 as described in Chap. 8) and packaging improvements (phase 6 as described in Chap. 9) have been finished.

After completing the learning stage, the GQM⁺Strategies grid will be updated and analyzed every 6 months as part of a set of organization-wide improvement workshops with the top-level management of Company X.

The first cycle should be completed after 9 months even though not all strategies will likely be completed within that time frame. This is done to have a quick decision point for checking whether the organization is on the right track with its defined goals and strategies. Depending on the existing strategies, the organization can build upon initiatives that were already launched earlier.

3.5.4   Train People

The personnel assigned to implement GQM⁺Strategies require appropriate training (Table 3.3). To coordinate the initiative, Watson does not possess the appropriate expertise and therefore involves external experts to transfer GQM⁺Strategies into Company X. In the initial application, the external experts train all GQM⁺Strategies stakeholders in Company X. Watson, as future maintainer of the method, receives very comprehensive training and works directly with the external experts. Additionally, he learns how to conduct GQM⁺Strategies training. In the future, he will be responsible for training new GQM⁺Strategies stakeholders.

Table 3.3 Example: training GQM⁺Strategies at Company X

Person	Role in GQM⁺Strategies	Scope of training
Mr. Watson	Expert in the GQM⁺Strategies approach at Company X	• Training: Comprehensive tutorial on the GQM⁺Strategies approach (2 days) • Additional learning materials: Guidelines on training and applying the GQM⁺Strategies approach, description of the GQM⁺Strategies process • Handouts and templates, e.g.: Training slides, templates for documenting organizational GQM⁺Strategies grid, software tool supporting modeling and visualizing GQM⁺Strategies grids • Coaching: Mentoring during development and employment of the GQM⁺Strategies grid. While learning the method, the internal GQM⁺Strategies expert (Mr. Watson) is coached by external consultants
Mr. Smith	Responsible for in-house software development and IT support of business units	• Training on the GQM⁺Strategies approach (1 day) • Comprehensive training in implementing goal-oriented measurement
Mr. Davis	Responsible for insurance-related strategies of Company X	• Basic introduction to the GQM⁺Strategies approach
Mr. Clark	Main stakeholder of measurement initiative who sponsors (owns) the GQM⁺Strategies initiative	• Basic introduction to the GQM⁺Strategies approach

Phase 1: Characterize the Environment

4

In this phase, we characterize the context of the GQM⁺Strategies application by defining the organizational scope of the method's application and specifying the characteristics of the application environment. The environmental characteristics encompass actual and uncertain attributes of the method application environment that determine the applicability of the method and that should be considered when building and maintaining GQM⁺Strategies grids. Table 4.1 summarizes the objectives, inputs, basic activities, and outcomes of this phase. In the following sections, we will describe the individual activities of this phase in more detail.

4.1   Characterize the Environment

Using inputs from the initialization phase, the coordinator identifies characteristics that should be considered when building and maintaining the GQM⁺Strategies grids. Relevant characteristics include those aspects of the application environment that influence:

Table 4.1 Overview of the "Characterize environment" phase

Characterize environment of GQM⁺Strategies application	
Objective	Characterize the context of the GQM⁺Strategies application by refining the organizational scope of the method's application and specifying the characteristics of the application environment
Inputs	• Initial scope and plan for applying GQM⁺Strategies (output of the "0. Initialize" phase)
	• Description of the organizational structure (such as an organizational chart)
Activities	1. Characterize the environment
Outcomes	• Any updates to the scope of the GQM⁺Strategies and the related organizational chart during this cycle
	• Characteristics of the GQM⁺Strategies application environment: context factors and assumptions

V. Basili et al., *Aligning Organizations Through Measurement*, The Fraunhofer IESE Series   25
on Software and Systems Engineering, DOI 10.1007/978-3-319-05047-8_4,
© Springer International Publishing Switzerland 2014

- Applicability of GQM$^+$Strategies: Environmental characteristics that potentially constrain or facilitate the usage of GQM$^+$Strategies, e.g., availability of documented organizational structure, existence of process documentation, availability of appropriate personnel, or availability of measurement data
- Definition of the rationale for selecting the organizational goals and strategies: Environmental characteristics provide a rationale for selecting appropriate organizational goals and strategies. Explicitly documenting such rationales not only makes the process of defining goals and strategies transparent but also facilitates organizational improvement when some goals or strategies fail. For example, if an unsuccessful strategy was based upon assumptions that turn out to be wrong, then improvement actions should be directed toward revisiting these assumptions and selecting alternative strategies

The characteristics encompass known and expected attributes of the application environment, in particular:

- *Context factors* refer to actual characteristics of the application environment. Context factors can be objective facts about the environment or they can be considered as facts because there is sufficient evidence based upon observation. Example context factors include application domain, organizational processes, and available measurement data, market trends, and competition
- *Assumptions* refer to uncertain characteristics of the application environment or guesses made to allow moving forward. Defining organizational goals and strategies often requires making certain assumptions because appropriate environmental characteristics are not objectively known and relevant evidence is missing. Example assumptions might include estimated baseline, personnel skills, usefulness of a new technology, and cost of introducing new processes, future market trends, and behavior of competitors

Context factors are typically known by the organization. Assumptions, on the other hand, represent information we need to define a goal or select a strategy but whose value we are not sure of at the time, so we must guess the values of these variables. An assumption might be a baseline we need for comparison but do not know, or the value expected from a particular strategy. Assumptions are explicitly expressed in the interpretation model as they need to be evaluated as an explanation of the resulting success or lack thereof of the goal or strategy.

In the "Characterize environment" phase of GQM$^+$Strategies, we define an initial set of context factors and assumptions. In this phase, we typically focus on generic characteristics that determine the feasibility of applying GQM$^+$Strategies. This initial set can then be refined in the "Define Goals, Strategies, and Measurement" phase, where specific environmental characteristics are determined to support decision-making about lower-level organizational goals, strategies, and their linkages.

Note that in some cases an assumption may become a context factor after the assumption is validated following the collection of a sufficient amount of evidence. For instance, we may only postulate that our customers are satisfied with our products because of the high sales level. Yet, without collecting appropriate evidence, this should be considered as an assumption, for example, because our product might be the only one on the market and customers may simply be forced to buy it—which does not necessarily imply that they are satisfied with it. The assumption may become a context factor if we obtain appropriate evidence, for example, through a customer satisfaction survey. Or, if we assume a particular baseline set of values for evaluating whether some goal has been achieved, we can replace that assumption with real data over time as baselines are built.

We may employ a variety of techniques for gathering context information, including focus groups, group brainstorming meetings, reading organizational documents, and individual interviews. The choice of elicitation methods depends on the number of people involved, the time constraints, and the availability of existing information. Example questions to answer while identifying relevant context factors for the scope of the GQM$^+$Strategies application include:

- What are the relevant characteristics of the environment in terms of business context?
- What are the characteristics of the products or services provided?
- What processes, tools, and technologies are employed?
- What is the size of the organization? Example size measures can be number of people employed, number of projects performed, revenue, and team size per project
- What characterizes the customers of the organization? Do you sell to multiple customers or a single customer?
- Are you contracted for your work? Do you contract out to other organizations?
- Is your organization at the top, middle, or bottom of the corporate structure?
- Is your organization at the top, middle, or bottom of the contract chain?
- Is your software embedded or user-intensive?
- Is your software mostly greenfield or legacy/COTS/reuse-driven?
- Is your software casual-use or mission-critical?
- What factors influence income sources and business model? For example, what factors influence profitability?
- What are the critical aspects of the internal and external interfaces of the organization? For example, what are the constraints of the contract chain, that is, interfaces to involved suppliers and acquirers?
- What are the elements of your existing measurement programs, for example, goals, models, measures, and measurement data?
- What baselines exist?
- What are your organizational principles?
- What are the key elements of your work environment? For instance, is the work atmosphere collaborative or competitive?
- Is your organization risk-averse, risk-neutral, or risk-driven?

In order to identify relevant assumptions, we may ask similar questions. But in this case we analyze environmental characteristics for which we have little or no empirical evidence. Example assumptions may refer to such aspects as technologies, market, customers, our organization, workforce, available baselines and data, etc.

4.2   Example

In order to illustrate the "Characterize environment" phase, we continue with the example of Company X. Let us remember that Company X decided to apply GQM⁺Strategies in order to establish a system of key performance indicators (KPIs) for the purpose of quantitatively evaluating the success (or failure) of their organizational strategies.

4.2.1   Characterize the Environment

The scope initially defined in the "Initialize" phase (Sect. 3.2) was already sufficiently detailed and did not have to be refined in this phase. Further characteristics of the GQM⁺Strategies application environment at Company X include:

- Aspects that may constrain or facilitate the applicability of GQM⁺Strategies:
  - Availability of measurement data: The Software Development group collects basic measurement data such as project effort, software size, or defect attributes
  - Commitment: Business units within the scope of the GQM⁺Strategies application are committed to actively participate in the related activities
- Aspects that may influence the selection of organizational strategies:
  - Software application domain: Insurance software
  - Software development project type: 80 % maintenance, 20 % new projects
  - Software development processes: Mainly Rational Unified Process (RUP). Agile development with Scrum (Schwaber 2004) has already been piloted in selected software development projects of other business units of Company X
  - Software quality assurance: Inspections using Checklist-Based Reading (CBR) (Fagan 1976) have been used for assuring the quality of software requirements and design specifications in selected software development projects of the Insurance Services business unit

Phase 2: Define Goals, Strategies, and Measurement

5

In this phase, we derive the GQM⁺Strategies Grid. In particular, we specify and align organizational goals and strategies within the GQM⁺Strategies scope, and we quantify goals using GQM graphs. Table 5.1 summarizes the objectives, inputs, basic activities, and outcomes of this phase. In the following sections, we will describe the individual activities of this phase in more detail.

5.1 Identify Existing Assets

It is a rather rare situation that a company defines its strategic measurement program from scratch. Typically, at least some goals, strategies, and performance indicators (measures) are already defined within the scope of the GQM⁺Strategies

Table 5.1 Overview of the "Define Goals, Strategies, and Measurement" phase

Define goals, strategies, and measurement	
Objective	Define the GQM⁺Strategies grid using existing assets where possible. This means defining and aligning organizational goals and strategies, documenting rationales in the form of context factors and assumptions, and defining the appropriate measures and interpretation models
Inputs	• Scope of the GQM⁺Strategies application and the related organizational chart • Characteristics of the GQM⁺Strategies application environment: context factors and assumptions

Activities	1. Identify existing assets
	2. Select relevant assets
	3. Build up GQM⁺Strategies grid
	  (a) Elicit specific context and assumptions
	  (b) Define organizational goals
	  (c) Make strategy decisions
	  (d) Refine GQM⁺Strategies element
	  (e) Define GQM graphs
	4. Review and adjust grid

Outcomes	• The full GQM+Strategies grid for the proposed application scope

V. Basili et al., *Aligning Organizations Through Measurement*, The Fraunhofer IESE Series   29
on Software and Systems Engineering, DOI 10.1007/978-3-319-05047-8_5,
© Springer International Publishing Switzerland 2014

application. The objective of this step is to identify and gather existing assets that may be reused while constructing the GQM⁺Strategies grid. In particular, we are interested in such assets as goals, strategies, measures, measurement processes, and interpretation models. An example approach for identifying existing assets might be a group meeting with representatives of all organizational units identified within the scope of the GQM⁺Strategies application. Typically, we start such a meeting by asking about the top-level goals and then continue in a top-down manner across the organizational structure, asking about strategies, goals, measures, and interpretation models. We try to associate each identified asset (at least informally) with the appropriate organizational units specified within the GQM⁺Strategies application scope and try to link these assets to each other. For example, we try to link related goals and strategies to each other and associate them with existing measures (performance indicators). Example questions we may ask in order to guide the identification of existing assets include:

- Are there organizational goals or objectives? What are they?
- Are there goals in any other organizational units?
- What data is currently being collected?
- Is there a measurement database?
- Are there defined measurement procedures?

5.2   Select Relevant Assets

After identifying existing assets, we assess their relevance in terms of their up-to-dateness and feasibility of reuse within the GQM⁺Strategies grid (i.e., their relevance with respect to the scope). The objective of this step is to avoid spending effort on considering irrelevant (thus useless) assets in the subsequent grid development steps. For example, we may rate organizational goals with respect to their adherence to the defined GQM⁺Strategies application scope, rate strategies with respect to their suitability within the defined context, and rate measures with respect to their suitability regarding the goals and the current state of the art in measurement. Thus, we are able to immediately exclude some assets from further consideration and keep only those we may want to consider as we move through the grid derivation. It is advisable to document (e.g., maintain a list) those relevant assets.

5.3   Build Up the GQM⁺Strategies Grid

The GQM⁺Strategies grid development process (Fig. 5.1) consists of two procedures for modeling grid elements: one associated with GQM⁺Strategies elements and one with GQM graphs. These two modeling procedures can be performed asynchronously as long as a GQM graph is not developed before its GQM⁺Strategies element. For example, we may specify a GQM graph for each

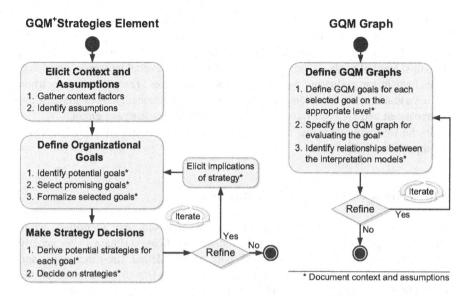

Fig. 5.1 Grid development process

element as we define it. Alternatively, we may specify any set of elements (i.e., goals and strategies) before defining the associated GQM graphs.

The grid development process suggests a top-down specification of organizational goals and strategies. In practice, the top level in the grid may not always be the highest level of the organization. We can start at any organizational unit, depending on where in the organization the application of GQM⁺Strategies is selected to be engaged. We will refer to that as the *top-level scoped*. Typically, we would proceed down from there. However, since all goals should be connected and aimed at satisfying the top-level organizational goals, we may try to solve the issue, making a connection between the top-level organizational goals and the top level of the goals that are within our scope. We may want to do this to demonstrate how the top-level goals from our scope contribute to the top-level organizational goals. For the sake of simplicity, we describe the grid development process in the typical top-down manner, starting from top-level business goals within the scope (i.e., goals on the top-level scoped). For each top-level goal in the grid, the two grid development subprocesses are performed to define, respectively:

1. Lower-level goals and strategies (GQM⁺Strategies elements)
2. Measurement goals, questions, and metrics (GQM graphs)

The process stops when we have reached a point where there are no longer any logical goals or strategies to be expanded and all goals have an associated GQM measurement graph. During this process, relevant assets that have been identified before can be considered for reuse. In this case, we try to align them according to the structure of the GQM⁺Strategies grid. After defining a grid element and its associated measurement at the top level, the grid development process iterates through all the organizational units we specified in the "Specify scope" activity (Sect. 3.2). For each organizational unit, we define and align the next level of goals. This next level of goals is determined by the preceding level of strategies, providing a mechanism for evaluating the results of those strategies. The process stops when we have reached a point where there are no longer any logical goals or strategies to be expanded and all goals have an associated GQM measurement graph.

In the following sections, we present the individual steps of the grid development process in more detail.

5.3.1   Elicit Context and Assumptions

In addition to the generic context and assumptions we identified while characterizing the context of the GQM$^+$Strategies application (Phase 1), we specify context factors and assumptions, which both help to define, limit the scope, and form a rationale for the goals and strategies we select at each level of the GQM$^+$Strategies grid. For example, for the top-level business goal, the context factors and assumptions will typically refer to the external constraints and opportunities and will be related to the company's vision and mission statements. External constraints and opportunities include such aspects as existing competitive (or substitute) products, the bargaining power of the suppliers, and market trends. Internal constraints and opportunities include such aspects as level of staff competence, technological advances, and existing infrastructure.

While identifying relevant context characteristics, we should differentiate between what we factually know (so-called context factors) and what we believe to be true but have little or no evidence about. This distinction will help later on (in Phases 4, 5, and 6 of the GQM$^+$Strategies process) to properly interpret the measurement data and find potential causes of failed strategies and missed organizational goals. For example, one of the actions after a strategy fails is to check whether it was selected based on certain assumptions and whether these assumptions actually turned out to be true.

In the next steps of the grid development process, we adjust the context factors and assumptions in order to explicitly document the rationales for defining specific goals and selecting specific strategies. In other words, eliciting relevant context factors and assumptions is part of each step of the grid development process— whenever we make a decision about defining a specific grid element, the associated rationales should be documented.

5.3.2   Define Organizational Goals

5.3.2.1 Identify Potential Goals
Top-down grid development starts with the definition of relevant top-level goals. In the subsequent steps, we derive organizational goals from the higher-level

strategies in the goal-strategy hierarchy. Top-level goals represent the goals at the highest level of the scoped suborganization. If the scope is the entire organization, the top-level goals will be the highest-level business goals of the organization. If the scope is a part of the entire organization (e.g., a selected business unit), the top-level goals will be the goals defined at the highest level of this suborganization. These top-level goals are considered as root goals within a GQM⁺Strategies grid. For an entire organization, candidate top-level goals are typically defined by management as part of strategic planning. These organizational goals are typically related to the company's vision and mission statements and refer to the state the entire company wants to achieve within a certain time period.

Goals for the entire organization typically exist, but might not exist in an operational form. Example high-level, nonoperational goals might be:

- Increase revenues
- Improve operating profits
- Increase bookings
- Improve asset management
- Improve customer relations
- Improve operations management
- Improve human resource strategies and leadership
- Improve quality

However, as stated above, one does not have to start with the entire organization; it is sufficient to start with the part that was chosen in the scoping, i.e., the top-level goals within the application scope. To frame the top-level scoped goals, we might want to first identify those organizational principles we do not want to change, i.e., aspects of our organization we want to keep as is. Thus, we might ask questions like:

- What are the key elements of our environment? E.g., transparency, employee satisfaction, controlled risk, learning environment, work atmosphere collaborative versus competitive, etc.
- Is our organization risk-averse, risk-neutral, or risk-driven?

These questions help us to understand when a goal might create a conflict with our organizational principles. To help in the goal elicitation process, we might begin with some simple questions like:

- What do we want to happen next?
- Where do we see our organization being in 2, 5, 10 years?
- How do we want to grow, e.g., new customers, new competencies?
- How would we define success, e.g., do we want to improve some aspect of the business?
- Is there some specific, more detailed goal we want to achieve?

It can also help to consider the following classes of business goals:

- *Growth goals*, e.g., acquire new projects with current competence areas; expand existing projects set; evolve existing competencies; build new competencies
- *Success goals*, e.g., deliver good products to customers; control costs; shrink schedule; increase profits; get corporate visibility (awards, etc.), build core competence
- *Maintain goals*, e.g., transparency, employee satisfaction, controlled risk, learning environment (here we might want to measure to assure there is no decrease in these goals)
- *Specific focus goals*: make helpdesk more efficient, predict if proposed effort has a good ROI, increase integration with rest of the company

We identify an initial set of potential business goals, maybe using some of the questions posed above as a guideline. Initially, we may define multiple goals that the company stakeholders (who participate in the grid development) perceive as most promising. We prioritize the goals, identify initial conflicts, identify potential hierarchical relationships (some may actually be subgoals of others), formalize the goals with the highest priority and at the highest level in a hierarchy, and fill out the organizational goal template.

In order to ensure that the most appropriate goals and strategies are defined, approaches such as *SWOT* (Strengths, Weaknesses, Opportunities, and Threats) analysis (Humphrey 2005) or *Five Forces* analysis (Porter 2008) can be used. In SWOT (Table 5.2), the organization takes a look at its internal strengths and weaknesses, on the one hand, and at the external market conditions (opportunities and threats), on the other hand. Based on these two views, the organization may position its goals and strategies to exploit organizational strengths and market opportunities, taking into account limitations and threats.

In the Five Forces analysis (Fig. 5.2), the organization takes a look at the basic forces that shape the market. An explicit analysis of these forces supports the organization in understanding the structure of its industry and stake out a position that is more profitable and less vulnerable to attack. Five Forces analysis helps to (1) position the organization where the forces are weakest, (2) exploit changes in the forces, and (3) reshape forces in favor of the organization.

Porter (2008) gives an example of commercial aviation as the least profitable business due to all five forces being very strong. A brief analysis of the five forces shows that in the avionics business, "(1) established rivals compete intensely on price, (2) customers are fickle, searching for the best deal regardless of carrier, (3) suppliers—plane and engine manufacturers, along with unionized labor forces—bargain away the lion's share of airlines' profits, (4) new players enter the industry in a constant stream, and (5) substitutes are readily available—such as train or car travel."

Using an iterative approach, we define suitable strategies and lower-level goals for each top-level goal. We take advantage of existing assets to reuse/integrate goals and strategies already defined within the considered organizational scope. Detailed activities here include specifying strategies for higher-level goals,

Table 5.2 The SWOT analysis table

	Factors	
Context	Helpful/positive (support attainment of organizational goals)	Harmful/negative (prevent attainment of organizational goals)
Internal (internal characteristics of an organization)	**Strengths** (internal characteristics— capabilities of the business or organization that give it an advantage over competitors) Examples: patents, skilled employees, access to new technologies, etc.	**Weaknesses** (internal characteristics— limitations of the business or organization that place it at a disadvantage relative to competitors) Examples: high employee turnover, high cost structure, limited access to distribution channels, etc.
External (external conditions of the market in which an organization acts)	**Opportunities** (external conditions that improve an organization's chances of increasing its business performance e.g., increasing profits) Examples: unfulfilled customer needs, emergence of new technologies, removal of legal constraints, etc.	**Threats** (external conditions that decrease the business performance) Examples: change in customer preference regarding the current product/services, emergence of substitute products/services, new legal barriers, etc.

Fig. 5.2 Five Forces analysis

specifying the corresponding lower-level goals, and formalizing goals. Note that GQM⁺Strategies explicitly documents the rationale behind goals and strategies and their relationships, and supports measuring the success of goals and strategies through goal-oriented measurement.

5.3.2.2 Select Promising Goals

While developing the grid, we should focus on a limited number of the most important goals, especially when developing such a grid for the first time. For this purpose, we prioritize potential goals and select a subset of the most important ones (within the scope of the GQM⁺Strategies application). Typically, we consider

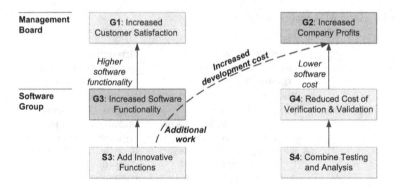

Fig. 5.3 Example goal dependencies

promising goals with respect to their feasibility, benefit, and cost. For example, we focus on goals that have the greatest positive impact on business success associated with feasible costs. The process of goal selection is a very interactive process, requiring input from various units of the organization.

For each selected top-level goal, we document the context factors and the assumptions that led to the selected top-level goals.

5.3.2.3 Document Selected Goals

Finally, we document each selected goal by using the organizational goal template illustrated in Table 2.1 in Sect. 2.2. During goal formalization, we again revise the context factors and assumptions, and document the relevant rationales that led to each specific goal aspect documented in the goal template. For example, we document the reason why we decided on the particular values of a goal's magnitude and time frame.

While specifying the organizational goals, we should consider their mutual dependencies and document potential relationships in the goal formalization template. Explicitly considering goal dependencies allows us to avoid situations in which apparently independent high-level goals lead to strategies that jeopardize the attainment of other goals (other than those from which they were derived). Figure 5.3 illustrates example goal dependencies between two business-level organizational goals: "G1: Increased customer satisfaction" and "G2: Increased company profits." Business goal G1 is refined (through corresponding strategies) into an organizational goal at the software development unit, namely, goal "G3: Increased functionality." Goal G3 is based on the assumption that software products that offer more innovative functionalities will lead to gains in customer satisfaction. The strategy (S3) selected for achieving goal G3 is quite straightforward and consists of adding innovative functionalities to the existing software product. Business goal G2 is refined into an organizational goal at the software development unit, namely goal "G4: Reduce cost of V&V." This goal is based on the assumption that the cost of software verification and validation (V&V) can be reduced while maintaining the quality of the delivered software product. In other words, it is assumed that the cost efficiency of V&V can be increased while maintaining its effectiveness in assuring the product's quality. This goal is to be achieved by following strategy S4 of combining testing and analysis activities. The rationale behind this is that software analysis techniques, when applied in early phases, prevent slippage of software defects into later phases. Reducing defect slippage, in turn, will generally have a positive effect on company profits because less faulty products will require less rework (although some investments to reduce defect slippage might initially be needed).

Yet, there is potential conflict between software unit goals and business goals. Since implementing innovative functionalities implies additional effort for achieving the increased functionality, (G3) will most likely involve increased software development costs, which in turn is in conflict with the increased profits business goal (G2). In this situation, G3 in conflict with G2 given strategy S3.

5.3.3   Make Strategy Decisions

5.3.3.1 Derive Potential Strategies

In this step, representatives of the corresponding units of the organization derive potential strategies for their higher-level goals. Strategies represent ways of achieving the goals. Usually we can identify a number of alternative or collaborative strategies for achieving one goal. In the case of *alternative strategies*, succeeding in one alone suffices for achieving the associated goal. In case of *collaborative strategies*, all strategies must succeed in order to achieve the associated goal. Collaborative strategies are more common than alternative strategies as the latter add cost.

5.3.3.2 Decide on Promising Strategies

In the end, we decide on one or more of the most promising strategies. We select strategies based on their feasibility, cost, and likelihood of success. Decisions regarding particular strategies should be based on and documented with clear rationales (context factors and/or assumptions).

5.3.3.3 Elicit Implications of Strategy

On the lower levels of the grid hierarchy, goals are derived from strategies. In order to define appropriate goals, we consider the implications of the strategies. For each strategy, we define at least one goal that operationalizes the successful implementation of the strategy on the current grid level. For example, if the strategy is "Achieve a certain level of software reliability through testing (i.e., test reliability in)," then the corresponding goal should quantitatively evaluate whether software reliability has actually been tested in.

5.3.4   Refine GQM⁺Strategies Element

We continue iterating through goal and strategy elicitation steps until the GQM⁺Strategies element is complete. The element is complete if it contains all relevant goals and strategies within the scope of the GQM⁺Strategies application, starting from the top business level down to the lowest elements of the organization's operational units. Operational units refer to units that actually implement the strategies in their daily work.

5.3.5   Define GQM Graphs

Using an iterative approach, we define a GQM graph for each goal of the GQM⁺Strategies Element. Detailed activities include defining measurement goals, deriving GQM graphs, and defining interpretation models.

The GQM approach (Basili and Weiss 1984), which (as explained earlier) is what GQM⁺Strategies is built upon, is a mechanism for defining and evaluating a set of operational goals using measurement. It represents a systematic approach for tailoring and integrating goals with models of the software processes, products, and quality perspectives of interest, based upon the specific needs of the project and the organization.

Once goals and strategies in the GQM⁺Strategies element part of the grid have been defined, it is then necessary to apply GQM to those goals to plan their evaluation in the GQM graph part of the grid. This involves, for each goal in the grid, the following activities: (a) developing a set of well-defined measurement goals for the quantities of interest in the GQM⁺Strategies goal, e.g., customer satisfaction, on-time delivery, improved quality, schedule; (b) generating questions (based upon models) that define those goals as completely as possible in a quantifiable way; (c) specifying the metrics that need to be collected to answer those questions and to track process and product conformance to the goals; (d) developing mechanisms for data collection; (e) collecting, validating, and analyzing the data in real time to provide feedback for corrective action; and (f) analyzing the data in a postmortem fashion to assess conformance to the goals and make recommendations for future improvements. Activities (a), (b), and (c) are all performed as part of the "define goals, strategies, and metrics" phase in the GQM⁺Strategies process. Activity (d) is performed as part of the "Choose Process" phase, activity (e) is performed as part of the "Execute Process" phase, and activity (f) is performed as part of the "Analyze Outcomes" phase.

The process of setting goals and refining them into quantifiable questions is complex and requires experience. In order to support this process, a set of templates for setting goals and a set of guidelines for deriving questions and metrics were developed (Basili and Rombach 1988). These templates and guidelines reflect our experience from having applied the GQM approach in a variety of environments.

In the following paragraphs, we will briefly discuss steps (a) defining measurement goals, (b) generating questions, and (c) deriving appropriate metrics, using

Table 5.3 GQM goal template

Analyze some	**Object of the study**: processes, products, other experience models
To	**Purpose**: characterize, evaluate, predict, motivate, control, improve, etc.
With respect to	**Focus**: cost, correctness, defect removal, changes, reliability, user friendliness, etc.
From the point of view of	**Viewpoint**: user, customer, manager, developer, corporation, etc.
In the following context	**Environment**: problem factors, people factors, resource factors, process factors, etc.

abstraction sheets. Steps (d) to (f) are addressed in the appropriate sections: (d) developing mechanisms for data collection in Sect. 6.2, (e) collecting, validating, and analyzing the data to provide feedback for corrective action in Sect. 7.2, and (f) analyzing the data to assess conformance to the goals in Sect. 8.2.

5.3.5.1 Defining Measurement Goals

Measurement goals may be defined for any object, for a variety of reasons, with respect to various models of quality, from various points of view, relative to a particular environment. The goal is defined by filling in a set of values for the various parameters in the template. As stated above, the measurement goal is systematically documented using the GQM goal template. The template specifies the measured *object* and its *attributes*, the *purpose* of measurement, the *viewpoint* that measurement represents, and the *context* in which measurement takes place.

Table 5.3 presents the GQM goal template. The **object of study** can be anything we want to analyze, and so we need a model of that object. For example, if the object is a process, then we want a model of the process itself. But there are many other aspects of the object of study that are important. For a process, aspects of importance include: how well the process is performed (performance conformance) and how that conformance will be evaluated, how well the people applying the process understand the domain to which the process is being applied, etc. So models of training, experience, ability of the people in performing the process, etc. are important to develop and measure.

The **purpose** of the study reflects the level of maturity required for the evaluation. For understanding or characterization purposes, a model of the object and any data we collect helps to provide us with some insight, but an evaluation purpose requires some basis for comparison (historical database) or some absolute measure. If the purpose is prediction, then we need a pattern in the data that allows us to develop a consistent model based upon factors that we have available or can reasonably estimate. Motivation, control, and improvement are purposes that require a reasonably accurate model that represents a true understanding of the object or quality we are modeling, else we are encountering risk.

The **focus** represents the specific aspect or attribute of the object of study that we are interested in. The focus implies the type of underlying model that is needed to guide the analysis of the measurement data. The author may choose more than one model, e.g., both defects and changes in a software system might be relevant, but have different models describing them.

The **stakeholder** is the party wanting the information. The stakeholder's point of view determines such things as when the information should be available, its level of granularity, its acceptable accuracy, etc. Taking the stakeholder needs into account helps the author pick the appropriate models. The author should put himself/herself in the mindset of the stakeholder so that all aspects of the analysis are performed from that point of view.

The **environment** aspect of a goal defines the context of the study by describing all aspects of the project so it can be categorized correctly and the appropriate set of similar projects can be found as a basis of comparison. Types of factors include: process factors, people factors, problem factors, methods, tools, constraints, etc. (Basili 1981). In general, the environment should include all those factors that may be common among similar projects and become part of the database for future comparisons. Thus, the environmental factors, rather than the values associated with these factors, should be consistent across several goals within the project and the organization. Some factors may have already been specified as part of the particular object or model under study and thus appear there in greater depth and granularity.

The set of variables in the template is integrally related. We typically start with the object of study and decide on the focus. This combination generates the requirements for a model. A potential set of models may already exist, e.g., there are several models that deal with the reliability (focus) of a product (object), or we may need to create one from scratch, e.g., for the effectiveness (focus) of a technique like reading (object). Our model selection is limited by its purpose. For example, if the purpose is to characterize the object, then all that is required is a set of models of the focuses of interest, e.g., size or number of defects or the product. If the reason is to evaluate the object with respect to a certain focus, then an evaluative model must be chosen along with an evaluation algorithm. The model will likely involve a comparison of the current state with past states of similar objects, e.g., fewer defects produced in the final product than usual when applying a particular technique. The selection of the model is greatly influenced by the stakeholder's needs. For example, if the stakeholder is the project manager, requiring immediate feedback, a model offering less accurate information might be acceptable. If the stakeholder is the corporation trying to decide if a new process is cost- and quality-effective so that it can be applied throughout the corporation, then a model that is more accurate and offers a longitudinal study over several projects would be appropriate. And clearly the context variables both limit the model and provide input to the model selected.

The simplest goals are characterizing goals. Examples include: *Analyze a set of software products in order to characterize them with respect to development error rates, cost in staff months, % of code reused from the point of view of the organization relative to the environment in which the software products are developed.*

5.3.5.2 Generating Questions

Guidelines exist for generating questions, models, and measures for various sets of objects of study. For example, if the object of study is a process, then we need to define the process and isolate the measurable aspects of the process. We need a definition of the focus or quality perspective of interest and a mechanism that allows us to interpret the result of applying the model to the object of study. This interpretation model can serve as a visualization or descriptive model of the results of the measurement for a characterization goal, an evaluation model judging whether the goal has been achieved, or a predictive model for estimating the entity of interest.

If the object of study is a product or set of products, as in the example above, we would expect to see a definition or characterization of the product or product set, a definition of the focus or quality perspective of interest, and an interpretation model that allows us to visualize, evaluate, predict, or control. These steps are easy for a characterization goal.

If the model chosen has a set of assumptions, then those assumptions should be checked for the particular environment. The checking of the assumptions can be part of the interpretation model. If the model is questionable, then a second model might be applied to help evaluate the relevance of the original model for the environment. If there are concerns about the accuracy or validity of the data collected, then the validity of the data should be checked.

5.3.5.3 Specifying the Metrics

The metrics are typically directly defined by the questions. The questions specify what metrics are required to answer the questions and the metrics in turn define what data needs to be collected. Sometimes the metrics are simply the data collected itself, e.g., number of lines of code as a metric for size, and sometimes they are combinations of sets of data, e.g., defects per line of code as a metric for defect density. Each question might require several metrics in combination as an answer. These are the metrics needed to build and interpret the model.

Abstraction Sheets

To help elicit and provide a clearer picture of a GQM goal, to help identify models for the perspective of interest and formulate questions, we can use a GQM abstraction sheet as proposed by Gresse et al. (1995) and Briand et al. (1996). The abstraction sheet helps elicit and structure information and assists in constructing, refining, and reviewing GQM goals, questions, and metrics. It also helps reveal dependencies between questions. There are four quadrants to an abstraction sheet:

1. Quality focus: What are the possible metrics for measuring the focus of the object of interest according to the project members? This provides some insights into the model that should be used and helps lay out the questions that are necessary to apply the model.
2. Baseline hypothesis: What is the project members' current knowledge with respect to these metrics? Their beliefs are documented as "baseline hypotheses"

Object	Purpose	Quality focus	Viewpoint	Context
Delivered product	Understanding	Reliability	Project team	A specific company producing shrink wrapped software

Quality focus (Questions and metrics)	Variation factors
Number of failures ▪ By severity ▪ Number of faults	Level of reviewing

Baseline hypotheses	Impact on baseline hypotheses
Distribution of failures by severity ▪ Minor 60 % ▪ Major 30 % ▪ Fatal 10 %	The higher the level of code review, the fewer minor failures will be detected after release

Fig. 5.4 Example: abstraction sheet for measuring top-level business goal

of the metrics. This may be available from actual data on past projects or it may represent some form of expert opinion, i.e., assumptions of what might be true.

3. Variation factors: Which context factors does a project member expect to be of influence on the metrics? This provides insights into what other information is important for understanding the baseline hypotheses.

4. Impact on baseline hypothesis: How could these variation factors influence the actual measurements? What kind of dependencies between the metrics and influencing factors are assumed? This provides insights into what other data are needed for interpreting the model and the metrics.

So, for a goal like: "*Analyze the product for the purpose of understanding the reliability from the point of view of the project team,*" we might fill out the abstraction sheet presented in Fig. 5.4. For a measure of the quality focus we suggest considering the number of failures. These can be further differentiated by severity, i.e., only examining the most severe failures. Based upon experience and intuition, the baseline hypothesis might be that the distribution of failures by severity level is 60 % minor, 30 % major, and 10 % fatal. The major factor that would influence this distribution might be selected as the level of inspection and review of the code, with the impact that more reviewing results in fewer minor failures detected after release.

5.4 Review and Adjust Grid

After we complete the GQM⁺Strategies grid, we review it individually and discuss potential findings in a group meeting. We recommend inviting to the meeting people who were not involved in the grid development but who are affected by the content of the grid (e.g., in that they will be involved in realizing strategies defined in the grid). During the review meeting, the coordinator of the

GQM⁺Strategies application walks though the grid and explains its elements to the other participants, who may ask questions. The review should focus on the completeness and consistency of the grid. The meeting participants should check whether the linkages between the goals and strategies are logical and whether the grid elements are supported by sufficient rationale (in particular, whether the documented assumptions are realistic). Issues that are identified during the session are immediately discussed and their resolution is planned; some issues might be addressed right away by adjusting the grid appropriately, whereas other issues may require additional work after the meeting (e.g., repeating some steps of the grid development procedure).

5.5 Example

Company X developed their GQM⁺Strategies grid in a series of workshops, which involved the method experts and representatives of business units from the scope of the method application. Experts moderated the workshops and facilitated grid development, whereas company representatives specified and discussed the elements of the grid.

5.5.1 Identify Existing Assets

The building of the GQM⁺Strategies grid at Company X started with a joint workshop aimed at identifying existing assets. At the beginning of the workshop meeting, the experts explained the goals and the organization of the workshop. The participants then performed a brainstorming session in which they identified the goals, strategies, and metrics already defined in Company X according to their knowledge, either explicitly or implicitly. For example, some metrics are defined explicitly in a systematic measurement program, or implicitly through the data collected in the Customer Relationship Management and Bug Tracking Systems. There are some goals and strategies already in existence.

5.5.2 Select Relevant Assets

Next, the workshop participants reviewed the set of previously identified assets and selected the relevant ones according to the defined scope. For Company X, the participants selected the top-level organizational goals from which they would start modeling the GQM⁺Strategies grid. After deciding on the most relevant top-level organizational goals, the participants selected the associated assets (e.g., goal, strategies, and metrics) and tried to sort and link them to each other in a structured way. On the one hand, they looked for relationships between goals and strategies, and for the underlying rationales (context and assumptions). On the other hand, they

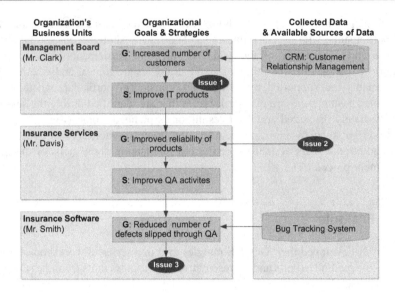

Fig. 5.5 Example: results from selecting relevant assets

captured metrics that had already been defined in Company X. Figure 5.5 illustrates an example result of the relevant assets.

After agreeing upon a set of existing assets that are relevant with respect to the scope of the planned GQM$^+$Strategies application, Mr. Clark, Mr. Davis, and Mr. Smith perform an analysis of the possible relationships and issues (see Fig. 5.5). With respect to the linkage between measurement data and organizational goals, the CRM system can support them in evaluating the number of customers in their different business areas, and their bug-tracking system can support them in evaluating defect slippage through their different QA stages. However, (*Issue 2*) measurement data is missing for quantitatively evaluating the attainment of the goal defined by insurance services ("Improved reliability of products"). The main idea for increasing the number of customers was to deliver better IT products in terms of their reliability. However, (*Issue 1*) the rationale for this strategy is not clear. Moreover, it is not clear whether this strategy is sufficient for increasing the number of customers or whether other strategies should be considered. Mr. Clark and Mr. Davis agree that additional strategies might be necessary. In order to improve the reliability of their products, the Insurance Services business unit might have to improve their QA activities, implying that the Software Development group might have to reduce the number of defects slipping through software quality assurance. The issue (*Issue 3*) to be solved by Mr. Smith is to select an appropriate strategy because the current software development approach is missing a strategy for reducing defect slippage. All the issues identified during this step (see Table 5.4 for an overview) will have to be resolved later on, when modeling the comprehensive GQM$^+$Strategies grid.

Table 5.4 Example: issues in initial set of existing assets

Issue	Description
Issue 1	The rationale for the strategy is not clear. It is not sure that improving insurance products is a sufficient strategy for getting more customers in the insurance area
Issue 2	It is not clear whether or not data is available for evaluating reliability on the customer's side
Issue 3	It is not clear what strategies should be performed to decrease the number of defects slipped

5.5.3   Build Up GQM⁺Strategies Grid (Management Board)

After identifying and selecting relevant assets, a series of workshops were devoted to developing a complete GQM⁺Strategies grid. For this purpose, the experts took the top-down approach in which they started with top-level organizational goals of the management board and went "down" through the organizational structure, defining associated strategies, goals, and GQM graphs at lower-level units in the organizational structure.

5.5.3.1 Elicit Context and Assumptions

The workshop sessions started with the definition of general context characteristics. The participants agreed on a few generic characteristics of Company X that determine the company's goals and strategies. These context factors were defined under the label **CA1** and included the following:

- Company X provides banking and insurance services to their customers.
- X directly sells services via the Internet without local sales agents.
- X has a lot of customers in the banking area, but only few in the insurance area.

5.5.3.2 Define Organizational Goals

Representatives of the company's management board decided to start with a single top-level business goal of increasing the number of customers in the insurance business area. The asset analysis shows that this was already an existing goal and therefore was important to the organization. Table 5.5 documents the formalization of the goal.

5.5.3.3 Define GQM Graphs

The top-level organizational goal was then quantified using the GQM approach. First, the experts defined an appropriate measurement goal. For this purpose, they used information that had already been specified while formalizing the organizational goal. Figure 5.6 illustrates the synergies between the specification of the organizational goal and the measurement goal.

Table 5.5 Example: formalization of the NC-G goal of the management board

NC-G: Increased number of customers in the insurance business area	
Object	Customers in insurance area
Focus	The number
Magnitude	10 % or more
Time frame	By the end of next fiscal year
Organizational scope	Management board
Constraints	While maintaining cost
Relationships	–

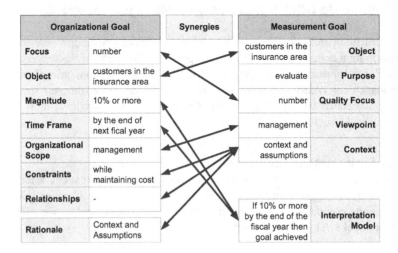

Fig. 5.6 Example: deriving the measurement goal from the organizational goal

For the measurement goal, appropriate metrics were defined using the classical GQM approach: The workshop participants asked relevant questions with respect to the measurement goal and defined metrics that provided data to answer those questions. In order to elicit more information about the GQM measurement goals, the experts used an abstraction sheet where they documented the baseline hypotheses with respect to the organizational goal and model for interpreting the measurement data. Figure 5.7 documents the GQM graph for the top-level organizational goal. The organizational goal was measured directly in terms of the number of customers in a given year. For the GQM⁺Strategies approach, the classical abstraction sheets were extended for evaluations by adding an interpretation model. This model specified a state that is desired so that the underlying organizational goal can be considered as having been attained based on the metrics defined in the quality focus and variation factor areas. So in Fig. 5.7, NC-G-I represents the interpretation model for NC-G.

The baseline hypothesis was that in fiscal year 2011, the insurance area had 5,000 customers. Consequently, in order to achieve the top-level organizational

Object	Purpose	Quality focus	Viewpoint	Context
Customers in insurance area	Evaluate	Increased number of customers by 10 % by the end of the next fiscal year	Management	CA1

Quality focus (Questions and metrics)			Variation factors
NC-G-Q1: What is the increase in the number of customers in a particular fiscal year? ▪ Cus(Y): Number of customers in year Y (e.g., in the next fiscal year 2012)			–

Baseline hypotheses	Impact on baseline hypotheses
Cus(2011) = 5000	–

Interpretation models
NC-G-I: Cus(2012) / Cus(2011) ≥ 1.1

Fig. 5.7 Example: abstraction sheet for measuring goal NC-G

goal, this number must increase by at least 10 % to 5,500 or more customers in the next fiscal year 2012, that is, goal NC-G is achieved if $Cus(2012)/Cus(2011) \geq 1.1$. Figure 5.8 presents an example visualization associated with the measurement of the top-level organizational goal.

It should be noted that if the goal is not met, we need to understand why and what needs to be changed to make the goal achievable. This involves examining whether the various subgoals were achieved and if not, why not. We have to analyze such things as the strategies (not effective?), the subgoal magnitudes (too high or too low?), and the assumptions so that we can fix the problem in real time, if possible. We will deal with this more specifically when we discuss the subgoals.

5.5.3.4 Make Strategy Decisions

After specifying the top-level goal of the management board, the participants looked for effective strategies for achieving the goal. Typically, a number of alternative strategies can be implemented to achieve the same goal. In order to select the most effective, feasible strategy, the context of the particular organization (its internal and external constraints and capabilities) should be considered. For this reason, the workshop participants started by considering relevant context factors and assumptions. After a brief brainstorming, they came up with one context factor that should be kept in mind when looking for potential strategies to achieve the top-level organizational goal:

- **Context CA4**: The services of Company X are built upon an enterprise information system (IS) that is composed of different software components (of which 60 % were developed in-house by the company's Software Development group).

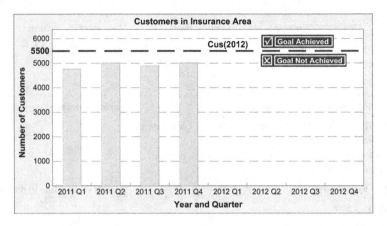

Fig. 5.8 Example: interpretation model of goal NC-G

One of the consequences of context factor CA4 is that Company X potentially has the ability to adjust their enterprise information system (because they developed most of it in-house). Having this fact in mind, the workshop participants discussed potential strategies for increasing the number of customers in the insurance area by 10 % or more. In the end, they identified three strategies:

- **Strategy NC-S1**: Improve the IT products (that support insurance services)
- **Strategy NC-S2**: Improve customer interaction processes
- **Strategy NC-S3**: Intensify marketing

Since implementing all identified strategies would be too expensive and was not deemed necessary for achieving the top-level goal, the participants had to decide on a subset of strategies. For this purpose, the participants considered further aspects of the Company's context, in addition to context factor CA4. In order to decide on the most promising, yet still feasible, strategies, the participants made two assumptions:

- **Assumption CA2**: To get more customers in the insurance area, the quality of the IT products has to be improved.
- **Assumption CA3**: To get more customers in the insurance area, the quality of the customer interaction processes has to be improved.

Based on these assumptions, strategies NC-S1 and NC-S2 were chosen to increase the number of customers in the insurance area by 10 % (i.e., in order to achieve the goal of the management board) (Fig. 5.9).

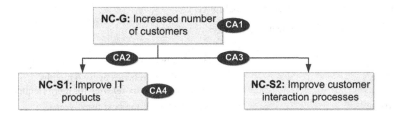

Fig. 5.9 Example: grid excerpts related to the management board

5.5.4   Build Up GQM⁺Strategies Grid (Insurance Services)

In the next iteration, goals and strategies related to the Insurance Services business unit were defined and aligned with the goals of the management board. For each strategy defined at the management board, its implications with respect to the Insurance Services business units were elicited.

5.5.4.1 Elicit Context and Assumptions
Before deciding on appropriate goals for improving IT support and customer interaction processes for insurance services, several context factors and assumptions need to be considered based on information from the help desk.

- **Context CA5**: Customers complain that it takes too long to deliver new features (react to the market) and to fix existing bugs.
- **Context CA6**: Customers complain that the IT products they have to deal with are not reliable.
- **Context CA7**: Customers complain about many issues related to the customer interaction process (such as inconsistent communication, mistakes in customer profiles, etc.).

5.5.4.2 Define Organizational Goals
Based on the specified context, the Insurance Service business unit defined three goals. In order to address improvement of the IT products (NC-S1), two goals were defined:

- **Goal FF-G**: Faster delivery of new features and fixes
- **Goal PR-G**: Improved reliability of products

In order to address the goal of improving customer interaction processes, one goal was defined:

- **Goal CI-G**: Improved customer interaction processes

Tables 5.6, 5.7, and 5.8 document the organizational goals defined for the Insurance Services business unit.

Table 5.6 Example: formalization of goal FF-G

FF-G: Faster delivery of new features and fixes	
Object	Enterprise IS
Focus	Time to deliver new features and bug fixes
Magnitude	Regular feature releases every 6 months and monthly bug fix releases (or more frequently)
Time frame	By the middle of the next fiscal year
Organizational scope	Management of the insurance services business unit
Constraints	While maintaining cost
Relationships	–

Table 5.7 Example: formalization of goal PR-G

PR-G: Improved reliability of products	
Object	IT products
Focus	Reliability
Magnitude	20 % fewer customer complaints
Time frame	By the middle of the next fiscal year
Organizational scope	Management of insurance services business unit
Constraints	While maintaining cost
Relationships	–

Table 5.8 Example: formalization of goal CI-G

CI-G: Improved customer interaction processes	
Object	Customer interaction processes
Focus	Quality
Magnitude	By having 20 % fewer customer complaints
Time frame	By the middle of the next fiscal year
Organizational scope	Management of insurance services business unit
Constraints	While maintaining cost
Relationships	–

5.5.4.3 Define GQM Graphs

In the next step of grid development, the goals for the Insurance Services business unit were made measurable by specifying appropriate GQM questions, abstraction sheets, and interpretation models.

G-FF: Faster Delivery of New Features and Fixes

For this goal, two relevant questions were defined, asking about the number of feature releases (F_Rel) and the number of bug-fix releases (BF_Rel) in the considered time span (T). Figure 5.10 presents an abstraction sheet for evaluating the decrease in time for delivering new features and bug fixes (i.e., for evaluating attainment of goal FF-G).

Object	Purpose	Quality focus	Viewpoint	Context
Enterprise IS	Evaluate	Time for delivering new features and bug fixes	Management of Insurance Services business unit	CA5-CA7

Quality focus (Questions and metrics)	Variation factors
FF-G-Q1: How many feature releases have been created in the first half of the fiscal year? ▪ **F_Rel(T)**: Number of feature releases in time span T (e.g., half a year) **FF-G-Q2**: How many bug fix releases have been created in the first half of the fiscal year? ▪ **BF_Rel(T)**: Number of bug fix releases in time span T (e.g., half a year)	–

Baseline hypotheses	Impact on baseline hypotheses
F_Rel(2011H2) = 1 BF_Rel(2011H2) = 5	–

Interpretation models
FF-G-I: F_Rel(2012H1) $\geq$ 1 AND BF_Rel(2012H1) $\geq$ 6

Fig. 5.10   Example: abstraction sheet for measuring goal FF-G

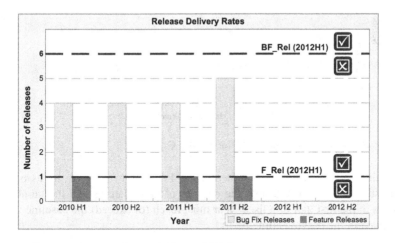

Fig. 5.11   Example: interpretation model for goal FF-G

In the text that follows, we use a special notation expressing the first and second half of a year, e.g., 2012H1 means the first half of year 2012 and 2012H2 means the second half.

In order to collect appropriate data for answering the measurement questions, two corresponding metrics were defined. Figure 5.11 illustrates a simple model for

Object	Purpose	Quality focus	Viewpoint	Context
IT products	Evaluate	Reliability	Management of Insurance Services business unit	CA5-CA7

Quality focus (Questions and metrics)	Variation factors
PR-G-Q1: How many customer complaints exist regarding product reliability? • **CC_PR(T)**: Number of complaints about product reliability in time span T (e.g., half a year)	–

Baseline hypotheses	Impact on baseline hypotheses
CC_PR(2011H2) = 1500	–

Interpretation models
PR-G-I: CC_RP(2012H1)/CC_RP(2011H2) ≤ 0.8

Fig. 5.12 Example: abstraction sheet for measuring goal PR-G

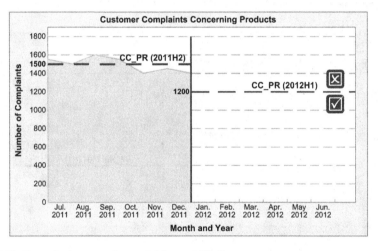

Fig. 5.13 Example: interpretation model for goal PR-G

interpreting the resulting measurement data. In order to achieve the associated organizational goal (FF-G), both the number of new features and the number of bug fixes in the first half of a fiscal year must reach (or exceed) the baseline values determined in the previous time period.

PR-G: Improved Reliability of Products

For this goal, one relevant question we can ask is about the number of customer complaints regarding product reliability. Figure 5.12 presents an abstraction sheet for evaluating the improvement of the reliability of products (i.e., for evaluating attainment of goal PR-G).

In order to collect appropriate data for answering the measurement questions, one corresponding metric was defined. Figure 5.13 illustrates a simple model for

Object	Purpose	Quality focus	Viewpoint	Context
Customer interaction processes	Evaluate	Quality	Management of Insurance Services business unit	CA5-CA7
Quality focus (Questions and metrics)			**Variation factors**	
CI-G-Q1: How many customer complaints exist regarding the interaction processes? ▪ **CC_IP(T)**: Number of complaints about the interaction processes in time span T (e.g., half a year)			–	
Baseline hypotheses			**Impact on baseline hypotheses**	
CC_IP(2011H2) = 700			–	
Interpretation models				
CI-G-I: CC_IP(2012H1)/CC_IP(2011H2) ≤ 0.8				

Fig. 5.14 Example: abstraction sheet for measuring goal CI-G

interpreting the resulting measurement data. In order to achieve the associated organizational goal (PR-G), the number of customer complaints during the first half of the year 2012 must be reduced by 20 % or more compared to the second half of the year 2011; this means a reduction from 1,500 complaints to 1,200 complaints or less.

G-CI: Improved Customer Interaction Processes

For this goal, one relevant question we can ask is about the number of customer complaints with respect to the integration process with Company X. Figure 5.14 presents an abstraction sheet for evaluating the improvement of the customer interaction processes by means of a deceased number of corresponding customer complaints (i.e., for evaluating attainment of goal CI-G).

In order to collect appropriate data for answering the measurement question, a corresponding metric was defined. Figure 5.15 illustrates a simple model for interpreting the resulting measurement data. In order to achieve the associated organizational goal (G-CI), the number of customer complaints in the first half of the year 2012 must be reduced by 20 % or more compared to the second half of the year 2011; this means a reduction from 700 to 560 complaints or less.

5.5.4.4 Make Strategy Decisions

After specifying goals for the Insurance Services business unit, the participants looked for effective strategies for achieving these goals. After a brief brainstorming session, Company X came up with the following:

- **Assumption CA8**: The delay of software development and IT projects is mainly responsible for not being able to deliver new features and bug fixes faster.
- **Context CA9**: Customers complain about inconsistent and incomplete information during their interaction with Company X.

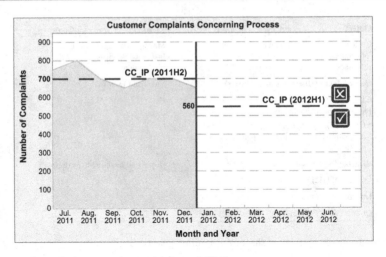

Fig. 5.15 Example: interpretation model for goal CI-G

Having these aspects in mind, the workshop participants discussed potential strategies for achieving the goals based on the following strategies:

- **Strategy FF-S**: Increase the productivity of development projects (to achieve goal FF-G of delivering new features and bug fixes faster)
- **Strategy PR-S**: Improve QA activities (to achieve goal PR-G of reducing customer complaints regarding product reliability)
- **Strategy CI-S**: Provide more complete and consistent information (to achieve goal CI-G regarding customer interaction processes)

Company X decides to follow all three strategies and to use only one strategy per goal. Figure 5.16 illustrates the first two levels of the grid developed until this point.

Table 5.9 specifies example relationships regarding the attainment or nonattainment of a goal of a specific organizational unit. For instance, achieving all goals of the Insurance Services business unit (FF-G, PR-G, and CI-G) but not achieving the goal of the management board (NC-G) would indicate that the two strategies (NC-S1, NC-S2) defined for achieving the top-level goal were not sufficient or not effective. One potential reason for this might be that the strategies were based on wrong assumptions. On the other hand, achieving the goal of the management board even though one or more goals of the Insurance Services business unit were not achieved would indicate that the strategies were not necessary (or at least their scope was too broad) or that the magnitude of one or more goals of the Insurance Services business unit was higher than necessary.

Alternatively, the interpretation of goal attainment can be represented in text form—as a set of *If-Then-Else* conditional statements. Table 5.10 illustrates the alternative interpretation for evaluating the attainment of the organizational goals at Company X.

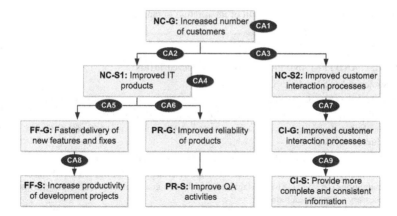

Fig. 5.16 Example: grid excerpts related to the management board and the Insurance Services business unit

Table 5.9 Example: interpretation of goals related to the management board and the Insurance Services business unit

Organizational Goals				Potential cause and possible solutions
NC-G	FF-G	PR-G	CI-G	
1	1	1	1	• Strategies NC-S1 and NS-S2 were successful
1	0	0	0	• Strategies NC-S1 and NS-S2 were not necessary • Magnitudes of FF-G, PR-G, and CI-G were higher than necessary (check magnitudes) • Check why (root causes) NC-G was achieved anyway
1	Any of goals = 0			• All strategies (NC-S1 and NC-S2) were not necessary • The scope of the strategies was too broad • Magnitudes of the sub-goals not achieved were higher than necessary (check magnitudes)
0	0	0	0	• Enforce strategies • Question all assumptions and check context factors
0	1	1	1	• Strategies NC-S1 and NC-S2 not sufficient (or not effective) • Assumptions CA2 and CA3 wrong • Magnitudes of one or more sub-goals FF-G, PR-G, and CI-G were not high enough
0	One or more sub-goals = 0			• Other/alternative strategies are necessary • Magnitudes of the achieved sub-goals were not high enough

0 – goal achieved, 1 – goals not achieved

Table 5.10 Example: alternative form of interpreting organizational goals

IF Cus(2012) / Cus(2011) ≥ 1.1 **THEN** <u>NC-G achieved</u>
IF (NC-G **AND** FF-G **AND** PR-G **AND** CI-G) achieved **THEN** Strategies NC-S1 and NC-S2 were successful. **ELSE IF** NC-G achieved **AND** (FF-G **AND** PR-G **AND** CI-G) **not** achieved **THEN** Strategies NC-S1 and NS-S2 were not necessary **or** Magnitudes of FF-G, PR-G, and CI-G were higher than necessary (check magnitudes) → Check why (root causes) NC-G was achieved anyway **ELSE IF** NC-G achieved **AND** (FF-G **OR** PR-G **OR** CI-G) **not** achieved **THEN** Both strategies were not necessary **or** the scope of strategy NC-S2 was too broad (check assumptions CA5 and CA6) **or** Magnitudes of the sub-goals not achieved were higher than necessary (check magnitudes).
IF Cus(2012) / Cus(2011) < 1.1 **THEN** <u>NC-G **not** achieved</u>
IF (NC-G **AND** FF-G **AND** PR-G **AND** CI-G) **not** achieved **THEN** Strategies NC-S1 and NC-S1 need to be enforced. **ELSE IF** NC-G **not** achieved **AND** (FF-G **AND** PR-G **AND** CI-G) achieved **THEN** Strategies NC-S1 and NC-S2 not sufficient (or not effective) **or** Assumptions CA2 and CA3 wrong **or** Magnitudes of sub-goals FF-G, PR-G, or CI-G were not high enough **ELSE IF** NC-G **not** achieved **AND** (FF-G **OR** PR-G **OR** CI-G) **not** achieved **THEN** Other/alternative strategies are necessary **or** magnitudes for the achieved sub-goals were not high enough.

5.5.5   Build Up GQM⁺Strategies Grid (Software Development Group)

In the next iteration, goals and strategies related to the Software Development group of Company X were defined and aligned to the other units. For each strategy defined by the Insurance Services business unit, its implications with respect to the Software Development group were elicited.

5.5.5.1 Elicit Context and Assumptions

Before deciding on appropriate software support goals, relevant representatives of the Software Development group considered several context factors and assumptions:

- **Context CA10**: Many software defects injected in early phases of software development slip to the customer.
- **Context CA11**: The existing information system does not ensure the exchange of consistent and complete information with the customers.

Table 5.11 Example: deriving goals for the Software Development group

Strategies of Insurance Services business unit	Goals of Software Development group
Strategy FF-S: Increase productivity of development projects	**Goal PP-G**: Increased productivity of development projects
Strategy PR-S: Improve QA activities	**Goal DS-G**: Decreased number of defects slipped
Strategy CI-S: Provide more complete and consistent information	**Goal IQ-G**: Improved information quality of IS

Table 5.12 Example: formalization of goal PP-G

PP-G: Increased productivity of development projects	
Object	Software maintenance and new development projects
Focus	Productivity
Magnitude	10 % increase (in terms of the amount of functionality delivered per person-hour)
Time frame	By the middle of the next fiscal year
Organizational scope	Management of software development group
Constraints	While maintaining the quality and functionality of the software
Relationships	Supported by "DS-G: Decrease defects slipped" less slippage → less rework effort → more effective work → higher productivity

Table 5.13 Example: formalization of goal DS-G

DS-G: Decrease number of defects slipped	
Object	QA activities (verification and validation)
Focus	Percentage of defects slipped
Magnitude	Decrease by 10 % per QA stage
Time frame	By the middle of the next fiscal year
Organizational scope	Management of software development group
Constraints	–
Relationships	Supports goal "PP-G: Increase productivity of development projects" less slippage → less rework effort → more effort of work → higher productivity

5.5.5.2 Define Organizational Goals

With the identified context factors and assumptions in mind, the workshop participants identified potential improvement goals. Table 5.11 summarizes the defined strategies of the Insurance Services business unit and corresponding goals derived for the Software Development group.

After considering feasibility, costs, and benefits, Company X decided to select all three goals defined for the software development unit. Tables 5.12, 5.13,

Table 5.14 Example: formalization of goal IQ-G

IQ-G: Improved information quality of IS	
Object	Enterprise IS
Focus	Information quality
Magnitude	Providing 20 % more complete and 10 % more consistent information
Time frame	By the middle of the next fiscal year
Organizational scope	Management of software development group
Constraints	–
Relationships	–

and 5.14 document the goals defined for the Software Development group of Company X.

5.5.5.3 Define GQM Graphs

In the next step of the grid development, the goals defined for the Software Development group were made measurable by specifying appropriate GQM abstraction sheets and interpretation models.

PP-G: Increased Productivity of Development Projects

For this goal, one relevant question was defined regarding development productivity. It asks about the average amount of functionality (in terms of function points count) delivered per person-hour of effort in the specified time span (T). Moreover, the workshop participants identified several variation factors that may influence development productivity. These factors encompass such aspects of the software development project as project type, programming language, or age of the software application (in the case of a maintenance or enhancement type of project). Figure 5.17 presents an abstraction sheet for evaluating the decrease in time for delivering new features and bug fixes (i.e., for evaluating attainment of goal PP-G).

In order to collect appropriate data for answering the measurement question, an appropriate productivity metric was defined. To evaluate goal attainment, we defined a simple interpretation model based on the median value of productivity. However, since the decision makers might also be interested in the distribution of the productivity value, in particular boundary values, the abstraction sheet defines a few more measures, such as lower and upper quartiles or minimum and maximum values. Using these values, we can visualize the distribution of productivity using box plots. Figure 5.18 illustrates the box plots that were used for interpreting the resulting productivity measurement data. In order to achieve the associated organizational goal (PP-G), the median productivity in the second half of a fiscal year must increase by 10 % (or more) compared to baseline values measured in the first half of a fiscal year. In addition to comparing the central tendency of productivity, the decision maker might want to look at the complete distribution of productivity. It can, for example, happen that although median productivity decreased by the required amount (10 %), the variance or extreme values of productivity increased. In such a case, the decision maker may want to adjust the interpretation model in the

Object	Purpose	Quality focus	Viewpoint	Context
Software maintenance and new development projects	Evaluate	Productivity	Management of Software Development group	CA8

Quality focus (Questions and metrics)	Variation factors
Per development project: **PP-G-Q1**: What is the productivity P per project? ▪ **FP**: Number of IPUG function points ▪ **PH**: Effort in person-hours of direct project effort ▪ **P** = FP / PH Across all development projects: **PP-G-Q2**: What is the distribution of productivity across projects finished in time span T (e.g., within the previous half year)? ▪ **P_Min(T)**: Minimum of P values for projects in T ▪ **P_Max(T)**: Maximum of P values for projects in T ▪ **P_Q1(T)**: Lower quartile of P values for projects in T ▪ **P_Q2(T)**: Median of P values for projects in T ▪ **P_Q3(T)**: Upper quartile of P values for projects in T	Per development project: ▪ **PP-G-VF1**: Project type (new development, maintenance, integration) ▪ **PP-G-VF2**: Implementation language (C#, Java, PHP, others) ▪ **PP-G-VF3**: Development approach (plan-based, agile) ▪ **PP-G-VF4**: How old is the application? (#years)

Baseline hypotheses	Impact on baseline hypotheses
P_Q2(2011H2) = 0.25	Not defined yet

Interpretation models
PP-G-I: P_Q2(2012H1)/P_Q2(2011H2) ≥ 1.1

Fig. 5.17 Example: abstraction sheet for measuring goal PP-G

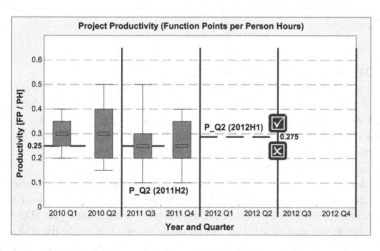

Fig. 5.18 Example: interpretation model for goal PP-G

Object	Purpose	Quality focus	Viewpoint	Context
QA activities (V&V)	Evaluate	Percentage of defects slipped	Management of IT department	CA10
Quality focus (Questions and metrics)			**Variation factors**	
Per development project: **DS-G-Q1**: What percentage of defects has slipped from phase P? ▪ **DD(P)**: Total # defects detected in phase P ▪ **DI(P)**: Total # defects injected in phase P ▪ **DS(P)**: Total # defects slipped from phase P = DI(P) - DD(P) ▪ **DSR(P)**: Ratio of defects slipped from phase P = DS(P) / DI(P) **DS-G-Q2**: What is the average slippage across all phases? ▪ **DSR_AVG** = Average of DSR(P) for all phases P Across all development projects: **DS-G-Q3**: What is the average slippage across all projects? ▪ **DSR_AVG(T)**: Average slippage for all projects finished in time span T (e.g., half a year)			Per development project: ▪ **DS-G-VF1**: Project type (new development, maintenance, integration) ▪ **DS-G-VF2**: Development approach (plan-based, agile) ▪ **DS-G-VF3**: How old is the application? (#years)	
Baseline hypotheses			**Impact on baseline hypotheses**	
DSR_AVG(2011H2) = 80			Not defined yet	
Interpretation models				
DSR_AVG(2012H1)/DSR_AVG(2011H2) ≤ 0.9				

Fig. 5.19 Example: abstraction sheet for measuring goal DS-G

future by considering other parameters of productivity distribution in addition to the simple median.

DS-G: Decreased Number of Defects Slipped

For this goal, several relevant questions were defined asking about the flow of defects through development phases and the percentage of defects that slipped through each individual phase. Moreover, the workshop participants identified selected variation factors that may influence defect slippage. Figure 5.19 presents an abstraction sheet for evaluating the decrease of defect slippage (i.e., for evaluating attainment of goal DS-G).

In order to collect appropriate data for answering the measurement questions, appropriate metrics were defined. Figure 5.20 illustrates a description of what is being measured. In order to achieve the associated organizational goal (DS-G), the average defect slippage ratio (DSR_AVG) in the second half of the fiscal year must be reduced by 10 % (or more) compared to the ratio in the first half of the fiscal year. So in the example in Fig. 5.20 the value of DSR should be less than or equal to 77.4 % (i.e., 86 % reduced by 10 %).

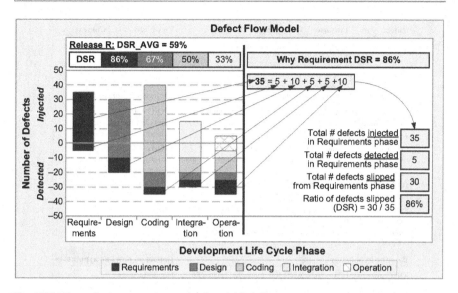

Fig. 5.20 Example: interpretation model for goal DS-G

IQ-G: Improved Information Quality of IS

For this goal, two relevant questions were defined asking about the completeness and consistency of information in the Enterprise Information System. Moreover, the workshop participants identified variation factors that may influence the quality of the information in the Enterprise IS. Figure 5.21 presents an abstraction sheet for evaluating the improvement of the information quality in the Enterprise IS (i.e., for evaluating attainment of goal IQ-G).

In order to collect appropriate data for answering the measurement questions, two corresponding information quality indices were defined. Figure 5.22 illustrates a simple model for interpreting the resulting measurement data. In order to achieve the associated organizational goal (IQ-G), the information completeness index and the information consistency index in the second half of a fiscal year must increase by at least 20 % and 10 %, respectively, compared to the first half of a fiscal year.

In order to properly interpret the information quality index (IQI) data, we define two variation factors: the percentage of information units in the Enterprise Information System that were assessed regarding IQI (i.e., which IQI data was considered) and the overall number of information units in the Enterprise Information System. The first factor (IQ-G-V1) gives us a measure of the sample size and allows us to evaluate the credibility of the IQI data. For example, let us consider information quality measured in two time spans: IQI(T1) = 90 % and IQI(T2) = 50 %. At first glance we may conclude that information quality has decreased dramatically. If we consider that in time span T1, the sample size was 20 %, whereas in time span T2, the sample size was 70 %, we may conclude that the IQI values for T1 and T2 are not directly comparable because they refer to quite different sample sizes and possibly scopes. So the high information quality observed in T1 may have been due

Object	Purpose	Quality focus	Viewpoint	Context
Enterprise IS	Evaluate	Information quality	Management of Software Development group	CA9, CA11

Quality focus (Questions and metrics)	Variation factors
IQ-G-Q1: What is the completeness of the information in the Enterprise IS? ▪ **IQI_Comp(T)**: Information quality index (IQI) for completeness in time span T (e.g., half a year) = # of complaints identified as completeness problems in time span T. **IQ-G-Q2**: What is the consistency of the information in the Enterprise IS? ▪ **IQI_Cons(T)**: Information quality index (IQI) for consistency in time span T (e.g., half a year) = # of complaints identified as consistency problems in time span T	▪ **IQ-G-V1**: % of information units in Enterprise IS classified by the IQI ▪ **IQ-G-V2**: Overall number of information units in Enterprise IS

Baseline hypotheses	Impact on baseline hypotheses
IQI_Comp(2011H2) = 70 % AND IQI_Cons(2011H2) = 80 %,	Not defined yet

Interpretation models
IQ-G-I: IQI_Comp(2012H1)/IQI_Comp(2011H2) ≥ 1.2 AND   IQI_Cons(2012H1)/IQI_Cons(2011H2) ≥ 1.1

Fig. 5.21 Example: abstraction sheet for measuring goal IQ-G

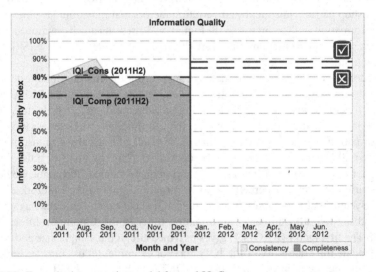

Fig. 5.22 Example: interpretation model for goal IQ-G

to the limited sample size. The second variation factor (V1-G-IQ) helps us understand why small sample sizes might have been selected.

Table 5.15 Example: deriving strategies for the Software Development group

Goals of Software Development group	Strategies of Software Development group
Goal PP-G: Increased productivity of development projects	**Strategy PP-S**: Introduce agile development[a]
Goal DS-G: Decrease number of defects slipped	**Strategy DS-S**: Introduce inspections after requirements specification
Goal IQ-G: Improved information quality of IS	**Strategy IQ-S**: Increase IT support of customer processes

[a]In large- and medium-size software organizations, it might be unrealistic to introduce agile development within 6 months. For Company X, it was expected to be feasible because of Assumption CA12

5.5.5.4 Make Strategy Decisions

After specifying the goals for the Software Development group, Company X looked for effective strategies for achieving these goals. The workshop participants came up with three context factors they considered relevant:

- **Assumption CA12**: According to the experience from the recently run pilot project using Scrum in the banking business unit, agile development principles appear to be able to speed up software development. Moreover, a small software development group should be able to change to agile development within a relatively short period of time. Because it is not clear whether the experience from the banking business unit can be transferred directly to the Insurance Services business unit, this is modeled as an assumption.
- **Context CA13**: According to the analysis of the defect data, too many defects slip from the requirements stage to the coding and system testing phases. However, as data from representative pilot projects indicate, introducing inspections (Laitenberger 2002; Ciolkowski et al. 2002) has a positive impact on the number of defects found in the requirements specification early on.
- **Context CA14**: Not all of Company X's services to the customer are completely IT-supported; some have to be provided manually, which decreases information quality.

Based on these context factors and the assumption, the workshop participants came up with three potential strategies, one for each goal of the Software Development group. Table 5.15 summarizes these strategies.

Figures 5.23, 5.24, and 5.25 specify example relationships regarding attainment of the goals of the Software Development group and nonattainment of the associated goals of the Insurance Services business unit.

In Fig. 5.23, if neither the median development productivity increased by 10 % or more (i.e., if goal PP-G was not achieved) nor an increased percentage of feature releases and bug fixes could be delivered every 6 months or more frequently (i.e., if goal FF-G was not achieved), then the strategy of increasing development productivity (FF-S) needs to be enforced or we need to try to understand why the strategy was not successful. If, however, development productivity increased by at least 10 % (i.e., if goal PP-G was achieved), meaning that the strategy of increasing

FF-G: Faster delivery of new features and fixes CA8 **FF-S**: Increase productivity of development projects **PP-G**: Increased productivity of development projects	**Organizational goals**		**Potential cause and possible solutions**
	FF-G	**PP-G**	
	1	1	Strategy successful
	1	0	Check magnitudes (less was sufficient)
	0	1	CA8 is wrong Strategy is insufficient
	0	0	Enforce strategy or try to understand why strategy was not successful

Fig. 5.23 Example: interpretation of goals related to Insurance Services business unit and Software Development group (1)

PR-G: Improved reliability of products **PR-S**: Improve QA activities CA10 **DS-G**: Decreased number of defects slipped	**Organizational goals**		**Potential cause and possible solutions**
	PR-G	**DS-G**	
	1	1	Strategy successful
	1	0	Check magnitudes (less was sufficient)
	0	1	Strategy is insufficient or goal was to high
	0	0	Enforce strategy or try to understand why strategy was not successful

Fig. 5.24 Example: interpretation of goals related to Insurance Services business unit and Software Development group (2)

CI-G: Improved customer interaction processes CA9 **CI-S**: Provide more complete and consistent information CA11 **IQ-G**: Improved information quality of IS	**Organizational goals**		**Potential cause and possible solutions**
	CI-G	**IQ-G**	
	1	1	Strategy is successful
	1	0	Check magnitudes (less was sufficient)
	0	1	CA9 is wrong Strategy is insufficient
	0	0	Enforce strategy or try to understand why strategy was not successful

Fig. 5.25 Example: interpretation of goals related to Insurance Services business unit and Software Development group (3)

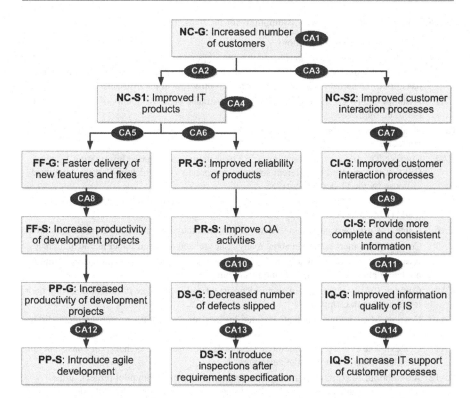

Fig. 5.26 Example: final grid

productivity (FF-S) was implemented but new features and bug fixes could still not be delivered at least every 6 months, then the strategy FF-S was not sufficient or the assumption about the delay of existing projects being mainly responsible for delivering new features and bug fixes late was wrong. In this case, additional and/or alternative strategies should be considered for achieving 6-month (or less) delivery cycles for new features and bug fixes. Finally, if 6-month delivery cycles were attained (i.e., if goal FF-G was achieved) despite the fact that development productivity did not increase by the required 10 % or more (i.e., if goal PP-G was not achieved), then the strategy of increasing productivity was right but the magnitude of productivity growth was probably too high; an increase of less than 10 % would be sufficient to achieve goal FF-G of the Insurance Services business unit.

In Fig. 5.24, if neither the number of customer complaints concerning reliability could be reduced by at least 20 % (i.e., if goal PR-G was not achieved) nor the rate of defects slipped through software quality assurance could be reduced by at least 10 % (i.e., if goal DS-G was not achieved), then the strategy of improving software quality assurance (QA) activities needs to be enforced or we need to try to understand why the strategy was not successful. If, however, the average defect slippage did decrease by 10 % (i.e., if goal DS-G was achieved) but the number of customer complaints regarding product quality did not decrease by 20 % (i.e., if

Table 5.16 Example: context and assumptions for the final grid

ID	Context factors and assumptions
CA1	Context: Company X provides banking and insurance services to their customers. Company X directly sells services via the Internet without local sales agents. Company X has a lot of customers in the banking area, but only few in the insurance area
CA2	Assumption: To get more customers in the insurance area, the quality of the IT products has to be improved
CA3	Assumption: To get more customers in the insurance area, the quality of the customer interaction processes has to be improved
CA4	Context: The services of Company X are built upon an Enterprise Information System (IS) that is composed of different software components (of which 60 % were developed in-house by the IT department)
CA5	Context: Customers complain that it takes too long to deliver new features (react to the market) and to fix existing bugs
CA6	Context: Customers complain that the IT products they have to deal with are not reliable
CA7	Context: Customers complain about many issues related to the customer interaction process
CA8	Assumption: The delay of software development and IT projects is mainly responsible for not being able to deliver new features and bug fixes faster
CA9	Context: Customers complain about inconsistent and incomplete information during their interaction with Company X
CA10	Context: Many software defects injected in early phases of software development slip to the customer
CA11	Context: The existing information system does not ensure the exchange of consistent and complete information with the customers
CA12	Assumption: According to the experience from the recently run pilot project, agile development principles should be able to speed up software development. Moreover, a small software development group should be able to change to agile development within a relatively short period of time. Yet this is not sure as agile principles were applied to a pilot project and have not been used regularly in ordinary projects
CA13	Context: According to the analysis of the defect data, too many defects slip from the requirements stage to the coding and system testing phases. However, as data from representative pilot projects indicate, introducing inspections has a positive impact on the number of defects found in the requirements specification early on
CA14	Context: Not all services of Company X are completely IT-supported; some have to be provided manually, which decreases information quality

goal PR-G was not achieved), then the strategy of improving QA activities (PR-S) was insufficient for achieving the goal (PR-G). Finally, if the number of customer complains decreased by 20 % or more (i.e., if goal PR-G was achieved), despite the defect slippage rate not decreasing by the required 10 % or more (i.e., if goal DS-G was not achieved), then the strategy of improving software QA was right but decreasing defect slippage by less than 10 % would be sufficient for achieving the goal of increasing the reliability of the IT products.

In Fig. 5.25, if the number of complaints regarding customer interaction process could not be reduced by at least 20 % (i.e., if goal CI-G was not achieved) and the Enterprise Information Systems were unable to provide 20 % more complete and 10 % more consistent information (i.e., if goal IQ-G was not achieved), then the

Table 5.17 Example: variation factors considered in the final grid

Variation factor (VF)	Organizational goals the VF is associated with
Project type (new development, maintenance, integration)	**PP-G**: Increased productivity of development projects **DS-G**: Decreased number of defects slipped
Implementation language (C#, Java, PHP, others)	**PP-G**: Increased productivity of development projects
Development approach (plan-based, agile)	**PP-G**: Increased productivity of development projects **DS-G**: Decreased number of defects slipped
Age of the application (# years)	**PP-G**: Increased productivity of development projects **DS-G**: Decreased number of defects slipped
% of information units in Enterprise IS classified by the IQI	**IQ-G**: Improved information quality of IS
Overall number of information units in Enterprise IS	**IQ-G**: Improved information quality of IS

strategy of providing more complete and consistent information (CI-S) needs to be enforced or we need to try to understand why the strategy was not successful. If, however, the quality of the information could be improved by the required thresholds (i.e., if goal IQ-G was achieved) but customer complaints regarding the interaction processes could not be reduced by at least 20 % (i.e., if goal CI-G was not achieved), then the strategy CI-S was insufficient. Finally, if the number of customer complaints regarding the interaction processes could be reduced by 20 % or more (i.e., if goal CI-G was achieved) although the quality of the information provided by the Enterprise IS did not increase by the required amount (i.e., if goal IQ-G was not achieved), then the strategy CI-S of increasing the completeness and consistency of information was right but smaller improvements would be sufficient for achieving goal CI-G.

5.5.6 Review and Adjust Grid

Once the grid was developed, the workshop participants checked the grid for completeness, consistency, and goal alignment, reviewing the context and assumptions. In this case, they did not find any deficiencies that required adjustments. Figure 5.26 illustrates the final grid developed during the workshop and Table 5.16 summarizes all context and assumptions specified within the grid. Finally, Table 5.17 summarizes the unique variation factors defined for the purpose of interpreting the measurement data associated with the organizational goals in the grid.

Phase 3: Plan Grid Implementation

In this phase, we operationalize the GQM+Strategies grid by preparing plans for implementing and deploying strategies (*Strategy Plans* for short) and for measuring the impact of the strategies on the attainment of organizational goals (*Measurement Plans* for short). Strategy plans refer to the setup of a couple of strategic projects in the organization that are responsible for implementing the defined strategies from the grid. Measurement plans refer to the setup or modification of measurement and control mechanisms. Thus, planning includes defining or adjusting procedures with respect to which activities are to be performed, by whom, when, how often, and how they will be performed, including the required infrastructure. Table 6.1 summarizes the objectives, inputs, basic activities, and outcomes of the "plan grid implementation" phase.

Organizational goals and strategies are the basis for *strategy planning*, that is, for setting up strategic projects as part of *strategy plans*. For example, if one organizational strategy was to introduce agile software development practices (Beck and Andres 2004), a strategic project would make sure that this strategy could be deployed in the organization. This could include, for instance, (1) evaluating

Table 6.1 Overview of the "plan grid implementation" phase

Plan grid implementation	
Objective	Specify plans for operationalizing the GQM+Strategies grid in the organization. This means preparing plans for implementing and deploying organizational strategies defined in the grid and for collecting, analyzing, and interpreting the measurement data according to the metrics and interpretation models specified in the grid
Inputs	• GQM+Strategies grid • Documentation of current work processes within the scope of the GQM+Strategies application (e.g., in the form of process models)
Activities	1. Develop strategy plans 2. Develop measurement plans 3. Train the personnel
Outcomes	• Strategy plans • Measurement plan

V. Basili et al., *Aligning Organizations Through Measurement*, The Fraunhofer IESE Series   69
on Software and Systems Engineering, DOI 10.1007/978-3-319-05047-8_6,
© Springer International Publishing Switzerland 2014

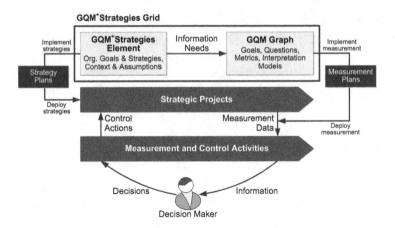

Fig. 6.1 Usage of strategy and measurement plans

which agile development process to use, e.g., Scrum (Schwaber 2004); (2) setting up pilot projects for evaluating the applicability of the new process; (3) adapting the process to the needs of the company; and (4) preparing the roll-out of the new development process within the organization.

GQM graphs are the basis for *measurement planning*, that is, for deriving plans for performing measurement and evaluating the success of the organizational goals and strategies. These plans are referred to as *measurement plans*. Measurement plans specify processes for acquiring data and then for extracting from it the information (knowledge) necessary for evaluating the success of organizational goals and strategies. Data acquisition processes include collecting, validating, and storing measurement data, whereas information/knowledge extraction processes include aggregating, analyzing, and interpreting the acquired measurement data. Measurement plans are then used for adjusting current measurement and control activities in the organization. These activities are performed in parallel with (business and supportive) processes, and their objective is to monitor and control the performance of those processes, and thus, the success of the associated strategies and goals.

Figure 6.1 illustrates the integration of the strategy and measurement planning. Measurement plans are employed (1) within strategic projects for collecting measurement data and (2) within measurement and control activities for extracting information (knowledge) needed by the decision makers for deciding about the performance of the work processes, i.e., the success of the organizational goals and strategies. Based on the outcomes of measurement and analysis, the decision maker takes control actions upon the strategic projects. Minor adjustments can typically be implemented immediately. Major adjustments that affect organizational strategies would typically require revising the GQM⁺Strategies grid and the corresponding strategy and measurement plans.

In the following sections, we will describe the strategy planning and measurement planning activities in more detail.

6.1   Develop Strategy Plans

This section deals with how to set up a few strategic projects to implement the strategies defined in the GQM⁺Strategies grid.

In the end, the defined strategies and the strategic projects will have an impact on all kinds of processes in an organization if the strategies are to be implemented sustainably in the organization. For example, let us consider the strategy of introducing a new software testing approach into a software development unit. This would include analyzing current testing processes (i.e., activities, inputs, outputs, and tools) and adjusting them according to the specification of the new testing approach. Implementing organizational strategies requires their integration into existing processes. In order to accomplish this, we must first identify which specific processes (i.e., activities or practices) should be executed in order to implement the strategies defined in the GQM⁺Strategies grid. For this purpose, we must analyze existing processes in order to decide which new processes should be added, how those processes should be embedded into the life cycle, and which existing processes should be replaced or modified so that they are properly integrated with the new processes. Process specification includes such issues as which activities are to be performed and by which organizational roles, which inputs and resources are required for performing these activities, and what outputs are expected. Additionally, we may specify prerequisites that must be met before the activity can start and the criteria that must be met before the activity can be considered complete (and before the following activity may start). Since people are typically unwilling to change their behavior, they will most probably not follow changed processes instantly. Therefore, it is not enough to merely communicate the change; rather, the change in the behavior of the process users must be facilitated and supported. Example means for supporting process change include information events, manuals, trainings, supervised applications, or a helpdesk that people can call if they are in trouble.

However, it is beyond the scope of this book to discuss change management of organizational processes. When developing strategy plans, we will simply focus on how to systematically set up strategic projects for implementing the strategies defined in the grid. For example, for each strategic project we must plan and schedule detailed activities, assigning necessary resources and budget, and ensure the appropriate infrastructure. Strategic projects may encompass one or more organizational strategies. Typically, a single strategic project would implement all strategies that affect a specific part of the organization in order to benefit from the synergies among these.

Planning and managing strategic projects involves a number of activities, such as assigning a project sponsor and defining a project manager, identifying appropriate work products and activities, estimating and scheduling activities, and assigning appropriate resources such as budget, personnel, infrastructure, tools, etc. For example, an important part of planning and monitoring a strategic project is risk management. We need to consider, for instance, whether there is a risk in implementing and deploying the goals and strategies as planned and what extra resources might be needed to achieve the correct grid as output, i.e., are more resources (e.g., people, money) needed for the project and is there a risk that the grid might not be perfect? A detailed discussion of these aspects is beyond the scope of this book. For more details, please refer to the project management literature—for example, best-practice guides such as *PMBOK—Project Management Body of Knowledge* (PMI 2013) or *PRINCE2—PRojects IN Controlled Environments 2* (OGC 2009).

6.2   Develop Measurement Plans

The second element in planning the application of the GQM$^+$Strategies grid is measurement planning. The resulting measurement plans are used to adjust the organizational measurement and control activities used to monitor the performance of the implemented strategies (i.e., business and supporting processes) and to evaluate the attainment of the organizational goals.

The basic input for measurement planning are the GQM graphs that specify the measurement goals (information needs), questions, metrics, and interpretation models. The outcome is a measurement plan that specifies: (1) how to obtain raw measurement data and (2) how to extract from this data the information needed to make decisions regarding organizational goals and strategies (i.e., how to fulfill the information needs represented by the measurement goals). Figure 6.1 presented the idea of implementing strategies and control mechanisms based on the strategy and measurement plans. On the left side of this figure, organizational strategies are implemented by adjusting and executing the appropriate business and supporting processes. The success of the strategies and attainment of the organizational goals is monitored by the appropriate decision makers (e.g., management) with the help of associated measurement and control mechanisms. The mechanisms are derived from the metrics associated with the organizational goals and strategies (right side of the figure). The measurement program provides the measurement data collected while implementing the strategies. These data are then analyzed according to predefined interpretation models and visualized, typically in the form of dashboards[1] (Eckerson 2005; Selby 2005), to the appropriate decision makers.

---

[1] According to Münch and Heidrich (2004), a dashboard is defined as a single point of project control and a means for process-concurrent interpretation and visualization of measurement data: It consists of (1) underlying techniques and methods for controlling software development projects, and additional rules for selecting and combining them, (2) a logical architecture that clearly defines logical interfaces to its environment, and (3) a supporting tool that implements the logical architecture.

Implementing the measurement plan consists of analyzing the current measurement processes in the organization and adjusting them where appropriate.

We will now discuss in more detail the key aspects of the measurement processes: (1) data collection, validation, and storage; (2) data aggregation, analysis, and interpretation; as well as (3) visualization and communication of the results.

6.2.1 Data Collection, Validation, and Storage

The first objective of a measurement plan is to specify *what* is to be measured. To identify which objects and which of their attributes need to be measured, we analyze the outcomes of work processes, documented, for example, in the form of process models. Objects represent any type of entity such as processes, products, resources, etc. Attributes correspond to the object's characteristics that are specified under the "Quality Focus" aspect of the measurement goal. Identifying objects and attributes provides insight on what exactly is to be measured and how soon it can be measured (i.e., when measurement data can first be collected). Next, the objective of a measurement plan specifies *who* is to collect it, *how* it is collected, and *when* it is collected, and how it should be interpreted. Note that data collection focuses on collecting data for *base metrics*, that is, metrics that refer to directly measurable attributes of objects. Data collection does not include obtaining data for *derived metrics*, that is, data that is produced from base metrics, for example, using a mathematical formula. Computing derived measures is part of the data aggregation step.

A key success factor for reliable measurement are defined and well-documented (1) work processes, which clearly specify process start and completion, e.g., through the specification of necessary and sufficient conditions for the start and completion of activities; (2) input and output process objects; and (3) roles. If they do not exist, it would be useful to build such documents, e.g., descriptive models, as accurately as possible. Well-defined and documented processes save a lot of trouble and cost when planning and executing measurement.

6.2.2 Data Aggregation, Analysis, and Interpretation

Planning the extraction of the information (knowledge) from raw measurement data includes aggregating measurement data, followed by analyzing and interpreting the aggregated data. Data aggregation refers to deriving complex measures based upon the base measurement data obtained directly during data collection. For example, development productivity is commonly derived by dividing some base measure of the size of the software by some base measure of the amount of effort spent producing the software ($Productivity = Size/Effort$).

Data analysis and interpretation refer to applying the interpretation models (defined in the grid) to the aggregated data, or metrics, to answer questions and evaluate the GQM measurement goals. For example, consider an organizational goal to increase development productivity by 10 % in the second half of the year compared to the first half and the corresponding measurement goal of evaluating the increase in productivity. The aggregated data required would be the productivity in the first and second halves of the year, say *ProdH1*, *ProdH2*, respectively. The appropriate interpretation model would check the percentage change in productivity $Change = ProdH2/ProdH1 \cdot 100 \%$. Interpretation of the measurement data can be supported by visualizing the data.

6.2.3 Visualization and Communication of the Results

Visualization and communication of the results refers to presenting the outcomes of measurement and analysis to the appropriate stakeholders (i.e., decision makers) in a timely and useful way in order to support them in making decisions regarding the success of organizational strategies and the attainment of organizational goals. The planning of visualization and communication encompasses the selection of appropriate visualization mechanisms and communication channels.

6.2.4 Identify Current Practices

Measurement plans can and should reuse existing measurement practices and processes. Therefore, the analysis of current work processes, which we discussed in the previous section, should also include the identification of current measurement practices and processes. Existing measurement processes should be adjusted in order to meet the measurement goals defined in the grid.

6.2.5 Adjust Current Practices

6.2.5.1 Plan Data Collection
A data collection plan should include all base metrics defined in the grid and should specify for each base metric several aspects summarized in Table 6.2 and discussed briefly in the following paragraphs.

What Is Measured? (Object and Attribute)
For each metric, the measurement plan specifies the artifact and the object's attributes that are measured. Example object attribute couples are developers' experience, code complexity, or testing effort.

Where Is Measurement Performed? (Scope)
This specifies the organizational scope of the data collection and analysis, that is, the organizational unit in which the measurement data is collected and analyzed. For example, certain data can be collected in the software development department

Table 6.2 Example tabular specification of a measurement plan

Base metric	What? Object	Where? Scope	When? Time/event	Where? Source	Who? Responsible	How? Means
LOC	Lines of software code	Software development unit	End of coding phase	SVN	Measurement expert	Automatic
PM Experience	Project manager's experience	Software development unit	Start of project	HR System	Human resources person	Manual

or in the marketing department, whereas other data can be collected throughout the organization.

When Is Measurement Performed? (Time)

For each metric, the measurement plan specifies the point in time when data should be collected, that is, when the required object is available and its property of interest (i.e., measured property) is known. Time can be specified in terms of calendar time, for example, "end of week." It can also be specified based on a trigger event, for example, at the end of a certain development phase or activity. The time aspect may also include specification of data collection *frequency*, such as "weekly," "monthly," "at the end of each iteration," etc.

Where Is the Source of Information? (Source)

For each metric, the measurement plan specifies the source from which the measurement data should be collected. This might be the place where the measurement object is stored. For example, in order to collect data on the complexity of the software code, we must measure the software code, which is stored in the SVN repository. The source may also refer to the place where the object is stored together with the characteristics we want to measure. For example, software defects are reported in the bug-tracking system together with characteristics that may include defect type, defect priority, defect severity, etc., so that we can access the bug-tracking system and extract the data from there. Another example might be developers' experience; this data is directly accessible from the human resources management system where the time each developer has worked in a given position is stored.

Who Is Responsible for Measurement? (Responsible)

For each metric, the measurement plan specifies the roles that are responsible for collecting valid measurement data. With respect to the specific responsibilities, we can distinguish three basic roles: provider, collector, and validator.

- The *provider* is the source of the information; the person or entity responsible for providing the measurement data.
- The *collector* is responsible for collecting the data and storing it in the measurement data repository for analysis and interpretation.

- The *validator* is responsible for validating the credibility of the measurement data supplied by the provider and acquired by the collector.

In practice, the provider and the collector can be the same person, depending on the actual source of the data. However, we recommend separating the validator role as it provides an independent check on the accuracy of the data. The provider, collector, and validator responsibilities can be realized, at least partially, by automatic tools. In such cases, the provider can operate and supervise the tools. For example, when measuring software code complexity, a person can play the role of provider and collector in that he/she operates the code measurement tools and supervises the measurement outcomes provided by the tool.

How Is Measurement to Be Performed? (Means)

For each metric, the measurement plan specifies the way measurement data is acquired. Two basic approaches are automatic and manual data collection. In *automatic data collection,* a tool is run on the measurement source and measures the properties of the measurement object (or it extracts the data already provided in the source). For example, we may run a static analysis tool on software code to collect the code's complexity, or we may run a query on a bug repository in order to collect the defect severity data. In *manual data collection,* a human (collector) acquires the measurement data, possibly with the use of simple tools such as questionnaires or web forms. For example, the collector sends a simple questionnaire to the software developers asking them about their experience (e.g., the number of years they have been working in a particular domain and in a particular position).

6.2.5.2 Plan Data Validation

Before measurement data can be stored or analyzed reliably, it has to first undergo a quality assurance process. The quality assurance process should be performed by a dedicated person (validator) who is independent of the person(s) who provided and collected the data. Table 6.3 summarizes the most common data integrity issues we should consider when validating measurement data:

Planning data quality assurance includes designing a checklist of potential data integrity issues and corresponding data analysis procedures, and preparing appropriate data analysis tools.

6.2.5.3 Plan Data Analysis and Interpretation

Data analysis includes such activities as data preparation, aggregation, analysis, and interpretation. Planning data analysis involves scheduling analysis procedures, selecting adequate tools, and ensuring appropriate resources and infrastructure.

Table 6.3 Common issues regarding integrity of measurement data

Data integrity issue	Potential countermeasure
Completeness: Not all data are collected as planned, which results in missing data in the database	• Repeat measurement (possibly post mortem) in order to collect missing data • Derive missing data from the available measurement data • Employ data imputation techniques to complete the data (i.e., techniques for imputing missing data based on the available data)
Internal consistency: Data points for the same attribute of the same object are not in a meaningful relation to each other	• Check the expected relationship between data points for the same attribute of an object. For example, the sum of daily work effort per person should be ≤ 12 h • Investigate potential causes of data inconsistency • Assess the correctness of measurements (data points) independent from each other, e.g., check if the collected data correspond to the defined metrics • Repeat measurement if inconsistent measurement data were collected
Plausibility: Data points for different attributes of the same object are not in a meaningful relation to each other	• Check the expected relationship between data points for various attributes of the same object. For example, the number of hazardous requirements cannot be larger than the total number of requirements • Investigate potential causes of data inconsistency • Assess the correctness of measurements (data points) for each attribute independent from each other, e.g., check if the collected data correspond to the defined metrics • Repeat measurement if inconsistent measurement data were collected

Abnormal data: Measurement data include outlier data	• Investigate the exact causes of outlier data in order to determine whether they are justified or not. If outlier data are not justified, consider the following:
	  – Recollect the outlier data and adjust it
	  – Exclude the outlier data

External consistency: Data points are not in a meaningful relation to the external world (external data and information sources)	• Check the plausibility of expected relationships (e.g., based on facts or on assumptions) • Check the validity of external data or information and the context from which they originate (Check how similar the contexts of internal and external data are) • Analyze data with respect to expected relationship, that is, which part of the data deviates from the expected values? • Investigate causes of inconsistency, for example, why does development productivity increase with increasing software size while common industry experience shows the opposite trend?

Data Preparation

Data preparation includes fitting the format of the measurement data to the aggregation, analysis, and interpretation techniques and tools. Example data preparation operations include:

- Changing representation format: This preprocessing activity refers to changing the data format. For example, project duration might be measured in terms of project start and end dates. The duration can then simply be computed by calculating the time span between the start and the end date. Yet, dates can be given using different notations, such as European (day–month–year) or US (month–day–year). Inconsistent formats are a common issue in a global development project.
- Capitalization: This preprocessing activity refers to changing the case of data strings. Although it may seem unimportant from the human analyst perspective, inconsistent capitalization of strings in the project measurement data may lead to serious errors when applying automatic analysis tools. Data analysis tools are typically case-sensitive when working with nominal or ordinal data. So the project phase ranges "requirements-testing" and "Requirements-Testing" may be treated as two different ranges of project phases.
- Concatenation and splitting: This preprocessing activity refers to joining multiple data fields into one or splitting one complex data field into several. For example, project measurement data may include a field that stores a list of programming languages used in the project. This one concatenated data field may be useless for the purpose of effort modeling and estimation. For instance, data for two projects might be "Java, C++" and "Java, C++, C." An analysis tool will consider these two projects as different, although in the latter case only a few lines of software code out of several thousand might have been implemented using "C." From the perspective of impact on development effort, considering these two projects as similar would, however, be more appropriate. In this case, we may want to split the programming language field into "primary" and "secondary" and set up thresholds on the minimal part of software that must be implemented using a given programming language in order to consider it as primary or secondary.
- Character clean-up: This preprocessing activity refers to removing extraneous characters that are not accepted by automatic analysis tools. Example characters include currency symbols such as dollar ($), euro (€), or yen (¥), which may be misinterpreted as non-numeric (e.g., control) symbols by certain analysis tools. In order to ensure that data fields representing monetary cost are treated as numeric fields, we should remove currency symbols. Note that before doing so we need to ensure that all values refer to the same currency. If not, we need to first convert all measurement to a common unit—in this case to a common currency.

Data Aggregation

Data aggregation includes deriving complex metric data based upon base metric data gathered during the data collection process. Planning data aggregation includes determining which data can and should be aggregated, how, when, and by whom. Typically, data aggregation will be performed by automatic tools, which are prepared during aggregation planning. For example, business intelligence (BI) solutions offer ready-to-use extract–transform–load (ETL) components that facilitate specifying which measurement data should be consolidated, when, and how. For example, planning aggregation will include specifying that "development productivity" data are to be derived using "software size" and "development effort" measurement through the simple mathematical operation of dividing size by effort.

Data Analysis and Interpretation

Data analysis and interpretation includes applying interpretation models defined in the grid (GQM Graph) for the collected measurement data. Planning analysis and implementation encompasses determining when, by whom, and how data will be interpreted and providing the interpretation results to the decision makers (specified in the GQM$^+$Strategies Element as one aspect of the organizational goal). The time of data interpretation is determined by the "time frame" aspect of the associated organizational goal. However, earlier analysis and interpretation can be useful for various purposes, e.g., for identifying risks and preparing the presentation format. The responsible person and the interpretation procedure are defined as part of the organizational work processes. The interpretation procedure and the techniques (including appropriate visualization means) are implemented using appropriate tools. For example, BI solutions offer customizable modules (Online Analytical Processing (OLAP) and reporting engines) that support analyzing the data and communicating the results (in a numerical and in a visual form) to the appropriate stakeholders (at predefined points in time as well as on demand).

Interpretation consists of two major parts, which might be seen as going through a grid horizontally and vertically (Fig. 6.2).

Horizontal Interpretation

Horizontal interpretation focuses on "GQM Graphs" and refers to interpreting the measurement data collected in the strategic projects according to the interpretation models defined in the GQM Graphs. During measurement specification, we go horizontally from measurement goals to question and metrics (G→Q→M). During data interpretation, we go the same way but in the opposite direction:

- From measurement to questions (Q←M): We use the measurement data for answering the questions defined in the GQM Graphs.
- From questions to measurement goals (G←Q): We use the answers to the questions in order to fulfill the information needs defined in the GQM Graph in the form of measurement goals.

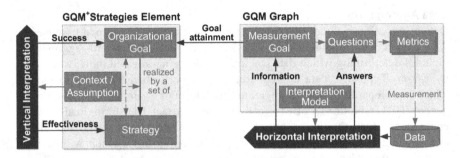

Fig. 6.2 Horizontal and vertical interpretation of analysis results

Horizontal interpretation of measurement data leads to a decision regarding the attainment of the organizational goals with which appropriate GQM Graphs and measurement data were associated. In general, horizontal interpretation is performed for each measurement goal according to the interpretation model defined for this goal. Yet, since GQM Graphs (and associated measurement goals) might be part of other, complex, graphs, the horizontal interpretation of a measurement goal may first require interpretation of the related measurement subgoals. A typical example in the context of GQM+Strategies is the "evaluation" measurement goal, which is broken down into multiple "characterize" measurement goals. For example, the measurement goal "G: Evaluate increase of development productivity" requires first that the baseline productivity from the past and currently observed productivity are characterized and then compared; this corresponds to two measurement subgoals: "G1: Characterize baseline productivity" and "G2: Characterize current productivity."

Vertical Interpretation
Vertical interpretation focuses on "GQM+Strategy Elements" and refers to interpreting the attainment of the organizational goals and the success of the strategies defined in the grid for achieving the goals. While interpreting the success of the goals and strategies, we look at the appropriateness of the defined organizational goals (e.g., regarding their scope, magnitude, and time frame), the validity of the hypothesized goal–strategy–goal relationships, the success of the selected organizational strategies, and the validity of the assumptions made while defining the grid.

6.2.5.4 Plan Visualization and Communication of the Results
In principle, visualization formats and communication mechanisms depend on the type and complexity of the information presented and on the stakeholders to whom this information is presented. Planning visualization and communication includes selecting and implementing approaches and tools that are most suitable for the intended stakeholders. These stakeholders are defined in the "Organizational scope" and the "Viewpoint" of the organizational goal (Table 2.1 in Sect. 2.2)

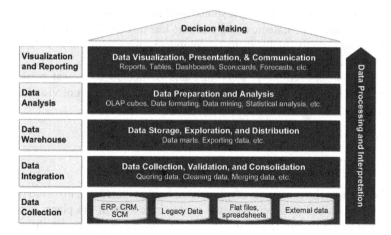

Fig. 6.3 Business intelligence architecture

and the measurement abstraction sheet (Sect. 5.3.5, Table 5.3), respectively. Exemplary visualization formats include pie charts, bar charts, histograms, radar charts, scatter plots, and tables.

6.2.6   Prepare Tools and Infrastructure

In order to minimize cost and maximize the reliability of the measurement, analysis, and interpretation, adequate technologies for data management and analysis should be used to support these activities. State-of-the-art business intelligence systems offer well-integrated and custom-configurable tools for the complete chain of data analysis, from data collection via validation, preprocessing, and analysis, to visualizing, reporting, and communicating the results. Figure 6.3 illustrates an example architecture of such a business intelligence system.

Most business intelligence systems consist of the following components:

- Data collection: Automated data collection tools, such as data miners that directly access internal or external data sources, and semiautomated tools, such as web forms or questionnaires.
- Data integration: Also known as extract–transform–load (ETL), this component supports the integration, aggregation, and validation of heterogeneous data from multiple independent data sources, as well as the loading of the data into a data warehouse.
- Data warehouse: The data warehouse represents a centralized database in which collected data is stored and maintained for analysis.
- Data analysis: Also known as Online Analytical Processing (OLAP), this component supports several multi-dimensional descriptive data analyses (i.e., slicing and dicing, pivoting, roll-up, and drill-down). Additionally, further analysis

tools are provided, such as simple spreadsheet tools that support the definition of customized analysis, statistical and machine learning packages that offer analysis to be used individually or to be combined into analysis flows. Advanced statistical packages are also provided sometimes.

- Visualization and reporting: Reporting and dashboard tools that present the outcomes of an analysis to interested stakeholders in the form of visualizations and reports.

6.3   Train Personnel

After the strategy and measurement plans have been prepared, the involved personnel should be trained in order to ensure proper execution of the plans. Personnel responsible for executing the strategies should become familiar with the process changes introduced due to the new organizational strategies. They should obtain training in the relevant tools that were introduced to support the execution of the work processes.

Personnel involved in measurement should obtain basic training motivating the use of goal-oriented measurement. Besides that, each person should get training appropriate to his/her responsibility, in particular:

- Providers: data supplying procedures and tools
- Collectors: advanced training in goal-oriented measurement, data collection methods and tools
- Validators: data preprocessing and cleansing techniques and tools
- Analysts: statistical and machine learning data analysis techniques and tools, data visualization
- Decision makers: interpretation of the analysis and interpretation results as well as use of the integrated approaches for presenting the measurement and analysis results (e.g., project dashboards)

6.4   Example

After specifying the GQM⁺Strategies grid, Company X prepared for its implementation by specifying the appropriate strategy and measurement plans and by training the personnel involved.

6.4.1   Develop Strategy Plans

Based on the newly defined strategies, the responsible managers of Company X took care of implementing them. They share the responsibility in the following way:

- Clark (CEO)
  - Strategy NC-S1: Improve IT products
  - Strategy NC-S2: Improve processes
- Davis (division manager of insurance services business unit)
  - Strategy FF-S: Increase productivity of development projects
  - Strategy PR-S: Improve QA activities
  - Strategy CI-S: Provide more complete and consistent information
- Smith (department head of software development group)
  - Strategy PP-S: Introduce agile development
  - Strategy DS-S: Introduce inspections after requirements specification
  - Strategy IQ-S: Increase IT support of customer processes
  The dependencies of the strategies defined above are as follows:
- Strategy NC-S1: Improve IT products
  - Strategy FF-S: Increase productivity of development projects
    (a) Strategy PP-S: Introduce agile development
  - Strategy PR-S: Improve QA activities
    (a) Strategy DS-S: Introduce inspections after requirements specification
- Strategy NC-S2: Improve processes
  - Strategy CI-S: Provide more complete and consistent information
    (a) Strategy IQ-S: Increase IT support of customer processes

This means that the leaf strategies that need to be implemented by strategic projects are basically the three strategies of the Software Development group listed below. All other strategies can be traced back directly to these three:

- Strategy PP-S: Introduce agile development
- Strategy DS-S: Introduce inspections after requirements specification
- Strategy IQ-S: Increase IT support of customer processes

In addition to strategic projects, the organization also needs to think about how to continuously monitor the goals related to these strategies. Therefore, a couple of additional measurement activities are defined. The concrete data that is required during these activities was specified in the measurement plans, which will be presented in the next section. Table 6.4 summarizes the setup of strategic projects and measurement activities.

6.4.2 Develop Measurement Plans

After adjusting the work processes according to the strategy plans, Company X integrated the measurement plans into these processes. In doing so, the existing means for measurement were identified and adjusted appropriately.

6.4.2.1 Identify Current Practices
The company did not perform measurement in the past; thus the measurement processes had to be defined from scratch.

Table 6.4 Strategic projects and measurement activities at Company X

Strategic project (P) and measurement activity (A)	Detailed activities	Responsible person
P1: Introduce agile	• Determine development project types that should make use of agile • Fully customize Scrum to the needs of the Insurance Services business unit of Company X • Train, pilot, and roll out Scrum to dedicated projects	Jones, IT project manager
P2: Introduce CBR	• Determine development project types that should make use of inspections • Integrate Checklist-Based Reading (CBR) (Fagan 1976) as an inspection technique into projects using a nonagile software development process • Train, pilot, and roll out CBR to dedicated projects	Thomas, IT quality manager
P3: Develop new CRM interface	• Design and implement new interface of the Customer Relationship Management System (CRM) • Train, pilot, and roll out new interface	Lewis, IT project manager
A1: Monitor management goals	• Collect, prepare, analyze, and interpret data related to Company's X management goals • Monitor attainment of business goals defined on Company's X management level	Clark, CEO
A2: Monitor insurance goals	• Collect, prepare, analyze, and interpret data related to insurance goals • Monitor attainment of the goals defined by the Insurance Services business unit	Davis, unit head
A3: Monitor software goals	• Collect, prepare, analyze, and interpret data related to the software development goals • Monitor attainment of the goals defined in the Software Development Group	Smith, group head

Table 6.5 Example: overview of measurement goals

Measurement goal (MG)	Short description
GQM-NC-G	Evaluate increase of number of customers
GQM-FF-G	Evaluate faster delivery of new features and fixes
GQM-CI-G	Evaluate improvement of customer interaction processes
GQM-PR-G	Evaluate improvement of reliability of products
GQM-PP-G	Evaluate increase of productivity of development projects
GQM-IQ-G	Evaluate improvement of information quality of Enterprise IS
GQM-DS-G	Evaluate decrease of number of defects slipped

6.4.2.2 Adjust Current Practices

Watson (company expert on GQM$^+$Strategies) set up data collection and analysis mechanisms for the measurement goals defined. Tables 6.5 and 6.6 summarize the measurement goals and metrics defined in the GQM$^+$Strategies Grid for Company X.

Table 6.6 Example: overview of metrics

MG	ID	Metric	Range	Scale type	Unit
GQM-NC-G	Cus(Y)	Number of new customers in year Y (e.g., next fiscal year)	N0	Ratio	Customers
GQM-FF-G	F_Rel(T)	Number of feature releases in time span T (e.g., half a year)	N0	Ratio	Releases
GQM-FF-G	BF_Rel(T)	Number of bug fix releases in time span T (e.g., half a year)	N0	Ratio	Releases
GQM-CI-G	CC_IP(T)	Number of complaints about the interaction processes in time span T (e.g., half a year)	N0	Ratio	Complaints
GQM-PR-G	CC_PR(T)	Number of complaints about product reliability in time span T (e.g., half a year)	N0	Ratio	Complaints
GQM-PP-G	P_AVG(T)	Average Function Points per person-hour of project effort in time span T (e.g., half a year)	R0	Ratio	FP/PH
GQM-IQ-G	IQI_Comp (T)	Information quality index (IQI) for completeness in time span T (e.g., half a year)	0–100	Ratio	%
GQM-IQ-G	IQI_Cons (T)	Information quality index (IQI) for consistency in time span T (e.g., half a year)	0–100	Ratio	%
GQM-DS-G	DSR_AVG (T)	Average ratio of defects slipped per overall defects introduced over all development phases (e.g., coding) for all releases in time span T (e.g., half a year)	R0	Ratio	%
GQM-DS-G	DT(P, R)	# defects detected in phase P for release R	N0	Ratio	Defects
GQM-DS-G	DS(P, R)	# defects slipped from P to P + 1 for release R	N0	Ratio	Defects
GQM-DS-G	DSR(P, R)	DT(P, R)/(DT(P, R) + DS(P, R))	R0	Ratio	%

N0 refers to the natural numbers including zero. N0 = {0, 1, 2, ...}
R0 refers to real numbers greater than or equal to zero

In order to collect and analyze the appropriate data, Watson defined a corresponding measurement plan. The plan specified what objects (and associated properties) are to be measured, the scope of measurement, the timing of the measurement activities, who is responsible for measurement, from where the measurement data are available, and how the measurement is to be performed. Table 6.7 summarizes the measurement plan prepared in a tabular form by Watson. Please note that the plan combines raw and derived metrics, that is, it represents a combination of plans for data collection and data aggregation. For example, for the number of complaints regarding reliability in time T (CC-PR(T)), at least the following raw metrics need to be measured: complaint identifier, complaint subject (e.g., reliability), complaint date. Deriving the CC-PR(T) measurement would then require executing an appropriate query on the complaints database. Such a query could be: "<u>count</u> unique complaints <u>where</u> *complaint_subject* = '*Reliability*' <u>and</u> *complaint_time* <u>in</u> (*start_date*, *end_date*)", where start_date and end_date determine the time span T during which reliability complaints are to be counted.

Table 6.7 Example: measurement plan

Metric	*What?* Object	*Where?* Scope	*When?* Time/event	*Who?* Responsible	*Where?* Source	*How?* Means
Cus(Y)	Customers of Company X	Management	Quarterly	Sales	Customer Relationship Management	Manual (inquiry)
F_Rel(T)	Feature releases in the release plan	Business unit	End of project	Product manager	Configuration Management	Automatic (query)
BF_Rel(T)	Bug fix releases in the release plan	Business unit	End of project	Product manager	Configuration Management	Automatic (query)
CC_IP(T)	Complaints regarding customer interaction	Business unit	Monthly	Help desk operator	Help desk	Automatic (query)
CC_PR(T)	Complaints regarding product reliability	Business unit	Monthly	Help desk operator	Help desk	Automatic (query)
P_AVG(T)	Productivity of development process	Software development group	End of project	Project manager	Questionnaire	Manual[a]
IQI_Comp(T)	Completeness of information	Software development group	Monthly	Project manager	Questionnaire	Manual
IQI_Cons(T)	Consistency of information	Software development group	Monthly	Project manager	Questionnaire	Manual
DSR_AVG(T)	Defect slippage of development process	Software development group	Quarterly	QA people	Bug tracking	Automatic (query)
DT(P, R)	Defects detected in release in development phase	Software development group	End of project	QA people	Bug tracking	Automatic (query)

| DS(P, R) | Defects in release slipped through development phase | Software development group | End of project | QA people | Bug tracking | Automatic (query) |
| DSR(P, R) | Defect slippage for release in development phase | Software development group | End of project | QA people | Bug tracking | Automatic (query) |

[a]Productivity of development process = Functional size of delivered software/Project effort. Functional size is measured manually using Function Points Analysis (ISO 2009). Project effort is reported manually by the project team members using appropriate questionnaires and is summed up by the project manager

	Information Quality Questionnaire (Information Unit Owner)

This questionnaire will focus on some attributes for all information units of all business processes. With the information of this questionnaire, we want to characterize and improve the uniqueness, completeness, consistency, and timeliness of information units.

The questionnaire is structured in five steps according to general information and relevant attributes for information quality. Please answer all questions in terms of your own information unit.

Please use only the yellow cells for your answers. If you have any further comments, please do not hesitate and use the comment column.

In the first step, we want to survey some general information about you and the information unit under investigation. The next steps focus on characterizing the uniqueness, completeness, consistency, timeliness, and confidentiality of the information unit.

For your information:
An Information Unit is a piece of critical information at Company X (like information about wells or oil and gas reserves) used in one or more business processes. Each information unit has one owner who maintains the information unit and is responsible for providing this piece of information at an appropriate level of quality. For a single information unit, there may be multiple users who make use of an information unit as part of a business process that has this information unit as input.

General

	General Information	Your answer:
G1.1a	Name of your information unit	
G1.1b	Give a short description of the information unit	
G1.2	Names of the business processes	
G1.3	Your name	
G1.4	Reporting time (year/month)	
G1.5	Current date (year/month/day)	

Uniqueness

This part of the questionnaire deals with uniqueness issues related to information quality.
Definition of Uniqueness: An information unit has a named unique source and every representation of that information unit has the same value.

	Questions:	Your answer:	Comments:
M1.1.1	In the context of your information unit: Is one defined unique source of the		
M1.1.2	What is the name of the unique source? If you don't know the name, please write "I don't know".		
M1.2.1	In the context of all replications of your information unit: Do you know about all		
M1.2.2	Please estimate the number of known replications.		
M1.3.1	What do you think: Does every representation (textual or in databases) of that information unit have the same value?		
M1.3.2	Please estimate the number of non-duplicates in your information unit.		
VF1.1a	Thinking about all replications of an information unit that are not replicated automatically: How often do replications have a time-stamp indicating the		
VF1.2	Are all replications that are not replicated automatically assured to be valid for		
VF1.3	Do you agree with the following statement: Replications should be updated as often as possible.		

...

Fig. 6.4 Example: Questionnaire for collecting "IQI" measurement data

6.4.2.3 Prepare Tools and Infrastructure

After planning the measurement, Watson prepared the tool support for collecting, analyzing, and interpreting the measurement data. Figure 6.4 presents the example questionnaire Watson designed using MS Excel for collecting measurement data information on an information quality index (IQI); this includes quality index data with respect to information completeness IQI_Comp(T) and information consistency IQI_Cons(T).

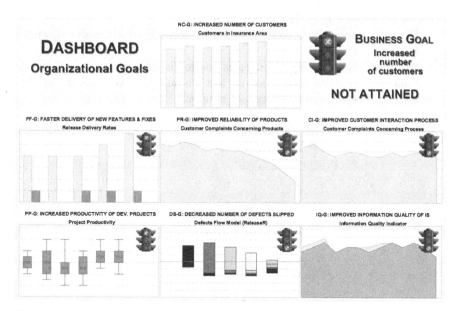

Fig. 6.5   Example: Tool support for visualizing the results of the analysis

Figure 6.5 illustrates an example dashboard for presenting the results of the data analysis in a visual form. The dashboard combines multiple graphs associated with a single interpretation model (e.g., associated with one organizational goal) in one view. This way a decision maker obtains the complete information (knowledge) he/she needs for assessing attainment of a goal all at once, yet in a form he/she can comprehend.

6.4.3   Train Personnel

In the training phase, Mr. Watson (company expert on GQM$^+$Strategies) conducted training for:

- The people who need to provide the data
- All stakeholders involved in the data interpretation (e.g., Mr. Clark, Mr. Davis, and Mr. Smith)
  The training included:
- Executing strategy plans, in particular:
  - Strategy PP-S: Agile software principles, processes, and tools
  - Strategy DS-S: Requirements inspection techniques and supporting tools
  - Strategy IQ-S: Customer-related processes, customer needs regarding IT support

- Executing measurement plan, in particular:
  - Measurement specification (i.e., what is to be measured and analyzed, when, by whom, and how)
  - Interpretation of the GQM$^+$Strategies grid for decision-making
  - Data supply, collection, analysis, and visualization components of the integrated business intelligence tool solution

Phase 4: Execute Plans

7

In this phase, the plans we prepared in the "Plan Grid Implementation" phase are executed, i.e., project strategies are implemented according to strategy plans and the measurement data are collected according to the measurement plans. Table 7.1 summarizes the objectives, inputs, basic activities, and outcomes of this phase.

Figure 7.1 illustrates the idea of two interlocking cycles. The outer organization-level learning cycle represents an improvement initiative within which a GQM⁺Strategies grid is defined, operationalized, and evaluated so that the organization can improve by achieving its goals and learn how to better apply the GQM⁺Strategies development process for the next larger cycle. The inner project-level cycle represents the deployment and application of the strategies in the individual units of the organization. The "Execute" phase consists of three major activities: (4.1) executing the strategies, (4.2) collecting and analyzing the data, and (4.3) feeding back the analysis results and making adjustments to the grid where necessary.

Table 7.1 Overview of the "Execute Plans" phase

Execute grid implementation plans	
Objective	Deploy and apply the strategies as specified in the Choose Process step, analyze their performance, and provide feedback based upon learning from the defined strategic projects
Inputs	• The GQM⁺Strategies grid • Strategy plans • Measurement plan
Activities	1. Execute strategies 2. Collect and analyze data 3. Provide feedback
Outcomes	• The results of the deployed and implemented strategies • The updated (if adjusted) GQM⁺Strategies grid, strategy plans, and measurement plans (adjusted as necessary) • Feedback: Experiences regarding the deployment and implementation of the organizational strategies • Measurement data

V. Basili et al., *Aligning Organizations Through Measurement*, The Fraunhofer IESE Series on Software and Systems Engineering, DOI 10.1007/978-3-319-05047-8_7,

Fig. 7.1 Organization-level and project-level cycles

The outer improvement cycle corresponds to an improvement program, whereas the inner cycle corresponds to one or more improvement projects. Within an improvement program, we characterize the enterprise environment (phase 1), define goals, strategies, and metrics (phase 2), and operationalize the strategies by defining appropriate strategy and measurement plans (phase 3). In phase 4, the strategies might first be deployed in a number of strategic projects and will then (if successfully deployed) be applied in daily operations. A single strategic project is typically realized within a particular organizational unit and deals with strategies associated with this unit. For example, strategies for introducing a new software testing approach and agile development processes will both be deployed in a strategic project realized in the Software Development group of the organization. The improvement program continues with phase 5, where the results from the deployed strategies are analyzed, followed by phase 6, where assets and knowledge from the improvement program are packaged. In order to keep continuously improving the organization, the next improvement program (outer cycle) is started in which the current goals and strategies are adjusted and new goals and strategies are deployed.

Ideally, a grid should not have unattainable goals or contain any inconsistencies, e.g., executing one strategy should not create a problem for executing another strategy. Such problems should have been identified and fixed in the "Define Goals, Strategies, and Measurement" phase, i.e., during grid development. However, while executing the grid, such problems might show up. Thus, project managers must monitor grid execution by analyzing the respective measurement data according to the measurement plan. Managers of strategic projects can react to problems by performing adjustments to their respective sections in the overall grid. These adjustments may lead to a request for more resources, for example. However, adjustments should be evaluated with respect to their complexity and achievability within the execute cycle. If an adjustment is so major that it requires the whole grid to be rethought or if the adjustment causes serious interference with the execution of other strategies, we might step out of the execute strategies phase and go to the analysis and package phase of the whole organizational life cycle.

All required adjustments should be consolidated and provided as feedback to higher-level organizational units as part of the organizational improvement cycle. This consolidated feedback contains information about the success of strategies, experiences gained during strategy execution, and (if appropriate) about local changes to the grid and its application plans (i.e., strategy application plans and measurement plans). This is a serious step, and an analysis with respect to resources and implications needs to be performed before this step is taken.

When to Continue the Organization-Level Improvement Cycle? The basic question raised here is when should a project-level improvement cycle be stopped and the leap be made to the organization-level improvement cycle? In general, there are two types of situations that can trigger a decision to leave the project-level execution cycle:

- Time-based: If the organization has defined a regular cycle time for the organization-level improvement cycle (such as once a year).
- Exception-based: During strategy deployment and implementation, there is a realization that something requires immediate management attention and has a substantial direct implication on the goals and strategies defined in the grid. Example situations include:
  - Unachievable goals or ineffective/unfeasible strategies (1) a goal as specified is unachievable using the associated strategy, (2) a strategy will not be effective or cannot be implemented as specified because the context has changed, or (3) a strategy cannot be deployed and applied without affecting another organizational unit. In such cases, if the changes cannot be made in real time without the approval of all related parties (stakeholders), we may have to make a major modification to the grid within an organizational improvement cycle and should thus move on to the analysis phase.
  - Insufficient resources: During strategy deployment and implementation, the allocated time or budget has been depleted even though no issues were identified that could not be solved with more time and resources. In such a case, a decision should be made to continue, i.e., more resources are made available and this will not affect the higher-level goals, or the execution phase should be left at the time because the resource limit is a serious constraint.

Table 7.2 Triggers for leaving or continuing the project-level improvement cycle

Trigger (Situation)	Response (Action)
Strategy does not bring expected effects with respect to accomplishment of the associated organizational goals.	Leave execution if currently executed strategies require changes that affect the complete improvement program (e.g., have an impact on the attainment of other goals). Continue execution if the lack of expected effects is caused by local constraints on the strategic project and if these constraints can be eliminated within local budget limits and without affecting strategies outside the project.
Deployment of a strategy requires more resources (e.g., time, manpower, or budget) than initially planned.	Leave execution if providing additional resources would mean taking (shifting) the resources from other strategic projects and would endanger their success. For example, taking human resources from other strategy projects would delay attainment of associated goals beyond the predefined time frame. Continue execution if extending resources (e.g., time, effort, or personnel) can be realized locally within the project without affecting other projects within the improvement program.
Application (usage) of a strategy increases consumption of resources (e.g., time, manpower, or budget) by more than expected.	Leave execution if the cost of applying a strategy significantly exceeds the foreseen resources and there is a risk that the cost of the strategy may exceed the benefits it entails— higher strategy application costs must be agreed upon and approved by the organizational management sponsoring the improvement program. Continue execution if there resources are available from other sources for applying the strategy.
Unexpected environmental constraints prevent deploying or applying a strategy.	Leave execution if the environment constraints affect the application of the strategy in these projects or in other projects (e.g., time, effort, or personnel). Continue execution if the constraints can be eliminated without affecting the goals and strategies.

Table 7.2 lists example situations (triggers) that require consideration and a decision as to whether to remain inside or leave the execution cycle.

7.1   Execute Strategies

Implementation of the strategies starts with the execution of business and supportive processes according to the plans prepared in the "Plan Grid Implementation" phase. Strategies are executed in a series of strategic projects. The scope of each strategic project is typically limited to particular units of the organization and implements business goals as well as business and supporting processes specific for these units. For example, the strategy of introducing agile software development affects all software development processes. These are specific to the software development unit and do not affect other organizational units, such as marketing or sales. Since deploying agile development is such a major modification, we may decide to first implement it in a number of less critical pilot projects in order to minimize the risk of a negative impact on the organization's business if the strategy should fail. Implementing agile development may require several learning cycles of its own.

7.2   Collect and Analyze Data

During execution, the project manager evaluates the success of the implemented strategies using the measurement data collected according to the measurement plans prepared in the "Plan Grid Implementation" phase. This includes collecting and storing the measurement data, validating the integrity of the data, and analyzing the measurement data. Figure 7.2 provides an overview of the data collection and analysis. Data providers and collectors report and gather data using tools. Measurements are performed according to the metric specifications and the measurement schedule defined in the measurement plans developed in Phase 3: "Plan Grid Implementation." The collected data are validated with respect to such issues as completeness and consistency and then stored in the measurement database. Potential deficits in data quality might be an indication of ineffective measurement planning and can be used for improving it (see dashed arrow in the figure). Finally,

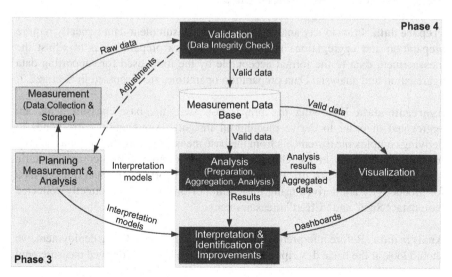

Fig. 7.2 Data collection and analysis

data are analyzed, visualized, and interpreted to extract information and gain the knowledge required for decision making, for example, for evaluating the success of organizational goals and strategies.

7.2.1 Collect Measurement Data

Data is continually collected during the deployment and implementation process. Data collection involves gathering measurement data either by running automatic measurement tools upon the appropriate artifacts or by directly acquiring data from data providers who deliver the appropriate data manually (e.g., using reporting tools). Measurement data are then stored in a central data repository.

7.2.2 Validate Measurement Data

As data is collected, the validator scrutinizes data integrity with respect to potential flaws such as incompleteness or inconsistency (refer to Table 6.3). Typically, after identifying potential threats to data integrity and discussing this with the data collectors, the latter should correct the data (collectors should correct data by themselves so that they can improve their data collection skills and avoid similar mistakes in the future). If particular data integrity problems reappear, then the associated data collection procedure and/or training should be reviewed and possibly improved, if necessary.

7.2.3 Analyze Measurement Data

Prepare data Prior to any analysis, validated measurement data typically require preparation and aggregation. The objective of data preparation is to adjust the measurement data to the format acceptable by the tools used for supporting data aggregation and analysis. Data preparation operations are discussed in Sect. 6.2.2.

Aggregate data Following the preparation step, the base measurements are aggregated in order to derive meaningful insights. Aggregation corresponds to deriving complex measurements from the base measures using the formulas defined for complex metrics in the GQM graphs. For example, if the complex metric "Productivity" is defined as "Productivity = Size/Effort," then measurement data for productivity are derived using this formula from two sets of directly collected base data: "Size" and "Effort" measurements.

Analyze data Before interpreting the data at various points during deployment, we should look at the basic descriptive statistics for the base and derived measurement

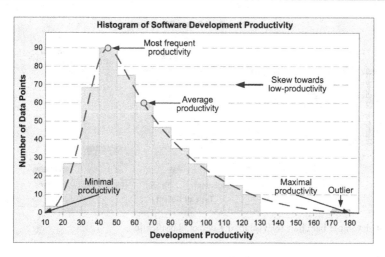

Fig. 7.3   Example descriptive statistics illustrated on the data histogram

data. Descriptive statistics are used for understanding the "nature" of data in terms of, for example:

- Range of values, i.e., minimum and maximum value
- Distribution of values across the range, e.g., in terms of variance, standard deviation, and skewedness
- Central tendency of the data, e.g., in terms of average value (statistical mean) or most frequent values (statistical mode)

Descriptive statistics help to identify data outliers (e.g., by analyzing the data distribution) and to aggregate the data (e.g., by computing the average value). Figure 7.3 illustrates example descriptive statistics on an example data histogram.

7.2.4   Visualize Measurement Data

Appropriate visualization can greatly improve quick and accurate insights into the nature of both base and derived measurement data. Examples of basic visualization means include histograms, scatter plots, bar charts, pie charts, and box plots. We will explain the most common visualization means in the next few paragraphs.

Bar chart   A bar chart displays rectangular bars with heights (for vertical bars) or lengths (for horizontal bars) proportional to the values they represent. Bar charts provide a visual presentation of categorical (nominal) data, which is a grouping of data into discrete groups. For example, Fig. 7.4 presents the grouping of defects according to the "Defect Type" and "Defect Qualifier" attributes defined in IBM's Orthogonal Defect Classification (ODC) (Chillarege et al. 1992). According to the

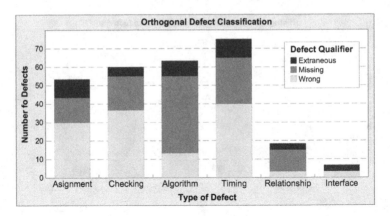

Fig. 7.4 Example bar chart for visualizing defect classification

ODC, the defect type "represents the nature of the actual correction that was made" and the defect qualifier "captures the element of either a nonexistent or wrong or irrelevant implementation." Each bar in the chart in Fig. 7.4 represents one defect type and the total bar height represents the number of defects of a certain type. Additionally, each bar is divided into three parts. Each part represents the portion of defects with a certain qualification according to the "Defect Qualifier." Notice that bar charts look similar to histograms, which we will present later in this section. Yet, unlike histograms, bars on a bar chart are separated to indicate that the values they represent are independent of each other.

Pie chart A pie chart is a circle divided into distinct sectors, each of which represents a proportion of data illustrated by the chart. The size of each sector (determined by the arc length of each sector and measured by a sector's area) is proportional to the quantity it represents. For example, Fig. 7.5 presents a combination of a pie chart and a bar chart for orthogonal defect classification (ODC) with respect to two aspects: "Defect Qualifier" and "Defect Source." According to the ODC, the defect qualifier "captures the element of either a nonexistent or wrong or irrelevant implementation," whereas the defect source describes the "development history of the defect." The pie chart in Fig. 7.5 shows a classification of all defects with respect to the defect qualifier. Each sector represents the number (and percentage) of defects of a particular qualifier. Notice that all sectors sum up to the total number of defects (i.e., to 100 %). Additionally, the largest sector representing defects qualified as "wrong" is further classified with respect to the defect source and visualized using a bar divided into sections that represents the quantities of defects from different sources.

Run chart A run chart (run-sequence plot) displays observed data in a time sequence. The horizontal axis in a run chart represents time and the vertical axis represents a variable of interest. The interval values represent the time elapsed between these values. Subsequent (over time) values of this variable of interest are

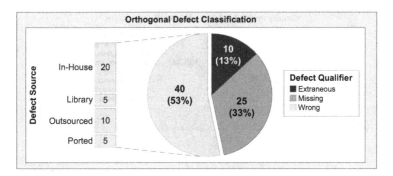

Fig. 7.5 Example pie chart for visualizing defect classification

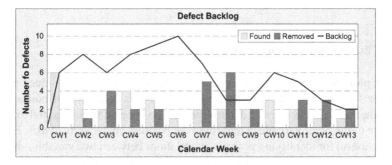

Fig. 7.6 Example run chart for visualizing the status of a defect backlog

connected with a curve. A trend plot offers a quick insight into the trends of the variable over time. For example, Fig. 7.6 illustrates a combination of a bar chart and a trend plot for visualizing defect detection and removal over time. The bar chart represents the number of defects found and removed (fixed) per calendar week, and the line represents the number of defects in the defect backlog per calendar week (i.e., defects that have been found but not removed yet).

Radar chart A radar chart is a chart that illustrates multivariate data in the form of a two-dimensional plot, in which values of three or more variables are represented by equiangular axes that start from the same point. For a single vector of data (i.e., a single observation), individual values are connected with a line. For example, Fig. 7.7 illustrates a radar chart that visualizes the results of assessing eight process areas defined by CMMI (2010). During the assessment, each process area is assessed in terms of the extent (in percentage) of implementing the practices defined for this area in the CMMI model. In Fig. 7.7, each axis represents one process area. The results of a single assessment are represented by a vector of eight values, which are connected with a line.

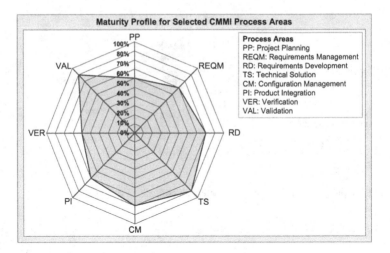

Fig. 7.7   Example radar chart for process maturity assessment results

Scatter plot   A scatter plot displays on Cartesian coordinates the values of two variables for a set of data. The data is displayed as a collection of points, each having the value of one variable determining the position on the horizontal axis and the value of the other variable determining the position on the vertical axis. Scatter plots are useful for identifying potential correlations between two variables, including functional relationships. They can also indicate data clusters and outliers. Figure 7.8 illustrates an example scatter plot for software size and defects. The horizontal axis represents the size of a software module measured in thousand lines of code (kLOC), and the vertical axis represents the number of defects found in that module. Looking at the plot we can immediately tell that there is a correlation between software size and number of defects. Moreover, the relationship is not linear, meaning that the number of defects increases disproportionally to the increase in software size. The fit line indicates that the relationship is most probably exponential, that is, an increase in a software module's size implies an exponential increase in the number of defects found in the module. Finally, the plot shows three data outliers. Data outliers can be investigated further by using box plots. In Fig. 7.10, we visualize the same set of data using a box plot and there we can see that the three outliers are actually two outliers and one extreme value.

Box plot   A box plot graphically represents groups of numerical data through their five descriptive statistics (Fig. 7.9): minimal value (min), lower quartile (Q1), median (Q2), upper quartile (Q3), and maximum value (max). A box plot may also indicate which observations, if any, might be considered outliers and extreme values (Fig. 7.9 illustrates how to determine these values). In this sense, a box plot implements an important principle of visualization, which is to focus the viewer's attention on what should be seen in the data. Figure 7.10 illustrates a box plot combined with a histogram, which show software defect density data. This is the same data set as in the scatter plot in Fig. 7.8, but the software size and defect data

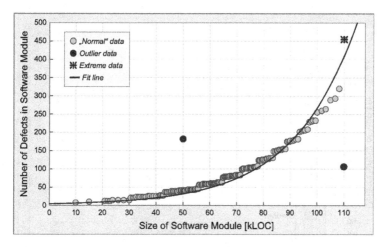

Fig. 7.8 Example scatter plot for visualizing software defects and size

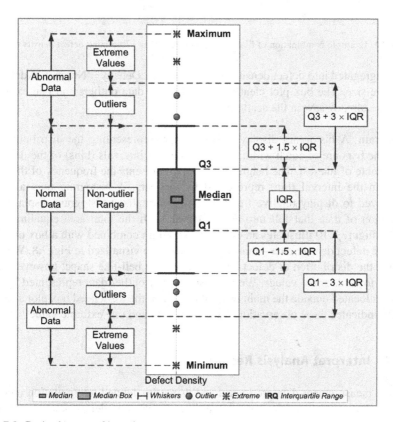

Fig. 7.9 Basic elements of box plot

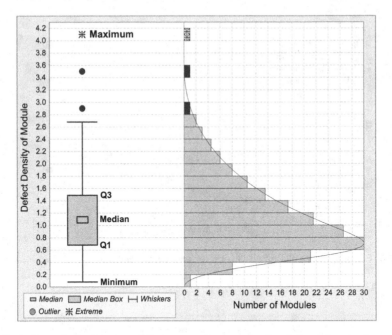

Fig. 7.10 Example combination of histogram and box pot for visualizing defect density

were aggregated into defect density such that Defect Density = Number of defects/ Software size. The box plot clearly shows the two data outliers and one extreme value we already saw in the scatterplot.

Histogram A histogram displays adjacent bars representing the distribution of data. The bars are of equal width, which represents intervals (bins) of the data for the variable of interest. The height of the bars represents the frequency of the data points in the interval (bin) represented by the bars. A histogram may also be normalized to display relative frequencies. A normalized histogram displays the proportion of data that fall into each interval, with the total area equaling 1 or 100 %. Figure 7.10 illustrates an example histogram combined with a box plot for software defect density data—the very same data we visualized in Fig. 7.8. We can see that the distribution of defect density data has a bell-like shape; however, it is skewed towards small values. We can also identify outlier data represented by the low bars located outside the main body of data. Yet, the associated box plot already clearly indicates these observations as two outliers and one extreme value.

7.2.5   Interpret Analysis Results

Finally, measurement data are interpreted using the defined interpretation models and baselines. For example, consider an interpretation model associated with the measurement goal of evaluating the increase in development productivity within the next year by 10 %. The interpretation model would compare the target productivity achieved in development projects performed in a recent year against the baseline productivity in subsequent years. Simple analysis would check if average productivity across target projects is 10 % higher than average productivity across baseline projects.

7.3 Provide Feedback

While deploying the strategies, feedback is performed to indicate how the implementation of the strategy is progressing and what adjustments need to be made. This should be done in as close to real time as possible. At various points in the deployment of the implementation process, the measurement data should be analyzed, identifying triggers that indicate feedback. These triggers can come from the recognition of problems requiring adjustments to the grid, strange trends like deviation from the plans or overspending of the predicted resources, etc. It is hard for team members to take the time for this observation and analysis, and this should therefore be performed by an oversight group, such as the Experience Factory Organization (Basili 1989; Basili et al. 1995).

Once strategy deployment is completed, it is time for a more detailed analysis and feedback as well as for packaging what has been learned for future grid implementations and organizational improvement. Refer to Chaps. 8 and 9 for a detailed discussion of how to analyze and package the results of the execution phase of the GQM$^+$Strategies learning cycle.

7.4 Example

7.4.1 Execute Strategies

In order to implement the GQM$^+$Strategies grid at Company X, three strategic projects and three major measurement and controlling activities were planned. Each strategic project and measurement activity was assigned to a project manager as described in the previous chapter.

7.4.2 Collect and Analyze Data

Mr. Watson, Company X's expert in GQM$^+$Strategies, plays the role of data collector and validator and acts as the oversight manager for monitoring intermediate feedback. The measurement program specifies several data providers who are to deliver measurement data to Mr. Watson. In particular:

Table 7.3 Issues related to strategic projects and measurement activities at Company X

Strategic Project (P) and Measurement Activity (A)	Issues
P1: Introduce agile	None
P2: Introduce CBR	Part way through the project it was realized that Checklist-Based Reading (CBR) would not be sufficient to decrease the number of slipped defects from the requirements document
P3: Develop a new CRM interface	Development of the new CRM interface has been completed and deployed according to the plan. Yet, the developers complained about insufficient involvement of the users in the development (especially regarding the requirements specification)
A1: Monitor management goals	None
A2: Monitor insurance goals	None
A3: Monitor software goals	During data analysis, it was revealed that the baseline data for information quality was wrong

- The Sales Manager provides customer data from the CRM system.
- The Product Managers provide data about feature and bug fix releases.
- The Service Desk Operators provide data about customer complaints.
- The Project Managers provide data regarding the functional size of the projects in terms of Function Points and effort required (in terms of person-hours).
- The Project and Product Managers provide information regarding the information quality index of the Enterprise IS.
- The Quality Assurance Team provides data from the bug-tracking system regarding the defects slipped.

Mr. Watson checks the integrity of the measurement data and gives feedback to the data providers. Next, if the measurement data successfully underwent validation, Mr. Watson analyzes it, looking for intermediate feedback triggers and using the predefined interpretation model to check attainment of the organizational goals addressed in the strategic projects. Table 7.3 summarizes the issues related to the strategic projects and measurement activities that Mr. Watson discovered.

7.4.3   Provide Feedback

Mr. Watson takes the feedback issues he identified following an early analysis of the measurement data and makes a real-time adjustment to the strategic project. He decides to switch from Checklist-Based Reading (CBR) to another reading approach, Perspective-Based Reading (PBR) (Basili et al. 1996), setting up training and deploying PBR for the rest of the project. He also fixes the baseline data problem. Both solutions appear to be effective, and the implementation progresses without further problems. Table 7.4 summarizes the two improvement actions and the persons responsible for executing the actions.

Table 7.4 Improvement actions after the feedback session

Strategy Project (P) and Measurement Activity (A)	Issue	Improvement actions
P2: Introduce CBR (Mr. Smith, Head of Software Development Group)	During piloting it was revealed that Checklist-Based Reading (CBR) was not sufficient to decrease the number of slipped defects from the requirements document.	Mr. Thomas (IT Quality Manager) talked to Mr. Smith (Head of Software Development group) in order to come up with an alternative strategy: • Mr. Smith decided to make a real-time modification to strategic project P2 and introduce an alternative requirements reading technique called Perspective-Based Reading (PBR). • Training was set up for PBR.
P3: Develop new CRM interface (Mr. Smith, Head of Software Development Group)	Developers complained about insufficient involvement of users in the development (especially for requirements specification).	Mr. Smith (head of software development group) talked to the manager of the CRM development project and to Mr. Davis (head of insurance services) in order to assess the root causes and the impact on the effectiveness of CRM system of the insufficient involvement of the CRM users during development. • They decided that the CRM interface would require major rework and that representatives of the insurance services business unit (users of CRM) needed to be involved in the reworked project. • The rework of CRM required setting up a new development project, which would require resources unavailable within the current "execute plans" phase. So, introducing sufficient IT to support the implementation of strategy IQ-S (i.e., supporting customer processes) had to be postponed and an alternative, probably less effective strategy should be implemented in the meantime to achieve goal IQ-G, i.e., improving information quality. • Because the time frame planned for implementing the strategies was almost up and all other strategies appeared to be successful, Mr. Smith and Mr. Davis decided to request a serious modification of the strategy IQ-S within the regular "analyze outcomes" phase.

(continued)

Table 7.4 (continued)

Strategy Project (P) and Measurement Activity (A)	Issue	Improvement actions
A3: Monitor software goals (Mr. Thomas, IT Quality Manager)	During data analysis, it was revealed that the baseline data for information quality was wrong.	Fix the baseline data • The cause of the problems with the baseline data was discovered and new baselines were generated.

At the end of the "execute plans" phase, it appeared that many of the goals had been achieved, but not all. Achieving the full set of goals required rethinking and developing a better strategy for improving the information quality. Note that it might have been possible to still achieve the top-level goal of increasing the number of customers. But in the next cycle, there is a chance to improve on what has been achieved in this "execute plans" phase by upgrading other strategies as well.

Phase 5: Analyze Outcomes

When we leave the "execute plans" phase, we proceed in one of the following states:

1. We completed the "execute plans" phase because of serious problem with respect to achieving subgoals, unsuccessful strategies, insufficient resources, etc., and because these issues were not fixable in real time. In this case, the "analyze outcomes" phase aims at discovering the root problems and considering ways to fix them and generate a new, improved grid with a higher chance of success. Once we understand how to adjust the grid, we can work on analyzing what we have learned to date to improve the grid development, implementation, and deployment processes for future evolutions of the grid or the development of new grids within the organization.
2. We completed the "execute plans" phase and successfully deployed the grid as originally specified or as modified in real time. In this case, the "analyze outcomes" phase aims at reviewing the analysis results and the feedback provided from the "execute plans" phase and at recording the lessons learned during the implementation and deployment of the strategies. For example, we write down the root problems of whatever changes we had to make (e.g., changes to the goals, strategies, or measurements) in order to avoid these problems in the future.

In this phase, we have the chance to analyze and visualize all the relevant measurement data that was collected in the "execute plans" phase as a whole, visualizing the final results and examining interpretations more deeply to better understand assessment of goal attainment. This step is performed in a postmortem fashion. Table 8.1 summarizes the objectives, inputs, basic activities, and outcomes of this phase. In the following sections, we will describe the individual activities of this phase in more detail.

In principle, the "analyze outcomes" phase consists of validating, analyzing, visualizing, and interpreting the data collected in the previous "execute plans" phase. Figure 8.1 provides an overview of the basic activities of Phase 4: "analyze

V. Basili et al., *Aligning Organizations Through Measurement*, The Fraunhofer IESE Series on Software and Systems Engineering, DOI 10.1007/978-3-319-05047-8_8,
© Springer International Publishing Switzerland 2014

Table 8.1 Overview of the "Analyze Outcomes" phase

Analyze outcomes of GQM⁺Strategies application

Objective	The objective of this phase is to analyze and visualize the data and other forms of feedback from the "Execute Plans" phase, leading to an evaluation of the process and the GQM⁺Strategies grid
Inputs	• Measurement data (collected through the "Execute Plans" phase) • The final version of the GQM⁺Strategies grid and the processes used • Feedback from the experiences to date
Activities	1. Validate and analyze the measurement data 2. Visualize and interpret the measurement data 3. Identify potential improvements
Outcomes	• Results of the analysis regarding the success of the strategies and attainment of the goals • Improvement potentials for future GQM⁺Strategies grids and processes

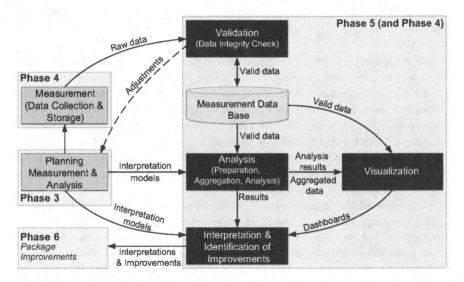

Fig. 8.1 Overview of data analysis and interpretation

outcomes." Major activities are represented by black rectangles. Gray rectangles represent activities performed in the previous phases of the GQM⁺Strategies learning cycle. The phase starts with the *Validation* of the base measurement data collected during the "execute plans" phase. Notice that if validation shows systematic deficits in the data, then this may provide a basis for adjusting the measurement and analysis plans (dashed arrow in the figure). After validation, the valid base data are input to analysis and visualization.

In the *Analysis* step, the measurement data are aggregated and processed according to the interpretation model defined in the "plan grid implementation" phase. For example, baseline and current development productivity is computed using software size and project effort data from the project before and after deployment of the corresponding organizational strategies.

In the *Visualization* step, we visualize the base measurement data, e.g., to observe trends in the data. For example, we may generate a scatter plot of size and effort data in order to see whether project effort is linearly or nonlinearly dependent on project size. We should also visualize the results of the analysis. For example, in order to assess a change in development productivity, we may draw a box plot of the baseline and current productivity.

In the final step, the *Interpretation* step, human decision makers take the outcomes of Analysis and Visualization and evaluate the attainment of the organizational goals according to the interpretation models defined in the "plan grid implementation" phase. Continuing the development productivity example, a decision maker takes the productivity statistics (e.g., mean, median, quartiles) and visualization (size-effort scatter plot, productivity box plot) and interprets these according to the interpretation model defined for evaluating a 5 % increase in development productivity. Such a model may simply compare the central tendency (e.g., mean) of the baseline and current productivity; it may also include performing statistical tests in order to check if the observed difference between baseline and current productivity is statistically significant.

The same step—validation, analysis, visualization, and interpretation—is also performed in Phase 4: "execute plans," but with a different focus. In the above description, the goal is to analyze the overall organizational goals, strategies, and GQM$^+$Strategies processes, while in Phase 4, it is about monitoring and controlling the strategic projects under development.

In the following sections, we will discuss the activities involved in more detail.

8.1 Validate and Analyze the Measurement Data

Prior to the analysis we should once again check that the repository data is valid and formatted consistently (e.g., that there is no inconsistency among the data from different strategic projects). If necessary, we may also need to further aggregate the data and recalculate the descriptive statistics.

8.2 Visualize and Interpret Data

The outcomes of the data analysis step are used to interpret the success of the goals and strategies defined in the grid. The results of the analysis are interpreted using the defined interpretation models and baselines. Visualization is an excellent way to support data analysis and interpretation to gain insights into the raw data, descriptive statistics, and analysis results. The objective of interpretation, like measurement in general, is to obtain sufficiently accurate information at a reasonable cost. That is why we should focus on the most relevant metrics and interpretation models. The focus of measurement and interpretation should be on addressing the most important effects while reducing the associated costs.

8.3   Identify Improvement Potentials

After interpreting the measurement data, we identify improvement potentials with respect to the grid, the GQM$^+$Strategies grid development process, and its implementation. We review the grid with respect to goal attainment and investigate potential causes of goals that were not achieved or were modified, and we collect feedback from the stakeholders who were involved in defining and implementing the grid. In the end, improvement potentials are discussed and prioritized. The highest-priority improvements are implemented in the subsequent cycle of the GQM$^+$Strategies learning loop. We perform both quantitative and qualitative analyses to complete the analysis process and identify potential improvements.

8.3.1   Analyze GQM$^+$Strategies Grid

The analysis of the GQM$^+$Strategies focuses on identifying improvement potentials with respect to (1) organizational goals and strategies, and (2) measurement specified for controlling the effectiveness of the strategies and attainment of the goals.

8.3.1.1 Attainment of Goals and Success of Strategies

At first we analyze the organizational goals and strategies with respect to the following aspects:

- Feasibility and suitability of the organizational goals, for example, with respect to scope, magnitude, and time frame
- Validity of the goal–strategy–goal relationships we hypothesized in the grid
- Effectiveness and sufficiency of the organizational strategies
- Validity of the assumptions made while defining the grid

8.3.1.2 Appropriateness of Measurement and Control Mechanisms

Next we analyze the defined measures and interpretation models with respect to the following aspects:

- Applicability and usefulness of the metrics and interpretation models used
- Feasibility and effectiveness of the measurement applied and of the controlling activities and mechanisms

Through the review of measurement, we try to make sure that information about achieving or not achieving an organizational goal was not based on improper or insufficient data or interpretation models. In such cases, we may, for example, come to the conclusion that the measured entities or attributes actually do not reflect the phenomenon we are interested in from the perspective of the organizational goals. For instance, the goal of increased development productivity may be interpreted as not being achieved because the productivity measurement did not consider the skills of the development team as a relevant aspect of productivity. Lower team skills would typically lead to a decrease in absolute productivity (e.g., the amount of software functionality delivered per unit of effort). Yet, it does not mean that the strategy selected for achieving the goal was not effective.

8.3.2 Gather Feedback from Relevant Stakeholders

In addition to the analysis of the GQM$^+$Strategies grid, we gather feedback from the relevant stakeholders involved in defining, implementing, and deploying the grid. One potential approach to this is the use of retrospective feedback sessions as proposed by Kerth (2001). The objective of a retrospective feedback session is to look back at the grid specification, implementation, and deployment activities and to improve the effectiveness of these activities in the future. Retrospectives explore what is working well on a project in order to ensure that good practices are reinforced and repeated. On the other hand, retrospectives also explore what is not working in a project and thus could be improved or avoided. Summarizing, the intent of retrospectives is to capture key lessons learned during the project in order to improve the effectiveness of strategies or future projects.

What Are Retrospectives and What Are They Not
"A retrospective is an opportunity for the participants to learn how to improve.
    The focus is on learning—not on fault-finding."
    The prime directive of project retrospectives formulated by Kerth (2001) is: "Regardless of what we discover, we must understand and truly believe that everyone did the best job he or she could, given what was known at the time, his or her skills and abilities, the resources available, and the situation at hand."

Detailed objectives of the project retrospective feedback session are:

1. Review the project from different perspectives.
2. Capture key lessons learned during the project. This includes answering the following questions:
   - What worked so well that it is worth noticing for the future as a best practice?
   - What did not work well and needs to be improved (done differently) in the future?
   - What was ambiguous or confusing and needs to be clarified in the future?
3. Document and report the feedback to the owner (sponsor) of the strategy introduction project and to the expert coordinating the GQM$^+$Strategies application in the organization.
4. Last but not least, build team collaboration and celebrate success.

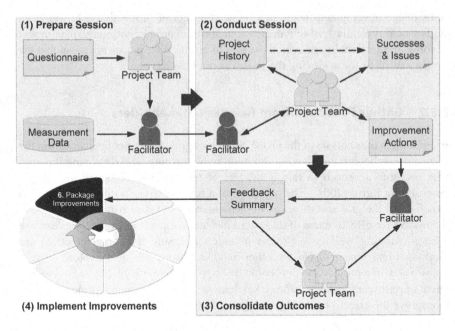

Fig. 8.2 Data collection and analysis

A classical project retrospective feedback session as proposed by Kerth (2001) consists of three major steps: preparing the session, conducting the session, and packaging the feedback gathered during the session. Figure 8.2 illustrates the procedure of a project retrospective. The consolidated outcomes of the feedback session are then input to the "package improvements" phase of the GQM⁺Strategies learning cycle in which we implement improvements to the grid as well as their implementation and deployment.

In the following paragraphs, we will briefly describe the activities within each phase of the project retrospective.

Step 1: Prepare Session

The objectives of the preparation are to gather input for the retrospective session and to arrange the session. Inputs to the session may include measurement data collected during the strategy introduction project and feedback from the project team members collected during the project, e.g., using questionnaires and forms on the project Wiki pages. Arranging the session includes selecting the session participants and planning the session in terms of duration, agenda, etc. The main activities performed in preparation of the feedback session include:

1. Select facilitator: The role of the facilitator is to moderate the group work during the feedback session and to synthesize its outcomes. For example, the facilitator ensures that every participant in the session has an opportunity to actively

participate and contribute. The facilitator should preferably be an external professional, independent of the project; if such a professional is not available, a member of the project team (typically a project manager) can assume the role.

2. Select session participants: Participants of the feedback session should represent different views on the project; they should represent different functions in the project (cross-functional team). A relatively small group of people (e.g., six to eight) is most effective. If there are more people working in the strategic project, then several small retrospective sessions can be organized (e.g., one for each strategy) in order to include everyone.

3. Plan duration and agenda: A session should not take much more than 2 h. In preparing the agenda, the facilitator should gather the aspects of the project for which lessons learned should be captured during the session, e.g., the effectiveness of the activities performed, common sources of project difficulties such as poor communication within the project team, poor planning and preparation of the project, insufficient consideration of project risks, insufficient resources, unclear project objectives, and misunderstood project roles.

4. Review feedback from comparable projects: If prior GQM$^+$Strategies improvement cycles exist, the facilitator may revisit feedback from similar strategic projects.

5. Collect inputs for the session: Inputs to the session may include quantitative measurement data collected during strategy deployment. Example input may include comparison of the planned and actually consumed effort for implementing the organizational strategies, e.g., using the earned value approach (refer to, e.g., Budd and Budd 2009). Inputs should also include issues discussed and reported during the project by the project team members. The facilitator synthesizes the available information and uses it during the session for stimulating team discussions.

Step 2: Conduct Session

The objective of the feedback session is to gather key lessons learned during the project, including project successes and difficulties. The main activities performed during the feedback sessions include:

1. Set the stage: The facilitator starts the session by explaining the goals, format, and agenda. Next, the facilitator establishes a safe environment for open dialog, e.g., by assuring the participants that anything said during the session will not be communicated outside, except for the explicitly defined and documented action plan and the lessons learned. The participants should agree that (1) everyone will be given an opportunity to speak and will be listened to; (2) the participants will respect each other's experiences and perceptions and avoid criticizing and blaming each other; and (3) the focus is on understanding problems, on learning, and on future improvements.

2. Create common perspective: To provide all participants with a common perspective, the facilitator presents the project status, quantitative project data, qualitative feedback collected prior to the session, and relevant information

from various prior deployments. The focus is on what was achieved, what was not, and on the actual resource expenditures (e.g., time, effort, and schedule) compared to the plan.

3. Generate insights: After presenting the project status, the facilitator asks the participants to share their insights regarding the project. The insight elicitation procedure consists of several steps:

   (a) Each participant is asked to write down, on separate cards, five things that went well and five things that did not go well in the project from his/her personal perspective.

   (b) Each participant then places the cards on the board and briefly describes for each of them why it is important.

   (c) The participants are asked to group the insights into affinity groups to create groups of similar insights. The facilitator talks about each group, finally arriving at a common view of the key insights for each group and a name for the group.

   (d) The participants prioritize the groups of insights.

   (e) Each group is discussed starting from the most important, and cause–effect diagrams might be drawn to identify the sources of success or failure (i.e., why some things went well whereas others did not). Each group discussion should end with a common understanding of the issue and agreement regarding its importance and potential causes.

4. Plan actions: Based on the project insights and their potential causes, the participants discuss potential actions. For things that went well, the participants identify best practices, for things that did not go well, they identify appropriate improvement actions. To plan improvement actions, the participants should specify at least the following: responsible person, goal of the action, activities to perform, and expected outcomes.

5. Close the retrospective: The facilitator closes the feedback session with a recap of the collective view on the project performance, the top insights, and the identified improvement actions. The participants are then given an opportunity to ask for clarifications or pose questions if agreement is missing on any of these items. A successful retrospective will conclude with agreement on all items. Finally, the facilitator collects feedback on the retrospective by offering each participant an opportunity to express his/her degree of satisfaction or perhaps offer improvement suggestions regarding the way the retrospective itself should be performed. It is up to the facilitator to document the outcomes of the session. This may mean saving electronic forms and notes, or taking a digital picture of the sticky notes on the board.

Example Questions to Provoke Retrospective Thoughts and Discussions
In order to provoke thoughts and discussions, the facilitator may prepare a catalog of questions prior to the session. Examples of questions might be:

(continued)

- Are you proud of the project results? If yes, what's good? If not, what's not so good?
- What was the single most frustrating part of the project?
- How would you do things differently next time to avoid this frustration?
- What was the most gratifying or professionally satisfying part of the project?
- Which methods or processes worked particularly well?
- Which methods or processes were difficult or frustrating to use?
- If you could change anything about the project, what would you change?
- What was the originally planned project schedule? What was the actual project progress?
- How accurate were the original estimates of project or activity effort and duration? What was over- or underestimated?
- How could we improve the estimates of size and effort to make them more accurate?
- Did we have the right people assigned to all project roles? Consider subject matter expertise, technical contributions, management, review and approval, and other key roles. If not, how can we make sure that we get the right people the next time?
- Were there early warning signs of problems that occurred later in the project? How should we have reacted to these signs? How can we be sure to notice these warning signs next time?
- Were project objectives, scope, constraints, and limitations made clear to all project team members from the beginning? If not, how could we have improved this?
- Were all team/stakeholder roles and responsibilities clearly delineated and communicated? If not, how could we have improved these?
- Were the expected project results, milestones, and specific schedule elements/dates clearly communicated? If not, how could we improve this?

Step 3: Consolidate Outcomes
The objective of the session packaging is to consolidate the outcomes of the feedback session, in particular the key lessons learned during the project and the improvement actions. The main packaging activities include:

1. Consolidate and document feedback and action plans: Immediately after the feedback session, the facilitator consolidates and documents the major outcomes of the session, which include: summary of the project (project scope and performance), list of lessons learned (successes and problems), and action plans.
2. Communicate feedback and improvement potentials: The facilitator communicates the outcomes of the feedback session to the stakeholders, e.g., the manager of the strategic project, the sponsor of the organizational improvement initiative, and the GQM+Strategies expert. Based on the feedback and the

scope of the improvement actions, the manager of the strategy introduction project and the GQM⁺Strategies expert may decide on which improvement to implement within the given strategy introduction project and which should be realized within the organizational improvement cycle.

Step 4: Implement Improvements

Issues and associated improvement potentials identified during the feedback session are input to the "package improvements" phase of the GQM⁺Strategies cycle (see Chap. 9). In this phase, the outcomes of the feedback session are analyzed together with the outcomes of the grid (i.e., the results of the analysis and interpretation of the measurement data). In the "analyze outcomes" phase, a subset of improvements that are perceived as the most relevant ones can be recommended for implementation and deployment; however, the final decision is made in the "package improvements" phase.

8.4 Example

After 6 months of implementing the grid in a series of three strategic projects, Mr. Clark (CEO) decides to reevaluate the overall grid based on the feedback from Mr. Smith and Mr. Davis on the issues, with a new implementation of the CRM interface (i.e., deployment of strategy IQ-S). For this purpose, the measurement data provided by the measurement and controlling activities (i.e., the governance activities) is analyzed and interpreted during a joint workshop. Table 8.2 summarizes the measurement and controlling activities from which data were used for interpreting specific organizational goals.

In the following paragraphs, we will present the results of the data analysis and interpretation.

8.4.1 Validate and Analyze Measurement Data

Data analysis and interpretation are performed upon the synthesized data collected in all governance activities. Before analysis and visualization tools were used to process the measurement data, they were validated with respect to potential flaws, in particular regarding completeness and consistency (internal and external). Mr. Watson (company expert in GQM⁺Strategies) validated the data and did not find any flaws.

8.4.2 Visualize and Interpret Data

Following the validation, the measurement data were processed using analysis and visualization tools. Base data were aggregated and presented using the dashboards prepared in Phase 4: "plan grid implementation." Figures 8.3–8.9 illustrate the

Table 8.2 Example: Considered governance activities and organizational goals

Source of measurement data (governance activity)	Interpreted organizational goals
A1: Monitor management goals (Clark, CEO)	• **GQM-NC-G**: Evaluate increase of number of customers
A2: Monitor insurance services business unit goals (Davis, head of insurance services business unit)	• **GQM-FF-G**: Evaluate faster delivery of new features and fixe GQM-PR-G: Evaluate improvement of reliability of products • **GQM-CI-G**: Evaluate improvement of customer interaction processes
A3: Monitor Software Development group goals (Smith, head of software development group)	• **GQM-PP-G**: Evaluate increase of productivity of dev. projects • **GQM-DS-G**: Evaluate decrease of the number of defects slipped • **GQM-IQ-G**: Evaluate improvement of IQ of Enterprise IS

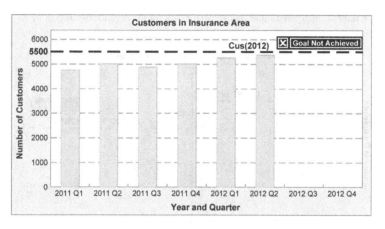

Fig. 8.3 Example: Interpretation of measurement data for the organizational goal NC-G

dashboards used for interpreting the organizational goals defined and implemented in Company X. In the next paragraphs, we will briefly interpret the results.

8.4.2.1 GQM-NC-G: Evaluate Increase of Number of Customers

The top-level business goal of Company X was (NC-G) to increase the number of customers in the insurance area in the year 2012 by 10 % compared to the previous year, 2011. In order to achieve this goal, the number of customers would have to increase from 5,000 to 5,500. Figure 8.3 illustrates the number of customers measured in each quarter across 2011–2012. In neither the first nor the second quarter of 2012 was the number of customers equal to or greater than the targeted 5,500. Therefore, the top-level business goal NC-G was not achieved.

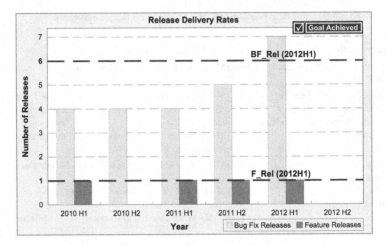

Fig. 8.4 Example: Interpretation of measurement data for the organizational goal FF-G

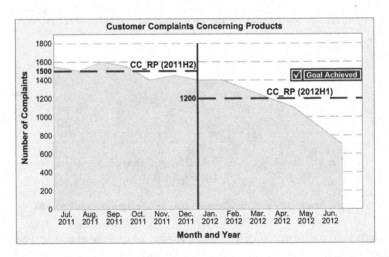

Fig. 8.5 Example: Interpretation of measurement data for the organizational goal PR-G

8.4.2.2 GQM-FF-G: Evaluate Faster Delivery of New Features and Fixes

The management of the insurance services business unit of Company X defined three goals to contribute to the attainment of the top-level business goal of increasing the number of customers. One goal was (FF-G) to release new features and bug fixes more frequently, specifically at least one new feature release every 6 months, and monthly bug fixes. Figure 8.4 illustrates the measured bug fixes and new feature releases throughout the years 2011 (baseline) and 2012 (target). In the first half-year period of 2012, the target values for new feature releases and bug fixes were reached or exceeded, respectively. Therefore, the insurance services business unit's goal FF-G was achieved.

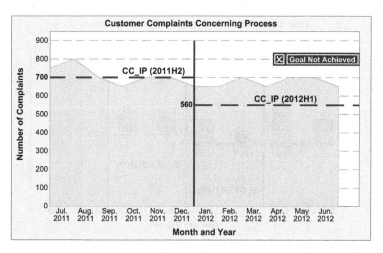

Fig. 8.6 Example: Interpretation of measurement data for the organizational goal CI-G

8.4.2.3 GQM-PR-G: Evaluate Improvement of Reliability of Products

The second goal defined by the management of the insurance services business unit was (PR-G) to reduce customer complaints concerning product reliability on an average of 20 % by the middle of the next fiscal year (2012). Figure 8.5 illustrates the measurement data collected during the baseline period, the second half of fiscal year 2011, and for the target period, the first half of fiscal year 2012. The insurance services business unit was able to reduce the average number of customer complaints regarding the reliability of products to below the target value of 1,200 complaints. Therefore, the insurance services business unit's goal PR-G was achieved.

8.4.2.4 GQM-CI-G: Evaluate Improvement of Customer Interaction Processes

Similar to the second goal, the third goal defined by the management of the insurance services business unit referred to customer complaints, but in this case complaints concerning the customer interaction processes. The goal was (CI-G) to have an average of 20 % fewer complaints of this nature by the middle of the next fiscal year (2012). Figure 8.6 illustrates the measurement data collected during the baseline period, the second half of fiscal year 2012, and for the target period, the first half of fiscal year 2012. The insurance services business unit was not able to reduce the average number of customer complaints regarding the customer interaction processes below the target value of 500 complaints. Therefore, the Insurance Services business unit's goal CI-G was not achieved. This was anticipated in the analysis done during the "execute plans" phase.

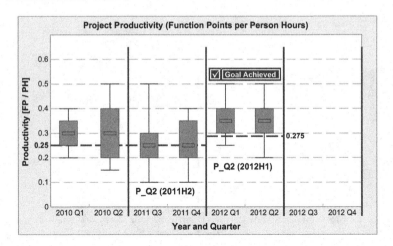

Fig. 8.7   Example: Interpretation of measurement data for the organizational goal PP-G

8.4.2.5 GQM-PP-G: Evaluate Increase of Productivity of Development Projects

The management of the Software Development group defined this goal in order to support attainment of the Insurance Services business unit goals (and the top-level goal of Company X). In order to support the insurance services business unit with more frequent delivery of new features and bug fixes (FF-G), the Software Development group defined the goal (PP-G) of increasing the productivity of development and maintenance projects by 10 % by the middle of the next fiscal year (2012). Figure 8.7 illustrates the basic statistics of the productivity measurements displayed in the form of box plots. Not only is the median located above the target threshold of 0.275 (as required by the defined goal), but the complete range of the nonoutlier productivity measurements is also located above the target threshold. Therefore, the Software Development group's goal PP-G was achieved.

8.4.2.6 GQM-DS-G: Evaluate Decrease of Number of Defects Slipped

In order to support the Insurance Services business unit by reducing the number of customer complaints concerning the reliability of their products (PR-G), the Software Development group defined the goal (DS-G) of decreasing the number of defects slipped through all quality assurance phases by 10 % by the middle of the next fiscal year (2012). Figure 8.8 illustrates the defect slippage for the baseline and target releases of the software product delivered by the Software Development group. According to the displayed measurement data and the computed defect slippage ratio (DSR), the Software Development group was able to reduce the overall number of defects slipped through QA by more than the required 10 % (from 59 % to 38 %). Therefore, the Software Development group's goal DS-G was achieved.

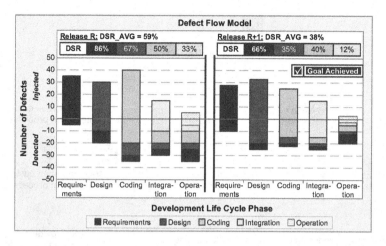

Fig. 8.8 Example: Interpretation of measurement data for the organizational goal DS-G

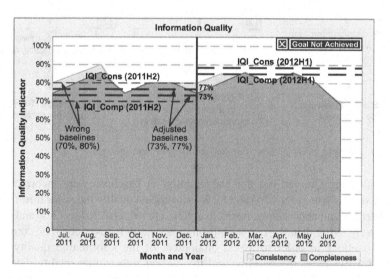

Fig. 8.9 Example: Interpretation of measurement data for the organizational goal IQ-G

8.4.2.7 GQM-IQ-G: Evaluate Improvement of IQ of Enterprise IS

In order to support the Insurance Services business unit in reducing the number of customer complaints concerning customer interaction (CI-G), the Software Development group defined the goal (IQ-G) of improving the enterprise information system to provide information of higher quality (for a definition of IQ, please refer to the "Example" section in Chap. 5, Fig. 5.21). Specifically, the Software Development group aimed at providing an Enterprise IS that provides 20 % more complete and 10 % more consistent information. In order to evaluate attainment of this goal, the Software Development group first measured the information baseline quality indicators for the second half of 2011. After the actual data had

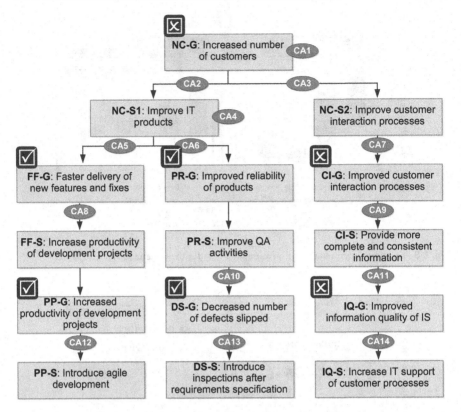

Fig. 8.10 Example: Interpretation of organizational goals and strategies

been collected, it turned out that the initially set baselines were incorrect. The initially set baselines of a 70 % and 80 % information quality index for information completeness and consistency, respectively, had to be corrected to 73 % and 77 %, respectively. After that, the current information quality indexes could be compared to the baselines in order to assess attainment of the information quality goal. Figure 8.9 illustrates the baseline and the current information quality data. The information quality collected for the first half of 2012 did not achieve the target values of 88 % (completeness) and 97 % (consistency). Therefore, the Software Development group's goal IQ-G was not achieved.

8.4.2.8 Summary: Interpretation of Organizational Goals and Strategies

Summarizing, Company X was not able to achieve its management-level business goal of increasing the number of customers by 10 %. Figure 8.10 illustrates the complete tree of goals and strategies with their status of attainment. The analysis of the goal attainment resulted in several observations:

Table 8.3 Example: Analysis of potential issues in the grid

Potential issue	Detail analysis
CA3, CA7, CA9, CA11, or CA14 are wrong	<u>Assumption CA3</u>: To get more customers in the insurance area, the quality of the customer interaction processes has to be improved. → Checked and found to be TRUE
	<u>Context CA7</u>: Customers complain about many issues related to the customer interaction processes. → Checked and found to be TRUE
	<u>Context CA9</u>: Customers complain about inconsistent and incomplete information during their interaction with company X. → Checked and found to be TRUE
	<u>Context CA11</u>: The existing information system does not ensure the exchange of consistent and complete information with the customers. → Checked and found to be TRUE
	<u>Context CA14</u>: Not all services of X are completely IT-supported; some have to be provided manually, which decreases information quality. → Checked and found to be TRUE
Strategy IQ-S was not properly deployed and, consequently, strategy CI-S was not effective	• Strategy IQ-S was not properly deployed in that the developed CRM interface did not meet the requirements of the intended users. • The analysis of the root problem indicated the "execute plans" phase. It was confirmed that there was insufficient involvement of CRM users in the development project (especially in the requirements specification). • It was decided that an improved strategy must be developed or selected to perform a major rework on the CRM interface in order to properly realize goal IQ-G. • EITHER the existing strategy of increasing IT support of customer processes can be improved by doing a better job of capturing CRM user input and providing more resources from IT to increase the completeness and consistency of the information • OR, alternatively, different, more effective strategies are needed to achieve goals IQ-G and CI-G.
There was not sufficient time for achieving goal NC-G	• The application of strategies associated with goal NC-G had to be stopped (i.e., the "execute plans" cycle had to be left) before the time frame of one year planned for the goal because of the problems with the effectiveness of strategy IQ-S. • Consequently, there was not enough time for achieving goal NC-G, i.e., application of the substituted strategies at the late date did not allow goal IQ-S to be fully achieved. • Yet, there was a positive trend with respect to goal NC-G (number of customers in the insurance area) and there is a good chance that after adjusting the ineffective strategy IQ-S and continuing the (to date) effective strategies, goal NC-G can be achieved as planned, i.e., within the next half year.

- Information quality in terms of completeness and consistency could not be improved significantly.
- Customers keep complaining about the interaction processes.
- The number of customers increased (there is a positive trend), but not sufficiently.

Based on these observations, Mr. Watson (company expert in GQM$^+$Strategies) discussed potential improvements with the relevant stakeholders: Mr. Clark (CEO), Mr. Davis (Head of Insurance Services business unit), and Mr. Smith (Head of Software Development group).

8.4.3 Identify Improvement Potentials

8.4.3.1 Data Analysis and Interpretation
During a joint meeting, Davis, Clark, Watson, and Smith discussed potential reasons for why the organizational goals IQ-G and CI-G, and NC-G were not achieved. For example, they considered the associated strategies and assumptions as well as the organizational goals that were achieved. Table 8.3 summarizes the potential issues they identified.

8.4.3.2 Retrospective Session
In addition, Mr. Watson organized a feedback session with the persons responsible for performing the strategic projects and the measurement activities as well as those responsible for providing the measurement data. His objective was to obtain feedback from the people involved in the strategy projects on what went well and what went poorly while implementing and deploying the GQM$^+$Strategies grid. The session followed a standard procedure for project retrospectives (see Sect. 8.3.2). Mr. Watson played the role of the facilitator. As one input to the session, he presented the results of the grid interpretation to the participants. In addition to the feedback to the grid implementation and deployment activities, session participants discussed potential reasons for why selected goals were not achieved. The feedback session ended with several improvement actions that should be implemented locally within the corresponding strategic projects and measurement activities (without the need for modifying the GQM$^+$Strategies grid). Table 8.4 summarizes the most important points with respect to what went wrong during the strategic project and thus should be the subject of improvement in the future.

8.4.3.3 Improvement Potentials
The stakeholders decided to focus future improvement activities on achieving goal CI-G of reducing the number of customer complaints concerning the customer interaction processes. They believe that achieving the goal would suffice for achieving the company business goal of increasing the number of customers by 10 %. In order to achieve goal CI-G, three major improvements were proposed:

Table 8.4 Example: Potential improvement actions identified during retrospective session

What went wrong?	Potential improvement action
• <u>Limited availability of insurance services personnel</u>: During the development of the new CRM interface, the CRM users affected by (and interested in) the change to the interface could not be involved in development (especially in the requirements specification) because they were busy with insurance services activities.	• Provide resources (budget and time) to insurance services in order to support more involvement of the CRM users in the development of high-quality IT support.
• <u>Poor software project management processes</u>: The defined and documented project management processes are not available in the software development group.	• Define and deploy standard improved project management processes and set up Project Management Office (PMO) to support project managers in effectively managing the project (especially managing project risks).
• <u>Poor skills of software project managers</u>: The software project managers are missing skills required for effectively managing software development projects, especially for managing project risks and preventing project performance issues. Insufficient skills are particularly critical in contexts where prescribed project management processes are missing.	• Provide appropriate training to project managers, including integrated project management, scope management, time and cost management, quality management, human resources management, communications management, risk management, procurement management, and stakeholder management.

1. <u>Introduce quality assurance of information</u>: Until the IT-related strategy for increasing information quality starts working fully (i.e., until an appropriate, high-quality CRM interface is developed and deployed), the stakeholders decided to intensify manual checks of information quality. For this purpose, they want to assign more personnel for reviewing the information with respect to its completeness and consistency.

2. <u>Introduce systematic software project management</u>: The root problem of the ineffective strategy IQ-S and the feedback from personnel involved in the CRM interface development project convinced the management of Company X to improve project management processes in the software development group. An appropriate strategy should be added to the grid and implemented in the next improvement cycle.

3. <u>Allow more time for achieving goal NC-G</u>: The involved stakeholders believe that the increasing trend in the number of customers (NC-G) indicates that the strategy of improving the customer interaction processes (NC-S) actually works but requires more time (as originally planned in the goal's time frame) to provide the required effect of a 10 % increase in the number of customers.

Phase 6: Package Improvements

9

In this phase, we modify the GQM⁺Strategies grid in order to close the gaps identified in the previous phase. This includes performing the necessary changes to the plans to modify the goals' magnitude or time frame, revising the strategies and modifying any data collection or analysis procedures. If we were successful in achieving our goals and no gaps have been identified, the grid will be kept as is.

To improve our approach for achieving the next generation of business goals, we also use the lessons learned to improve our overall process for developing a grid, our processes for implementing the strategies, and the data collection and analysis processes. We also gain experiential knowledge about how various strategies relevant to our business can be improved and packaged.

Finally, we package, store, and communicate the outcomes of the phase for future use. Table 9.1 summarizes the objectives, inputs, basic activities, and

Table 9.1 Overview of the "package improvements" phase

Package improvements	
Objective	The objective of this phase is to package, store, and communicate the experiences gathered in the previous phases and to create a revised version of the GQM⁺Strategies grid as well as the related strategy and measurement plans. If we were successful in achieving our goals and everything worked out well, no changes to the grid are necessary.
Inputs	• The GQM⁺Strategies grid • Strategy plans • Measurement plan • Improvement potentials (based on lessons learned and analysis results) for developing future GQM⁺Strategies grids, plans for the application of strategies, and plans for measurement and analysis
Activities	1. Revise grid and plans (including processes) 2. Communicate outcomes 3. Manage experience (store grid, plans, lessons learned, and analysis results) 4. Initiate a new cycle
Outcomes	• Revised GQM⁺Strategies grid and processes (if required) • Revised strategy plans and processes (if required) • Revised measurement plan and processes (if required)

V. Basili et al., *Aligning Organizations Through Measurement*, The Fraunhofer IESE Series 127
on Software and Systems Engineering, DOI 10.1007/978-3-319-05047-8_9,
© Springer International Publishing Switzerland 2014

outcomes of this phase. In the following sections, we will describe the individual activities of this phase in more detail.

Based on the identified improvement potentials from the execution and analysis phases, the implications on the specification of the GQM$^+$Strategies grid as well as the strategy and measurement plans are analyzed and revised versions are created. The outcome is communicated to all stakeholders so that final feedback can be obtained. Then the grid and the plans are stored in an experience repository and a new cycle of the overall process is initiated, if necessary. The six phases of the GQM$^+$Strategies process represent a continuous improvement cycle that allows for quantitatively evaluating the most important goals and strategies of an organization.

The frequency of running through the whole cycle largely depends on the speed at which the organization wants to evolve and continuously improve. It also depends on the size of the grid that is modeled and on whether this grid captures the entire organization or only different parts thereof. A large organization probably wants to come up with a 5-year plan for goals and strategies and revise that plan every year. A small organization probably sets up a 2-year plan and revises their actions every half year. Every revision of plans and the corresponding decisions should be based on sound empirical data. Data collection is continuous and analysis is performed in as close to real time as possible during the execution phase so changes can be made in a timely fashion and can therefore be mapped to one cycle through the GQM$^+$Strategies process. This does not explicitly imply that the whole grid is changed each time we run through the process. Higher-level goals and strategies probably stay stable for a very long time, whereas lower-level goals tend to change more frequently.

In the following sections, we will discuss the major activities of the "package improvements" phase in more detail.

9.1   Revise Grid and Plans

As part of this step, the GQM$^+$Strategies grid and the related plans and processes are revised based on the recommendations given as part of the analysis phase:

- The company expert on GQM$^+$Strategies prepares a meeting with the top-level decision makers regarding the improvement recommendations in terms of the GQM$^+$Strategies grid, the measurement plan, and the strategy plan as well as related processes. During the meeting, the company expert presents the recommendations and the top-level decision makers prioritize the improvement recommendations, i.e., they determine which ones will actually be implemented in the next cycle leading to concrete actions.
- The company expert analyzes the implications of the **improvement actions on the grid** and performs one or more of the following actions:
  - Replace organizational goals related to improvement with goals related to maintaining the current level of performance if the improvement was

achieved. For instance, if the original goal was to have increased productivity and the goal was finally attained, it can be replaced by a goal that is just about maintaining the current level of productivity.

- Modify attributes of existing grid entities (such as goals, strategies, context factors, assumptions, measurement goals, questions, metrics, and interpretation models), e.g., if the magnitude or time frame of an organizational goal needs to be changed, the description of some entities can be improved, or an assumption can be proven and becomes a context factor.
- Remove obsolete grid entities. For instance, if a strategy is no longer needed, it can be removed from the grid. This also holds for all other grid entities that are derived from the removed entity and are not referenced from other entities.
- Add new strategies, context factors, assumptions, measurement goals, questions, metrics, and interpretation models, if needed. For instance, an additional strategy may be needed to fully achieve an organizational goal or a new context factor or assumption needs to be documented. Adding a new organizational goal should be avoided during this phase because it probably should involve other stakeholders and requires deeper discussion and a workshop on how to obtain that goal in the organization. That should normally be done as part of another cycle of the overall GQM⁺Strategies process.
- The company expert also analyzes the implications of the **improvement actions on the strategy plans** and performs one or more of the following actions based on the adapted GQM⁺Strategies grid:
  - Remove obsolete strategies from the plan and inform the responsible managers that the corresponding implementation projects or governance activities need to be stopped. This also holds for other activities derived from the obsolete strategy.
  - Modify existing strategies if changes regarding the schedule are required based on adaptations of the timespan of the related organizational goals and inform the responsible managers that the corresponding implementation projects or governance activities need to revise their schedule.
  - Add new strategies to the plan and inform the responsible managers that corresponding implementation projects or governance activities need to be set up.
- The company expert analyzes the implications of the **improvement actions on the measurement plans** and performs one or more of the following actions based on the adapted GQM⁺Strategies grid:
  - Remove obsolete metrics from the measurement plan and inform collection resources and stakeholders about the changes.
  - Modify existing metrics of the measurement plan and inform collection resources and stakeholders about the adapted procedures (for instance, the definition of a metric was changed or the data has to be retrieved from a different tool).

- – Add new metrics to the measurement plan, set up the corresponding tooling for collecting the measurement data, and inform collection resources and stakeholders about the changes.
- The company expert analyzes the implications of the improvement actions on the overall GQM⁺Strategies process (including all activities for constructing/ maintaining the grid and the plans, for carrying out these plans, for analyzing the data, and for packaging the results). For instance, this includes changing/ adapting the communication paths in the organizations, doing data analysis more frequently, or taking into account more/other stakeholders.

9.2   Communicate Outcomes

As part of this step, the revised GQM⁺Strategies grid and the related plans are sent to all stakeholders of the measurement initiative in order to inform everybody about the current progress and to get final commitment from top-level management.

At this stage, the company expert only performs minor changes to the grid and the plans (such as correcting spelling errors or resolving obvious inconsistencies). If critical feedback is obtained, the company expert goes back to the previous steps to revise the grid and plans again.

9.3   Manage Experience

As part of the third step, the GQM⁺Strategies grid and the plans as well as the related lessons learned and analysis results are persistently stored in the organization. There are multiple ways for storing models, experience, and knowledge in an organization, ranging from simple file structures or database systems to more advanced concepts. The concrete conceptual and technical implementation of that storage depends on the needs of the organization.

The experiences packaged include all the processes associated with the application of the grid, the new processes defined resulting from the deployment of the strategies, and the measurement approaches and data including new baselines.

In the simplest case, a directory under version control would be sufficient for technically storing and accessing the latest version of the GQM⁺Strategies grid and the plans.

A more advanced concept for managing experience in an organization and allowing for continuous improvement is the Experience Factory (Basili 1989; Basili et al. 1995). Figure 9.1 gives an overview of the basic logical structure. It supports an organization by analyzing and synthesizing all kinds of experience, acting as a repository for such experience, and supplying that experience to various projects on demand. A repository called the experience base contains all kinds of informal, formal or schematized, and productized models and measures of various software processes, products, and other forms of knowledge. The original focus was on supporting software development projects, but the general idea can be used in any

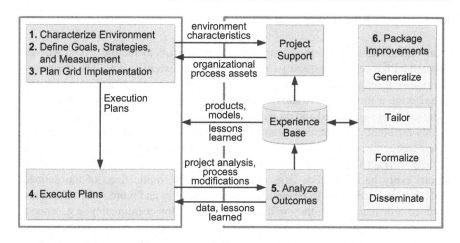

Fig. 9.1 Basic experience factory concepts

environment for packaging experiences as explicit models and reusing them systematically as part of future projects (e.g., strategic implementation projects).

The *Experience Factory* (*EF*) distinguishes between a project-specific and an
organization-wide part and follows the same basic phases as the overall
GQM$^+$Strategies process:

1. Characterize Environment: Understand the environment and retrieve experience
   appropriate to that environment (such as baselines).
2. Define Goals, Strategies, and Metrics: Define quantifiable and reasonable goals
   that have a strategic relevance to the organization.
3. Plan Grid Implementation: Choose the appropriate processes for obtaining the
   goals and evaluating their attainment (including techniques, methods, and tools).
4. Execute Plans: Perform the processes and collect the specified data.
5. Analyze Outcomes: Analyze the collected data to evaluate current practices and
   provide lessons learned for future improvements.
6. Package Improvements: Consolidate the experience gained in the form of new,
   or updated and refined, models and store it in the experience base.

9.4   Initiate New Cycle

The last step is about initiating a new iteration of the six phases of the
GQM$^+$Strategies process. The overall process defines an improvement cycle from
setting goals for the organization to evaluating their attainment and coming up with
concrete improvement actions. The whole process is driven by the company expert
on GQM$^+$Strategies, which imitates the process in concordance with top-level
management. Note that the characterization phase in the new cycle differs from
the characterization phase in the last cycle, as the organization has been changed by
that cycle.

9.4.1 Cycle Frequency and Intensity

If an organization is interested in continuous improvement, the cycle will be repeated with a certain frequency (*time-based improvement cycles*). The frequency of running through the whole cycle largely depends on the speed at which the organization wants to evolve and continuously improve. It also depends on the size of the grid that is modeled and on whether this grid captures the entire organization or only different parts thereof. A small organization will normally tend towards a higher frequency of improvement cycles (e.g., once or twice a year) because they are able to react fast. So they will probably set up a 2-year plan and revise their actions every half year. For large organizations, the implications of the defined goals and strategies need to be evaluated more carefully and more stakeholders are involved. For that reason, they will probably have a lower frequency, e.g., once a year for a 5-year plan.

Every revision of plans and the corresponding decisions should be based on sound empirical data. Data collection is continuous and analysis is performed in as close to real time as possible during the execution phase so changes can be made in a timely fashion and can be mapped to one cycle through the GQM⁺Strategies process. In different iterations, the different phases may be carried out with different intensity depending on whether and which parts of the grid, the strategy plan, and the measurement plan are actually affected and need to be changed.

Generally, there is a tendency that higher-level goals and strategies stay more stable than lower-level goals and strategies. For instance, if a higher-level goal is to remain competitive in terms of value delivered to our customers, this is probably a general goal that will remain stable throughout the entire lifetime of the organization. Lower-level goals and strategies for achieving that top-level goal may change over time depending on the change of the overall market addressed by an organization.

It should be noted that during the first cycle through the organization-level learning cycle, a great deal will be learned about the application of GQM⁺Strategies itself. The second cycle will certainly involve further learning but can take advantage of what has been learned from the first cycle, and the personnel will be more familiar and experienced with applying the approach.

Figure 9.2 gives an example of what the schedule of cycles of the overall GQM⁺Strategies process might look like. Let us assume a company that wants to revise their goals and strategies on a yearly basis. In year #1, the first regular cycle is conducted. The grid and the plans are worked out in the first 2 months. After that, the improvement initiatives are launched until the end of November. In December, analysis and packaging are performed. In year #2, two cycles are performed: one regular and one exceptional one. The regular one ends in May due to some critical event (such as the company needing to react to a new competitor). The company analyzes the current state of their goals and strategies in May and works out an extended grid from June to July. After that the reworked grid and plans are carried out until the end of the year. In year #3, another regular cycle is performed.

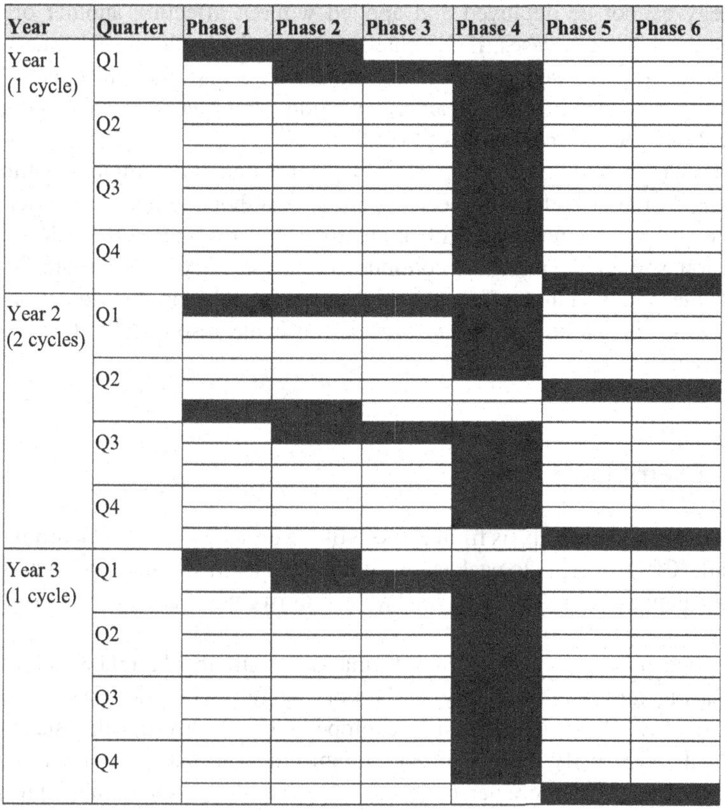

Year	Quarter	Phase 1	Phase 2	Phase 3	Phase 4	Phase 5	Phase 6
Year 1 (1 cycle)	Q1						
	Q2						
	Q3						
	Q4						
Year 2 (2 cycles)	Q1						
	Q2						
	Q3						
	Q4						
Year 3 (1 cycle)	Q1						
	Q2						
	Q3						
	Q4						

Fig. 9.2 Example of multiple cycles of the GQM⁺Strategies process

9.4.2 Exceptional Cycles

Normally, an organization will define an appropriate frequency of cycles of the GQM⁺Strategies process (e.g., once a year). The majority of time within one cycle is spent in Phase 4 on executing the strategy implementation projects and carrying out the governance activities, which includes analyzing the movement of the organization towards achieving their goals.

However, there may be situations in which an exceptional cycle is needed (*exception-based improvement cycle*) if something requires immediate management attention and has a substantial, direct implication on the goals and strategies defined in the grid. Example exceptional situations include:

- Unachievable goals or ineffective/unfeasible strategies: During strategy deployment and implementation, there is a realization that (1) a goal as specified is unachievable with the associated strategy, (2) a strategy will not be effective or cannot be implemented as specified because the context has changed, or (3) a strategy cannot be deployed and applied without affecting another organizational unit. In such cases, if the changes cannot be made in real time without approval of all related parties (stakeholders), we may have to make a major modification to the grid within an organizational improvement cycle and thus we should move on to the analysis phase.

- Insufficient resources: During strategy deployment and implementation, the allocated time or budget has been depleted even though no issues are identified that could not be resolved with more time and resources. In such a case, a decision should be made to continue, i.e., more resources should be made available and will not affect the higher-level goals, or the execution phase (Phase 4) should be left at the time because the resource limit is a serious constraint.

9.5   Example

After performing the analysis from Phase 5 of the organization-level learning cycle, Mr. Clark (CEO) decides to package what has been learned. The major outcomes of the analysis phase were the three following improvement recommendations:

1. Introduce quality assurance of information: Until the IT-related-strategy for increasing information quality starts working fully (i.e., until an appropriate, high-quality CRM interface is developed and deployed), the stakeholders decided to intensify manual checks of information quality. For this purpose, they want to assign more personnel for reviewing the information with respect to its completeness and consistency.
2. Introduce systematic software project management: The root problem of the ineffective strategy IQ-S and the feedback from the personnel involved in the CRM interface development project convinced the management of Company X to improve the project management processes in the software development group. An appropriate strategy should be added to the grid and implemented in the next improvement cycle.
3. Allow more time for achieving goal NC-G: The involved stakeholders believe that the increasing trend in the number of customers (NC-G) indicates that the strategy of improving the customer interaction processes (NC-S) actually works but requires more time (as originally planned in the goal's time frame) to provide the required effect of a 10 % increase in the number of customers.

9.5.1   Revise Grid and Plans

Mr. Watson (company expert in GQM$^+$Strategies) conducts a meeting with Mr. Clark (CEO) to summarize all outcomes and improvement recommendations of the analysis phase. Mr. Clark decides on implementing all recommendations.

After that, Mr. Watson analyzes the implications of the improvement actions on the grid:

- A second strategy needs to be added to goal IQ-G to achieve improved information quality until the appropriate IT support of customer processes is available:
  - IQ-S2: Manually check the information quality of information systems.
- An appropriate goal and strategy need to be defined in the software development group to improve the involvement of CRM users in the project (especially in the requirements specification) in which IT support for customer processes is developed.
- More time is needed for achieving NC-G, i.e., for increasing the number of customers, CI-G for improving the customer interaction processes, and IQ-G for achieving improved information quality. In consequence, the time frame attribute of the organizational goal definition is extended by 6 more months.
- Goals FF-G and PR-G of the business unit as well as goals PP-G and DS-G of the software development group have been attained. Nonetheless, the company wants to monitor that this level of performance is maintained in the future. As a consequence, the four goals are modified to maintain the current level of performance:
  - FF-G: Maintain delivery rate of new features and fixes
  - PR-G: Maintain reliability of products
  - PP-G: Maintain productivity of development projects
  - DS-G: Maintain number of defects slipped
- Strategies NC-S1, FF-S, PR-S, PP-S, and DS-S need to be adapted accordingly. NC-S1, FF-S, PR-S become maintenance strategies and the strategies of the software development group, PP-S and DS-S, can be removed because their implementation is done and because no specific actions are required right now to maintain the current level of performance:
  - NC-S1: Maintain quality of IT products
  - FF-G: Maintain productivity of development projects
  - PR-G: Maintain effectiveness of QA activities

An overview of the overall goals and strategies of the revised grid can be seen in Fig. 9.3. A complete list of the organizational goals is presented in Table 9.2. The changed parts of the organizational goal template compared to the original version of the grid are written in italic style.

However, even though the revised grid does not require defining additional metrics, the GQM measurement goals and the corresponding interpretation models need to be adapted in order to address the maintenance goals that are replacing some of the improvement-related goals in the grid. Table 9.3 gives an overview of the changes required.

Next, Mr. Watson revises the strategy plan based on the changes of the GQM⁺Strategies grid and summarizes the new responsibilities. The changed parts are written in italic style:

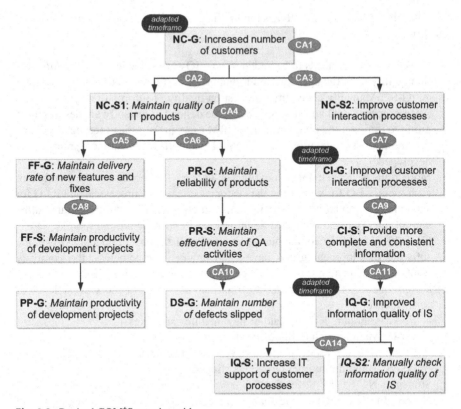

Fig. 9.3 Revised GQM⁺Strategies grid

- Clark (CEO)
  - Strategy NC-S1: Improve IT products
  - Strategy NC-S2: *Maintain* processes
- Davis (division manager of insurance services business unit)
  - Strategy FF-S: *Maintain* productivity of development projects
  - Strategy PR-S: *Maintain effectiveness* of QA activities
  - Strategy CI-S: Provide more complete and consistent information
- Smith (department head of software development group)
  - Strategy IQ-S: Increase IT support of customer processes
  - *Finished Strategy PP-S: Introduce agile development*
  - *Finished Strategy DS-S: Introduce inspections after requirements specification*
- Jones (help desk manager)
  - *New Strategy IQ-S: Manually check information quality of information*

Table 9.4 summarizes the revised strategic projects and measurement activities together with the responsible roles at Company X. The projects related to the finished strategies have been removed and a new project is initiated, led by

Table 9.2 Revised organizational goals

	Focus	Object	Magnitude	Time frame	Scope	Constraints	Relations
NC-G	Amount of	Customers in insurance area	10 % more	*Until Jan. 2013*	Management	While maintaining cost	–
FF-G	Time of delivering new features and bug fixes of	Enterprise IS	*Feature releases every 6 months and monthly bug fix releases*	*Continuously*	Management of insurance services business unit	While maintaining cost	–
CI-G	Quality of	Customer interaction processes	Having 20 % less customer complaints	*Until Jan. 2013*	Management of Insurance Services business unit	While maintaining cost	–
PR-G	Reliability of	IT products	*Maintain current level*	*Continuously*	Management of Insurance Services business unit	While maintaining cost	–
PP-G	Productivity of	SW maintenance and new development projects	*Maintain current level*	*Continuously*	Management of Software Development group	While maintaining quality and functionality	–
IQ-G	Information quality of	Enterprise IS	20 % more complete and 10 % more consistent information	*Until Jan. 2013*	Management of Software Development group	–	–
DS-G	Number of defects slipped through	QA activities (V&V)	*Maintain current level*	*Continuously*	Management of Software Development group	–	–

Table 9.3 Revised measurement goals and interpretation models

Measurement goal (MG)	Short description	Interpretation model (pseudo formula)
GQM-NC-G	Evaluate increase of number of customers	$Cus(2012)/Cus(2011) \geq 1.1$
GQM-FF-G	*Evaluate delivery of new features and fixes*	$F\_Rel(All) \geq 1$ AND BF_Rel $(All) \geq 6$
GQM-CI-G	Evaluate improvement of customer interaction processes	$CC\_IP(2012H2)/CC\_IP (2011H2) \leq 0.8$
GQM-PR-G	*Evaluate reliability of products*	$CC\_RP(All) \leq 1200$
GQM-PP-G	*Evaluate productivity of development projects*	$P\_Q2(All) \geq 0.275$
GQM-IQ-G	Evaluate improvement of information quality of Enterprise IS	$IQI\_Comp(2012H2)/IQI\_Comp (2011H2) \geq 1.2$ AND $IQI\_Cons(2012H2)/IQI\_Cons (2011H2) \geq 1.1$
GQM-DS-G	*Evaluate number of defects slipped*	$DSR\_AVG(All) \leq 60\,\%$

Table 9.4 Strategic projects and measurement activities at Company X

Strategic project (P) and measurement activity (A)	Detailed activities	Responsible person
P3: Develop new CRM interface	• Design and implement new interface of the Customer Relationships Management System (CRM) • Train, pilot, and roll out new interface	Lewis, IT project manager
PN: *Information quality training*	• Train people in manually checking information quality • Reassign resources to support manual check of information quality	*Jones, help desk*
A1: Monitor management goals	• Collect, prepare, analyze, and interpret data related to Company X's management goals • Monitor attainment of business goals defined on Company X's management level	Clark, CEO
A2: Monitor insurance goals	• Collect, prepare, analyze, and interpret data related to insurance goals • Monitor attainment of the goals defined by the Insurance Services business unit	Davis, unit head
A3: Monitor software goals	• Collect, prepare, analyze, and interpret data related to the software development goals • Monitor attainment of the goals defined in the Software Development group	Smith, group head

Mr. Jones (help desk manager), to train help desk members in manually checking information quality until the IT support is in place. Mr. Jones is informed by his department head to set up the new strategic project. Mr. Lewis (leader of P3) is informed about the updated schedule.

Last, Mr. Watson revises the measurement plan based on the changes of the GQM+Strategies grid and the revised strategy plan. He analyzes the overhead cost related to collecting the data and analyzes the feedback to optimize the data collection process. The conclusion is that no change to the way data is collected at Company X is currently required.

9.5.2 Communicate Outcomes

Mr. Watson sends the revised GQM+Strategies grid and the related plans to all stakeholders of the measurement initiative (Mr. Clark, Mr. Davis, Mr. Smith, and Mr. Jones) in order to inform everybody about the current progress and get final commitment from the CEO. The revised grid and plans are accepted by all involved parties.

In addition, the experiences gained by all stakeholders while applying GQM+Strategies are collected and packaged. The experience packaged involves two types of information:

• What they have learned about building the grid and going through the cycle so that they can be more efficient about it next time through. Issues might include improvement of the training as well as specific improvements to the various stages of the process, such as grid building and tool use, the planning process for execution, real-time feedback during the execution, and the analysis and packaging processes. If they are committed to applying GQM+Strategies, they need to evolve it into an efficient and effective process.
• What they have learned about applying the technologies and how they had to tailor and measure them for the organization. This would include the Scrum methodology and how it should be tailored and measured, Checklist-based and perspective-based reading and how it should be tailored and measured, etc. This might involve streamlining the process by adding or eliminating steps, improving the process specification and procedures, assessing the roles or assignment of roles, etc.

9.5.3 Manage Experience

Mr. Watson decides to set up a company-internal versioning repository for storing the latest version of the GQM+Strategies grid, the strategy plan, and the measurement plan. In order to increase overall commitment to the goals and strategies defined in the grid and to increase transparency regarding the currently ongoing initiatives, Mr. Clark decides that a new page to the company-internal Wiki shall be added, providing a summary of the currently pursued goals and strategies as well as the ongoing improvement initiatives.

9.5.4   Initiate New Cycle

The first iteration of the overall GQM$^+$Strategies cycle has been completed successfully. Mr. Clark decides that from now on, Company X will perform yearly workshops to revise the grid and the plans developed. Mr. Watson will be responsible for organizing these events and initializing the next cycle.

Part II

Industrial Applications and Relations to Other Approaches

In this part of the book, we discuss GQM⁺Strategies from the perspective of its application in daily practice. In particular:

- Chapter 10 discusses the industrial challenges addressed by GQM⁺Strategies. Furthermore, an overview of typical application scenarios as well as actual application cases of the approach in different industrial contexts are presented.
- Chapter 11 presents how GQM⁺Strategies relates to other approaches, such as organizational performance measurement and process improvement, which are already well established in the industrial world.
- Chapter 12 summarizes the current achievements and future developments regarding the GQM⁺Strategies approach.

Industrial Challenges and Applications 10

Success requires both the right strategy and operational effectiveness.

—Michael E. Porter, 1996

This chapter gives some insights into typical industrial challenges addressed by GQM⁺Strategies and highlights some industrial real-life applications of the approach. First, we will focus on typical usage scenarios and real-life challenges addressed by the different domains where the approach has actually been applied. After that, we will take a closer look at the specific challenges and industrial needs of IT and software development companies as this was defined as the initial focus and starting point of the GQM⁺Strategies approach. Finally, we will present three industrial cases in which the approach was applied:

- ECOPETROL S.A.: International gas and oil company (see Sect. 10.2)
- IPA: Japanese government agency for IT technology transfer (see Sect. 10.3)
- JAXA: Japanese aerospace agency (see Sect. 10.4)

10.1 Industrial Challenges

Basically, we can distinguish between three classes of challenges addressed by the approach based upon common challenges from our industrial applications:

- Alignment: The first major challenge lies in the consistent alignment of goals, strategies, and associated measurement data across different units of an organization. If this alignment is not present, an organization is not able to demonstrate the value of strategies in the context of its higher-level goals and make sure that the whole organization walks in the same direction. In terms of data collection, one will typically find different bits and pieces distributed across the organization, but these often do not contribute to an overall meaningful story. The GQM⁺Strategies grid supports an organization in identifying goals, strategies,

V. Basili et al., *Aligning Organizations Through Measurement*, The Fraunhofer IESE Series 143
on Software and Systems Engineering, DOI 10.1007/978-3-319-05047-8_10,
© Springer International Publishing Switzerland 2014

and measurement data and in defining clear rationale-based linkages between all elements (making use of context factors and assumptions). By doing this, existing gaps such as conflicting goals can be identified and corresponding improvement actions can be initiated. Furthermore, it makes sure that data is collected for a specific goal without causing unnecessary bloat.

- Communication: The second major challenge lies in being able to transparently communicate goals and strategies and the data needed for evaluating the attainment of goals so that the whole organization knows their role in attaining the top-level goals and can walk in the same direction. If no communication mechanism is available, there is a high risk that implicit, locally defined strategies will be followed, which may or may not contribute to the goals defined for units at higher levels in the organizational structure. Even without collecting any data, the GQM⁺Strategies grid itself can be used for communicating existing elements and for establishing a common understanding of the direction the organization wants to take.

- Decision-Making: The third major challenge lies in having a mechanism to support measurement-based decision-making. If no such mechanism is present, organizations tend to base their decisions on company-wide strategies or gut-feeling, instead of on a sound analysis of the measurement data available for making informed improvement decisions based on the outcomes of the analysis. The GQM⁺Strategies grid supports an organization in measurement-based decision-making by defining what data needs to be collected and how to analyze and interpret the data in terms of the defined goals and strategies. Furthermore, the defined rationales support the organization in picking appropriate alternative strategies.

Table 10.1 lists some common example questions an organization may have in the context of the sketched challenges when making use of the approach.

Over the last several years, various aspects of GQM⁺Strategies have been and are being applied in many different companies working in completely different domains and having different business models. Most commonly, the application has involved development of a grid or partial grid. Table 10.2 gives an overview of the different applications addressing the domains and business areas in which the approach was applied, the main motivation for making use of GQM⁺Strategies, and, finally, the concrete activities the companies performed as part of the overall application process and according to the specific needs they had. Although our scope was again on IT-based and software development organizations, it is equally useful in broader contexts, as the applications indicate. The main purpose of this list is not to give a complete list of all GQM⁺Strategies applications, but to highlight some typical application scenarios.

Table 10.3 maps the cases presented in Table 10.2 to the general classes of challenges identified in Table 10.1.

In Sect. 2.3, three basic parts of a typical process for applying and integrating GQM⁺Strategies in an organization have been introduced:

Table 10.1 Typical example questions in the context of industrial challenges

Challenges	Example questions	GQM$^+$Strategies-related actions
Alignment	Are my goals, strategies, and measurement data appropriate, complete, consistent, and well aligned?	Model existing goals, strategies, and measurement data as well as their linkage via the grid and identify issues (Alignment)
	How do I empower my units to come up with their own successful strategies contributing to my business goals?	Define top-level goals and strategies that all units should refer to and align with (Communication)
	How do I plan and control strategies in alignment with organizational goals?	Derive new strategies from organizational goals (Alignment)
	What is the value of my strategies towards organizational goals?	Show how existing strategies contribute to organizational goals (Alignment)
	How do I make sure that all suppliers and projects contribute to my organizational goals?	Align supplier- and project-related strategies with organizational goals (Alignment and Communication)
Decision-making	How do I monitor and control the attainment of goals and the success/failure of strategies?	Derive metrics from existing goals and strategies
	How do I come up with the right corrective actions?	Analyze the impact factors on your goals and define/adapt strategies
	How do I define realistic targets for goal attainment?	Analyze the trend in data and update the timespan for obtaining the target values
Communication	How do I make sure that everybody knows and understands one another's goals and strategies?	Document and publish existing goals, strategies, and measurement data internally

- **Develop**: The first part (phases 1 and 2) is the development of a hierarchical grid that aligns goals, strategies, rationales, and measurement.
- Implement: The second part (phases 3 and 4) involves the execution of the strategies and measurements defined by the grid, allowing us to check the attainment of the goals, the effectiveness of the strategies, etc.
- Learn: The third part (phases 5 and 6) involves learning from what was done by analyzing the results and improving the process for generating further goals and strategies.

In Table 10.4, a mapping of the cases shown in Table 10.2 to the parts of the GQM$^+$Strategies process actually performed is presented.

Although derived from experiences in the software domain, GQM$^+$Strategies is also intended to be applicable in other domains. For example, Sarcia (2010) applied GQM$^+$Strategies for strategic planning of military training programs. Most of the applications presented in Table 10.2 involve proprietary work, but we do have permission to provide insights into three cases, which will be presented in more detail at the end of this chapter.

Table 10.2 Practical applications of GQM$^+$Strategies

Business/domain	Motivation	GQM$^+$Strategies-related actions
Industry		
(I1) European telecommunications company	Control and steer strategic improvement programs Derive appropriate indicators for measuring success	Specify grid of organizational goals, strategies, and measurement goals Develop templates for KPI definition
(I2) European automotive supplier	Set up a CMMI-compliant measurement program	Specify goals and strategies for different business units Attach an existing GQM database to goals Develop release mechanisms for goals and strategies of different business units Develop tool support
(I3) European telecommunication network testing company	Evaluate cost, benefit, and schedule for modernizing existing product suite	Specify grid of organizational goals, strategies, and measurement goals Strategic decision-making
(I4) International telecommunication system provider	Increase the visibility at all organizational units of how strategic decisions impact operations	Specify grid of organizational goals, strategies, and measurement goals Strategic decision-making
(I5) Asian insurance company	Develop goals and strategies for new business domain	Specify the grid of organizational goals, strategies, and measurement goals Strategic decision-making
(I6) Japanese Aerospace Exploration Agency (JAXA)	Increase transparency when collaborating with external suppliers	Specify the grid of organizational goals, strategies, and measurement goals and share them with the external supplier
(I7) Asian system integrator in the banking and insurance domain	Demonstrate the value of activities in terms of business goals Select project proposals having the greatest value to the organization (portfolio management)	Specify grid of organizational goals, strategies, and measurement goals Specify alignment matrix between project goals and organizational strategies Develop indicators for prioritizing project proposals
(I8) ECOPETROL (international gas and oil company)	Demonstrate value of IT as information provider Link improvement activities to organizational goals	Specify grid of organizational goals, strategies, and measurement goals Develop KPI systems for measuring information quality and software quality Develop tool support
(I9) European banking software provider	Link monitoring and control mechanisms to organizational	Specify organization business goals

(continued)

Table 10.2 (continued)

Business/domain	Motivation	GQM⁺Strategies-related actions
	goals and derive appropriate improvement activities	Develop KPI systems for measuring performance of software development processes and projects, and of quality of software products
(I10) International container shipping company	Select appropriate improvement strategies for introducing new IT/SW technologies Define quantitative criteria for demonstrating the success of selected IT/SW technologies	Define IT/SW goals and align them to business goals of the organization Derive appropriate strategies and detailed goals for the IT unit Derive KPI system and quantitative criteria for evaluating success of IT/SW strategies and goals
(I11) US Federally Funded Research and Development Corporation (FFRDC)	Evaluate different strategies for developing new business opportunities	Define goals and alternative strategies for new business area Derive KPI system for evaluating success of strategies
Government		
(G1) Information-technology Promotion Agency, Software Engineering Center (IPA/SEC), Japan	Illustrate value of projects to overall goals and strategies	Specify grid of organizational goals and strategies Specify alignment matrix between project goals and organizational strategies Develop indicators for computing the value contribution of projects
(G2) Poznan University of Technology	Set up an indicator system for controlling the progress of meeting the required criteria for obtaining a national certificate of education excellence	Specify grid of organizational goals, strategies, and measurement goals Derive KPI system for controlling the progress of meeting the required excellence
Research		
(R1) ADiWa Logistics Software German Research Project	Align project objectives and business objectives of involved research and industry partners	Specify grid of organizational goals, strategies, and measurement goals
(R2) ARAMIS Embedded Systems German Research Project	Align project objectives and business objectives of involved research and industry partners	Specify grid of organizational goals, strategies, and measurement goals Derive evaluation goals and hypotheses from grid
(R3) MBAT Embedded Systems European Research Project	Align project objectives and business objectives of involved research and industry partners	Specify grid of organizational goals, strategies, and measurement goals Derive evaluation goals and hypotheses from grid

Table 10.3 Practical application and addressed challenges

Business/domain	Alignment	Decision-making	Communication
Industry			
(I1) European telecommunications company	✓		
(I2) European automotive supplier	✓	✓	
(I3) European telecommunication network testing company	✓		
(I4) International Telecommunication system provider			✓
(I5) Asian insurance company	✓		
(I6) Japanese Aerospace Exploration Agency (JAXA)	✓	✓	✓
(I7) Asian system integrator in the banking and insurance domain	✓		
(I8) ECOPETROL (international gas and oil company)	✓	✓	✓
(I9) European banking software provider	✓	✓	
(I10) International container shipping company	✓	✓	
(I11) US Federally Funded Research and Development Corporation (FFRDC)	✓	✓	
Government			
(G1) Information-technology Promotion Agency, SE Center (IPA/SEC), Japan	✓		✓
(G2) Poznań University of Technology	✓	✓	
Research			
(R1) ADiWa Logistics Software German Research Project	✓	✓	
(R2) ARAMIS Embedded Systems German Research Project	✓	✓	
(R3) MBAT Embedded Systems European Research Project	✓	✓	

Table 10.4 Practical application and addressed parts of the GQM$^+$Strategies process

Business/domain	Develop (1, 2)	Implement (3, 4)	Learn (5, 6)
Industry			
(I1) European telecommunications company	✓	✓	
(I2) European automotive supplier	✓	✓	✓
(I3) European telecommunication network testing company	✓		
(I4) International Telecommunication system provider	✓		
(I5) Asian insurance company	✓		
(I6) Japanese Aerospace Exploration Agency (JAXA)	✓	✓	
(I7) Asian system integrator in the banking and insurance domain	✓	✓	
(I8) ECOPETROL (international gas and oil company)	✓	✓	✓
(I9) European banking software provider	✓	✓	✓
(I10) International container shipping company	✓	✓	✓
(I11) US Federally Funded Research and Development Corporation (FFRDC)	✓		
Government			
(G1) Information-technology Promotion Agency, SE Center (IPA/SEC), Japan	✓	✓	
(G2) Poznań University of Technology	✓	✓	✓
Research			
(R1) ADiWa Logistics Software German Research Project	✓	✓	✓
(R2) ARAMIS Embedded Systems German Research Project	✓	✓	✓
(R3) MBAT Embedded Systems European Research Project	✓	✓	✓

10.2   ECOPETROL S. A., Columbia

"With GQM+Strategies, we were able to make the contribution of the information manage-
ment strategy to the business goals explicit."

Dr. Alexis Ocampo
Group Leader Enterprise Architecture
ECOPETROL, Columbia

10.2.1 Application Context and Objectives

In the year 2010, ECOPETROL, one of the worldwide leading companies in the oil
and gas industry, launched an initiative for better aligning its IT- and software-
related activities with its business goals. This initiative changed the traditional role
of IT from a classical service provider and easily replaceable cost factor to a central
information provider that contributes to the company's success by providing high-
quality information to support critical management decisions. In order to achieve
this, the goals and strategies of the IT department had to be mapped to the business
goals of ECOPETROL and their value had to be made more transparent in terms of
the overall organization. In addition, a system of indicators was developed to enable
the objective assessment of the success/failure of a strategy and its optimization
over time.

10.2.2 Solution Approach

The application of GQM+Strategies at ECOPETROL was conducted by Fraunhofer
IESE and CESE and included all six phases of the process but, for cost reasons,
focused on a very narrow path through the overall GQM+Strategies grid. The main
idea was twofold. First, the connection between several strategies of the IT department and the goals and strategies of the management had to be clarified. Second, we
wanted to examine the consequences of the defined IT goals and strategies of the
Software Factory, which had to implement these strategies. The Software Factory
(composed of external software development companies) is responsible for
maintaining and integrating existing systems as well as developing new IT-based
software systems.

- Characterizing: Defining the scope, characterizing the environment and context,
  and determining responsibilities were done in a joint workshop with different
  stakeholders from ECOPETROL. The participants were mostly from the IT
  department, plus representatives from the Software Factory and Fraunhofer
  measurement experts. The CIO was involved in checking and approving the
  final scope defined.
- Setting Goals: Grid development was also conducted in several workshop
  sessions on site, involving the IT department and the Software Factory.

Management-oriented goals and strategies were included based on a company-internal presentation. The whole grid was presented to the CIO and finally approved. The first sessions focused on building the hierarchy of goals and strategies. The later sessions focused on building a measurement and interpretation model for selected goals based on GQM Abstraction Sheets. Due to financial reasons, the focus was on goals related to improving and maintaining information quality. The remaining phases of the overall process focused on these subgoals only.

- Choosing Process: Based on the measurement model, a data collection questionnaire was designed.
- Executing, Analyzing, and Packaging: The questionnaire was piloted in a two-stage process. During the first piloting stage, a sample group filled out the questionnaire in an artificial environment without disturbing influences. Another sample group filled out the questionnaire in their real-life work setting. The understandability of the questionnaire was evaluated and improved based on the results of the laboratory study. The results of the field study were also used to analyze the quality of selected information units of individual business units. During the second piloting stage, the approach was applied in 13 different areas of the company. 86 information unit owners were interviewed to assess 184 information units (i.e., defined critical pieces of information that are formally tracked and maintained by the IT department). Measurement experts conducted these interviews in order to support the interviewees in answering the questionnaire and to collect feedback about the understandability and applicability of the questionnaire in practice. After piloting was completed, the information units will now be assessed by the corresponding owner without the support of a measurement expert. A tool will semiautomate the process and support the information unit owners in completing the questionnaire.

10.2.3 Results

Figure 10.1 shows excerpts from the first GQM$^+$Strategies model. At the business level, three goals and corresponding strategies were defined, starting with the very high-level goal (G1) of being among the top companies in terms of oil and gas reserves down to the lower-level goal (G3) of decreasing the analysis time needed for finding oil and gas reserves. At this stage, a strategy was defined to improve the quality of the information because providing high-quality data will support the decision-making process by decreasing the time needed to find new oil and gas reserves.

One central goal of the IT unit is to improve and maintain information quality (G4). The IT department provides and manages several information units (pieces of critical information) for other business units. As can be seen in the organizational goal template (Table 10.5), the major goal is to improve the quality of these information units by reducing the amount of critical information by 10 %.

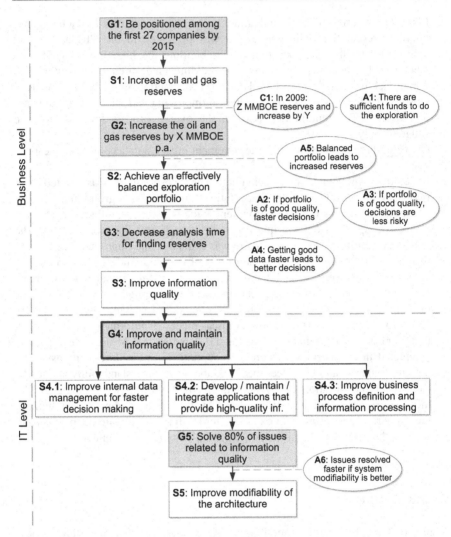

Fig. 10.1 ECOPETROL: Excerpts from the GQM⁺Strategies grid

Table 10.5 ECOPETROL: Example organizational goals

Organizational goal at ECOPETROL: Information quality	
Focus	Information quality (with the attributes: uniqueness, completeness, consistency, timeliness, and confidentiality)
Object	Information units of all business processes
Magnitude	10 % decrease of critical information units for each attribute and 10 % decrease of medium-critical information units for each attribute
Time frame	Every 3 months
Organizational scope	Information division for the upstream (related to exploration and production of oil and gas reserves)
Constraints	Use of resources for other activities
Relationships	Budget needs to be checked against revenue-related goals

Object	Purpose	Quality focus	Viewpoint	Context
Information unit	Evaluate	Uniqueness	Business / IT	(confidential information)

Quality focus (Questions and metrics)	Variation factors
Uniqueness: An information unit has a named unique source and every representation of that information unit has the same value. For each information unit (relevant for the decisions to be made): • **Q1.1**: Is one defined unique source specified? • **M1.1**: (yes/no/don't know) • **Q1.2**: Do you know about all replications of this information unit? • **M1.2.1**: (yes/no) • **M1.2.2**: Estimated # of known replications • **Q1.3**: Does every representation of that information unit have the same value (check a representative sample, 10% of # of known replications)? • **M1.3.1**: (yes/no/don't know) • **M1.3.2**: Estimated # of non-duplicates	• **V1**: Update Rate • **VM1.1**: Time between updates in minutes

Baseline hypotheses	Impact on baseline hypotheses
(confidential information)	(confidential information)

Interpretation models			
M1.1	*M1.2.1*	*M1.3.1*	*Assessment*
(all values)	(all values)	no / don't know	red (critical)
no / don't know	(all values)	(all values)	red (critical)
yes	no	yes	yellow (medium)
yes	yes	yes	green (uncritical)

Fig. 10.2 ECOPETROL: GQM abstraction sheet excerpts

The grid offers four different strategies addressing and operationalizing this goal. One of them (S4.2) was broken down to the level of improving the modifiability of software architectures (S5). The other refinements are not shown here.

The measurement goals focus on evaluating the improvement in terms of information quality. Figure 10.2 gives an example GQM Abstraction Sheet for analyzing the uniqueness of information units at ECOPETROL. An interpretation model was added at the bottom of the abstraction sheet to assess the data in the context of the organizational goal of improving and maintaining information quality. The lower part of the table gives a simple mapping between the metric values (M1.1, M1.2.1, and M1.3.1) and a color encoding scheme for critical ("red"), medium-critical ("yellow"), and uncritical ("green") information quality. Following this model, it is now possible to measure the attainment of the organizational goal by monitoring the number of critical, medium-critical, and uncritical information units over time.

Figure 10.3 shows a screenshot of the GQM$^+$Strategies tool capturing the excerpts of the grid that was obtained. The whole initial model included

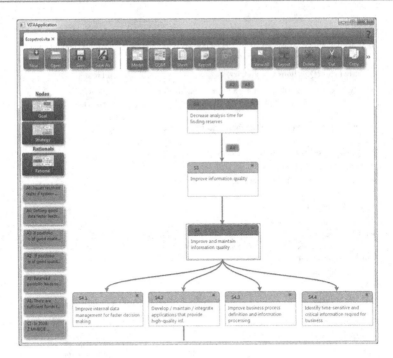

Fig. 10.3 ECOPETROL: Screenshot of the GQM⁺Strategies editor

5 organizational goals, 8 strategies, 5 measurement goals, and 24 metrics. The underlying formal model representation was used as a basis for maintaining and extending the grid in future iterations.

10.2.4 Costs and Benefits

Costs The total effort for this application of the approach amounted to approximately 16 person-days for Fraunhofer IESE and 4–5 person-days for each ECOPETROL participant (1 person-day corresponds to 8 h). Of that, 40 % was spent on building the grid and 60 % was spent on defining all indicators in details, defining the data collection questionnaires, and conducting a trial application.

Benefits The feedback given by the ECOPETROL participants was very positive. Some of the benefits mentioned include the following aspects:

- Contribution of the IT department: Using the GQM⁺Strategies model, ECOPETROL was able to connect the operational IT level (their actual work) to the more strategic business-oriented levels of the organization.
- Identification of basic metrics and data: Following a GQM-centric exercise, the engineers were challenged to revise their current work and to precisely define what is meant by quality aspects such as timeliness, consistency, completeness, or uniqueness.

- Making organizational goals operational: The approach also supported ECOPETROL in operationalizing the model and collecting the necessary data based on the questionnaire.
- Rationale-based linkage: ECOPETROL was able to identify the assumptions underlying the goals and strategies. The engineers usually identified risks related to a project, but never assumptions related to goals and strategies. This linkage helped the engineers to understand that value can be accomplished differently although the IT services are essentially the same.
- Transparent decision-making: The approach helped narrow down the space of alternatives for possible upstream activities that would demonstrate value. For example, prospect generation is an exploration activity that really pushes an oil and gas company forward. Other activities in exploration might not have this impact. Thus, engineers might answer questions like "What is the best activity for IT to focus on?" in order to demonstrate a quick and clear value to the business.
- Rectifying IT and development cost: Finally, ECOPETROL was able to demonstrate the value of IT-related activities. The model became a communication means for bringing together business and IT.

Future work regarding ECOPETROL will focus on completing the initial model and demonstrating the added value using quantitative evidence. The questionnaire for information quality is currently being applied in different business areas. Corresponding measurement instruments have to be developed for other business goals and must be integrated, so that their attainment can be evaluated systematically with respect to whether IT is providing the value that was promised.

10.3 Information-Technology Promotion Agency, Japan

"GQM⁺Strategies supported us and multiple other Japanese organizations in aligning IT- and software-related activities to the strategic needs of our business."

Katsutoshi Shintani
Senior Adviser, Software Engineering Center
Information-technology Promotion Agency, Japan

10.3.1 Application Context and Objectives

The GQM⁺Strategies approach was applied at the Software Engineering Center of the Information-technology Promotion Agency[1] (IPA/SEC) to evaluate the business value of new research and development projects. Specifically, IPA/SEC aimed

---

[1] Established in 1970, IPA promotes best IT practices within the Japanese industry. The principal fields of IPA's activities include IT Security, Software Engineering, IT Human Resources Development, and Open Software. In 2004, IPA established the Software Engineering Center (SEC), whose research and technology transfer activities focus on ensuring the development of highly reliable software in Japan.

at evaluating the contribution of new research projects to their business objectives and budget in order to decide about the optimal portfolio of research projects that generate minimal cost and support attainment of their business goals. This objective represented the interests of two groups of project stakeholders, who represent "opposing" perspectives:

- The *project initiator*, who proposes a new research and development project, must justify the project in terms of its business value.
- The *project owner*, who sponsors the new project, must decide whether to accept or reject the project. Regarding the complete project portfolio, the project owner must focus on projects with the highest business impact (support of business goals).

GQM⁺Strategies supports choosing the right project portfolio in that it provides a clear view on the alignment of candidate projects to the organizational goals. On the one hand, it helps decision makers assess the business value of each project independent of other projects. On the other hand, decision makers can assess redundancies between projects that implement the same business goal.

10.3.2 Solution Approach

The solution approach consisted of evaluating the alignment between project-specific goals and goals and strategies defined at the lower levels of the IPA/SEC grid. The primary objective was to assess the extent to which project-specific goals fit the operational-level goals and strategies defined in the grid, and thus the extent to which they contribute to the organizational business goals (defined at the top of the grid). The secondary objective was to revise the GQM⁺Strategies grid, for example, in order to make sure that all appropriate linkages were documented in the grid. With respect to the alignment between project and organizational goals and strategies defined in the grid, four generally possible situations were considered:

1. A project defines a goal that directly corresponds to one of the IPA/SEC goals. This is the desired situation in which project-specific goals clearly contribute to the business objectives defined in the IPA/SEC GQM⁺Strategies grid.
2. A project defines a goal that does not link to any of the IPA/SEC goals and strategies. This is the undesired situation in which a project-specific goal does not make a clear contribution to IPA/SEC's business goals. In this case, the project goal should be further justified or excluded. A project in which most or all of the goals do not make clear contributions to IPA/SEC's goals should not be included in the current portfolio.
3. A project defines a goal that does not directly correspond to any of IPA/SEC's goals. In this situation, there is no clear linkage between the project-specific goal and IPA/SEC's business goals. In such a case, one should first check whether the project-specific goal addresses one of the higher-level organizational strategies

defined in the grid (situation 4). If it does, then the project-specific goal should be linked to the appropriate higher-level strategy. Otherwise, an appropriate business justification for the project with respect to the specific goal must be provided. In other words, one should check whether the project-specific goal contributes to the business goals via organizational goals and strategies that exist in the organization but are not modeled in the grid.

4. A project defines a goal that links to one of IPA/SEC's strategies. In this situation, the project-specific goal directly addresses one of the higher-level organizational strategies defined in the grid; however, it does not correspond to any of the lower-level goals associated with the strategy. In this situation, one should first investigate why the goals associated with the strategy in the grid have not been used in the project. In particular, we should investigate whether the project-specific goal and the goals in the grid are complementary or redundant to each other. If necessary, the grid should be adjusted appropriately.

A project can be accepted for inclusion in the project portfolio if all its goals are aligned with business goals (situation 1 or 4) and if these business goals are not yet implemented by other projects.

Because the IPA/SEC grid ended with operational strategies, we reviewed projects with respect to their alignment with these strategies. In order to support the search for the optimal set of projects for inclusion in the IPA/SEC project portfolio, we created two simple tools: a *project alignment matrix* and a *strategy coverage matrix*.

10.3.2.1 Project Alignment Matrix

The *project alignment matrix* (Fig. 10.4) documents a set of reference strategies defined at the bottom, operational, level of the GQM$^+$Strategies grid and the goals defined within an individual project. The body of the matrix documents links between project-specific goals and reference strategies in that it specifies the rationale (context factor or assumption) that justifies a particular link.

10.3.2.2 Strategy Coverage Matrix

In order to support strategic alignment for a portfolio of multiple projects, we propose combining the project alignment matrices into a so-called strategy coverage matrix. A *strategy coverage matrix* (Fig. 10.5) is a two-dimensional matrix that

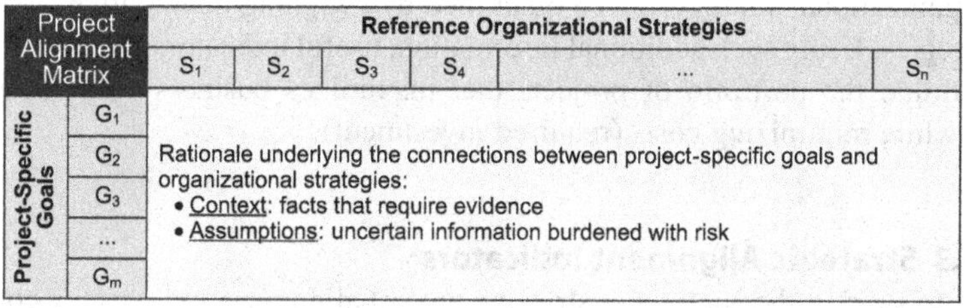

Fig. 10.4 Project alignment matrix

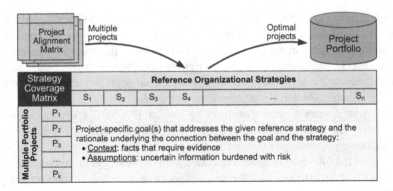

Fig. 10.5 Strategy coverage matrix

combines project alignment matrices across multiple candidate projects proposed in an organization. On the vertical axis, the matrix lists the projects, whereas on the horizontal axis, the organizational reference strategies are listed. The matrix body documents links between projects and strategies. The link between a project and a strategy is justified by documenting (1) the project's goals that address the strategy, as specified in the project's alignment matrix, and (2) the rationale—context and assumptions—of the goal-strategy relation.

We used the strategy coverage matrix to identify an optimal set of projects to be included in IPA/SEC's project portfolio. The optimal set of projects refers to a minimal set of projects (minimal in terms of number of projects and/or overall project budget) that cover all relevant organizational strategies. In practice, it may happen that not all strategies are covered by the proposed projects. In such a case, adjusting the goals of one or more projects or adding a new project in order to fill in the gap in strategy coverage should be considered.

Note that achieving 100 % strategy coverage maximizes the likelihood of achieving all business goals. Yet, this does not guarantee achieving the business goals due to the risks inherent in the goal-strategy chains documented within the organizational GQM$^+$Strategies grid.

The strategy coverage matrix can be extended by additional information to support better assessment of the business value delivered by the considered project. For example, for each project the estimated project cost and the extent to which it contributes to each strategy can be quantified. Moreover, the business relevancy of each organizational strategy can be quantified by assigning quantitative weights to the strategies. Using such additional information, useful indicators can be computed to determine the portfolio of projects that maximizes business value (expected return) while minimizing costs (required investment).

10.3.2.3 Strategic Alignment Indicators

In order to support the analysis of strategic project alignment and strategy coverage in a quantitative manner, we propose several simple indicators that can be easily derived from the project alignment matrix and visualized in order to support portfolio selection.

- Unaligned Project Goals: The percentage of project-specific goals related to a particular project that remain unaligned with any of the organizational strategies. The larger the number of project-specific goals that remain unaligned with the business objectives, the lower the potential business value of the project. Such a project generates large expenses for implementing its goals, yet it does not generate much added business value.
- Unaddressed Reference Strategies: The number of organizational strategies that remain unaddressed by any of the candidate (portfolio) projects. This indicator provides a quick look at the absolute count of reference strategies to be covered by a project in order to obtain 100 % coverage.
- Project Alignment: The overall percentage of project-specific goals that are aligned with reference strategies, over all proposed projects. This indicator provides information about how many project-specific goals are justified by their contribution to the business objectives.
- Strategy Alignment: The overall percentage of reference strategies covered by project-specific goals. This indicator quantifies the extent to which reference strategies are addressed by the projects and their specific goals.
- Unaligned Cost: The percentage of expenses for implementing project-specific goals that do not address any reference strategy, and thus do not generate any added business value. This indicator provides a quick look at the amount of money that is going to be potentially wasted to attain project-specific goals that do not contribute to the attainment of the organizational business goals.
- Cost Alignment: The percentage of the overall project budget that is spent on business-justified project goals. This indicator shows what part of the overall project expenses goes towards realizing the reference strategies. The remaining part is potentially wasted on attaining project-specific goals that do not contribute to the organization's business value.
- Alignment Certainty (Absence of Risk): The percentage of goal-strategy alignment links that are based upon empirical evidence (context information) as opposed to those based on assumptions. This indicator quantifies the probability of successful implementation of reference strategies that are addressed by project-specific goals.

10.3.3 Results

IPA/SEC defined three major strategies for achieving their business objectives. These three strategies were broken down into more operational strategies. In order to realize these operational strategies, and particularly to meet the operational strategies in one of the strategic areas of IPA/SEC, five research projects were proposed, each addressing one specific goal. In order to assess the strategic alignment of research at IPA/SEC, a one-day workshop was performed. The workshop participants consisted of one internal and four external or extended members of

Table 10.6 Project costs and strategy values at IPA/SEC

Strategy ID and strategy value									
Project		S1.1	S1.2	S1.3	S1.4	S2.1	S2.2	S2.3	S2.4	S3.1
ID	Cost[a]	100	100	100	100	100	100	100	50	300
P1	20	100	100	–	–	90	100	70	45	–
P2	10	–	–	70	70	10	–	–	–	–
P3	10	–	–	30	30	–	–	30	5	–
P4	10	–	–	–	–	–	–	–	–	–
P5	20	–	–	–	–	–	–	–	–	300

[a]Example project costs in million Yen (real cost not provided due to confidentiality reasons)

IPA/SEC, and two external GQM$^+$Strategies experts who moderated the workshop. In the first step, the reference strategies and the research project were documented in a strategy coverage matrix. Next, the workshop participants looked for links between project goals and reference strategies, and documented the underlying rationales. In addition, the workshop participants estimated the potential cost of each candidate project, assigned relative importance values to the reference strategies, and distributed importance values over the linked projects. Table 10.6 briefly summarizes the result of the cost-value assignments.

A visual analysis of the project alignment matrix indicated full coverage of IPA/SEC's research strategies. Yet, a few strategies were addressed by more than one project (and associated goal). This apparent redundancy was explained by the complementary character of the projects, which was quantified by the assigned contribution to strategy values.

The detailed analysis of the alignment was supported by computing several project alignment indicators (as discussed in the previous section). The full coverage of the research strategies observed qualitatively was confirmed quantitatively by the 100 % alignment between strategies and strategy values. However, since one research project (P4) was not aligned with any reference strategy, we could not talk about full alignment (*Project Alignment = 80 %*). Due to expenses on the unaligned project P4, the overall cost alignment dropped to 86 %. The IPA/SEC members agreed that business justification for this project requires further internal discussions. Finally, because some of the links were justified through assumptions, the alignment was burdened by some uncertainty (*Alignment Certainty = 86 %*). Finally, the relative business value of each research project was assessed by computing the ratio between the project's contribution to the strategy's value in million Yen of project costs. The most beneficial project was P2; the least beneficial one was the unaligned project P4.

10.3.4 Costs and Benefits

Costs The overall cost of employing GQM$^+$Strategies for selecting a project portfolio at IPA/SEC comprised approximately 7 person-days of IPA/SEC experts and 3 person-days of GQM$^+$Strategies experts. The cost of IPA/SEC included the participation of seven experts in a one-day project alignment workshop. The effort of the GQM⁺Strategies experts included effort spent by (1) two experts for moderating the one-day project alignment workshop and (2) one of the experts for analyzing and packaging the outcomes of the workshop.

Benefits IPA/SEC benefited from using GQM⁺Strategies in several ways:

- Project contribution: IPA/SEC was able to connect the operational project level to the strategic levels of the organization. This is especially important when it comes to multi-project alignment in larger organizations (project portfolios), where hundreds of projects (or project proposals) have to be evaluated regarding their contribution towards higher-level goals.
- Key performance indicators: Simple project alignment indicators allowed for easily identifying gaps and potential risks of the project alignment.
- Rationale-based linkage: IPA/SEC was able to identify the assumptions underlying the goals, strategies, and the links between them. Explicitly considering assumptions helped the project managers to quantify the risk of not achieving business goals because of some assumptions being actually wrong.
- Decision-making: IPA/SEC was able to focus and optimize those project goals that clearly contribute to the business objectives (e.g., IPA/SEC gained a clear rationale for rejecting projects that did not contribute to business goals).
- Rectifying cost: IPA/SEC was able to demonstrate the business value of project activities and argue for getting project funding.

10.4   Japanese Aerospace Exploration Agency, Japan

"The experience of using the GQM⁺Strategies approach at JAXA shows that the approach helps to clarify the relationship between activities of different organizational units on different levels of the organization, as well as to explicitly show the contributions of those activities to the attainment of top-level business goals."

Masafumi Katahira, Tatsuya Kaneko, Yuko Miyamoto
Japan Aerospace Exploration Agency (JAXA)

10.4.1 Application Context and Objectives

Alignment in a multiorganizational scenario can enhance the integration of different internal organizational units and external organizations, such as suppliers. Achieving such multiorganizational integration has become increasingly important for the Japan Aerospace Exploration Agency (JAXA) and was their reason for applying GQM⁺Strategies. For internal organizational units, an important aspect of integration is to clarify their contribution towards top-level business goals. With respect to the integration of external organizations, defining effective measurement systems in the context of distributed collaborations is important as a means for efficient control.

This GQM⁺Strategies application addressed the following objectives:

1. For distributed projects with external organizations, the goal was to align measurement needs and make them transparent.
2. For software process improvement within a JAXA-internal unit, the goal was to highlight its contribution to top-level organizational goals and make sure that these contributions are aligned.

Both objectives were addressed under the additional condition of maximizing measurement reuse by including and exploiting already existing assets.

10.4.2 Solution Approach

The focus of the application of GQM⁺Strategies at JAXA was on the first three phases (Initialize, Characterize Environment, and Define Goals, Strategies, and Measurement) of the GQM⁺Strategies process, that is, on developing the GQM⁺Strategies grid. Due to the distributed nature of our collaboration and the resulting schedule constraints, we proceeded in four main steps. The first step was a preparative step that included activities from the Initialize and Characterize Environment phases, followed by three iterations for the grid modeling phase (Define Goals, Strategies, and Measurement). Figure 10.6 illustrates the course of GQM⁺Strategies application at JAXA.

10.4.3 Results

For both objectives, the alignment to JAXA's top-level goals was relevant. Thus, modeling of these goals was necessary in order to ensure a goal-oriented procedure. Achieving integration in this multiorganizational scenario by using GQM⁺Strategies was possible by modeling the internal and external organizational units and, additionally, linking them to an appropriate interface (organizational level) at JAXA. Then the associated goals and strategies were refined for the organizational units.

Figure 10.7 presents the resulting GQM⁺Strategies grid with its levels and interfaces. This GQM⁺Strategies grid did not only provide the possibility of integrating the different types of organizational units but also captures the project and line organization of JAXA. The grid was refined from JAXA's organizational top level into two sub-trees (represented by "Project Organization" and "Line Organization" in Fig. 10.7), which were further refined into two and three further organizational levels, respectively. The two-level refinement of the Project Organization encompasses the project and supplier project levels. The three-level refinement of the Line Organization encompasses the unit, subunit, and operational levels. The project organization was modeled with the suppliers' project-level

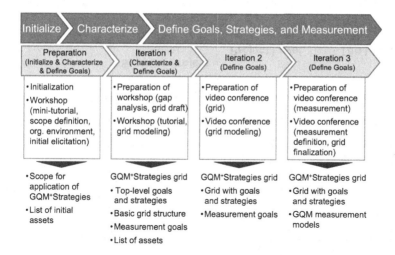

Fig. 10.6 JAXA: Overview of the application of GQM⁺Strategies

goals linked to the JAXA project-level goals, which in turn were linked to JAXA's top-level goals (see Fig. 10.7 on the right). Capturing the line organization required four levels. These include JAXA's top level, the unit level of each internal unit, a subunit level, and finally the operational level of each internal subunit (see Fig. 10.7 on the left).

Every interface creates several opportunities for interaction between the involved organizational units. For example, at an interface between JAXA and an external supplier, it is not only possible for JAXA to specify goals or success criteria of such collaborations, but, furthermore, the joint definition of measurement models can be used as a means for gaining better insights. This can be achieved through a better understanding of the actual realization of the defined goals made possible by analyzing the strategies that are pursued at the supplier organization to achieve success. This provides opportunities for insights that go beyond pure analysis of measurement data.

The overall GQM⁺Strategies grid contains a total of 23 GQM⁺Strategies elements, as well as 23 associated GQM graphs (i.e., measurement models) for evaluating the success of the GQM⁺Strategies elements.

In the following, we will provide a more detailed look at one part of JAXA's GQM⁺Strategies grid, which is illustrated in Fig. 10.7. We will discuss the line organization branch, which models the contribution of the software process improvement group to the overall goals at JAXA and in particular to those of JAXA's Engineering Digital Innovation Center (JEDI).

First, the JAXA top-level goal "Improve mission success" is refined into a goal that is most relevant for JEDI (unit level), which is the goal "Improve technology for JAXA development projects (G04)" (see Fig. 10.8). At the JAXA research department level (JEDI: unit level), the dissemination and effectiveness of technological improvement is monitored based on aggregated measures, which are composed from the results of the different JEDI research groups. Thus, JEDI's contribution is linked to

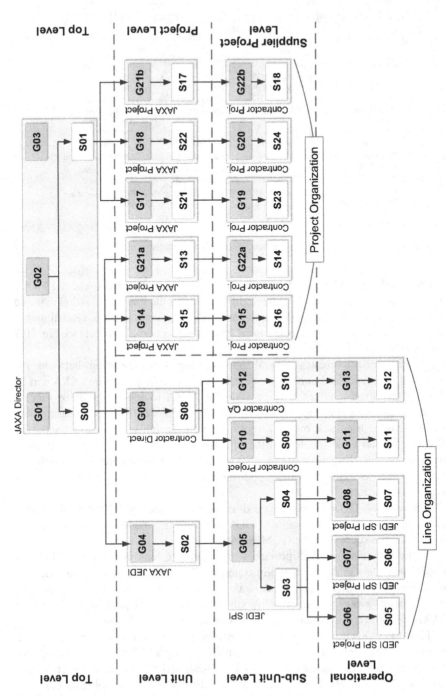

Fig. 10.7 JAXA: Structure of the GQM⁺Strategies grid

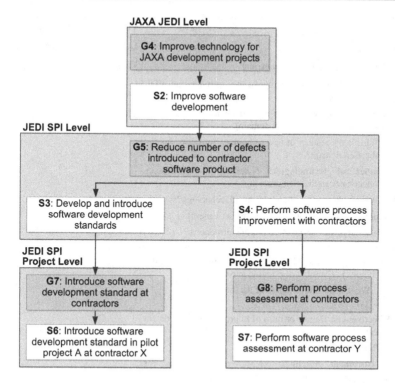

Fig. 10.8 Goals and strategies at the unit (JEDI), subunit (JEDI SPI), and operational (JEDI SPI Project) levels

one top-level business goal. The general JEDI goal was additionally refined into a software-specific strategy, "Improve software development (S2)." This strategy was further refined on the level of the software process improvement group (subunit level). At this level, the goal "Reduce number of defects introduced to contractor software product (G05)" was refined based on the higher-level strategy. The aerospace domain is known for its high safety and reliability requirements with respect to both hardware and software products. JAXA acquires most of its technology and software from external suppliers and projects are thus mainly conducted in a distributed collaboration setting. In this context, JAXA promotes the usage of specific software development processes as a means of constructive quality assurance and defect reduction. Based on this, the JEDI SPI goal was refined into two strategies (S3 & S4) for the software process improvement group. Based on these strategies, the GQM⁺Strategies grid was further refined on the operational level. Software process assessment is performed as one of this group's operational activities to achieve the SPI group-level goal "Reduce number of defects introduced to contractor software product." This operational activity was aligned with the SPI group-level strategy within the grid. Additionally, explicit alignment from the top-level business goals to the operational-level goals was achieved, as a consistent and traceable link within the grid was refined.

Object	Purpose	Quality focus	Viewpoint	Context
Technology	Evaluate	Improvement	JAXA JEDI	JAXA Project
Quality focus (questions and metrics)			**Variation factors**	
Q1: What is the technological improvement provided by JEDI per application domain?			-	
• **Technology improvement:** Sum (Impact) / number of technologies (per application domain)				
Q1.1: What is the number of new technology introductions per application domain?				
• **Number of technologies:** Number of technologies introduced per application domain				
Q1.2: What is the impact of an introduced technology?				
• **Impact:** Dissemination* Average (effectiveness)				
Q1.2.1: What is the dissemination of the introduced technology?				
• **Dissemination:** (Number of introductions of a specific technology) / (Number of possible introductions)				
Q1.2.2: What is the effectiveness of the introduced technology?				
• **Effectiveness:** Degree or ratio of improvement (e.g. defect reduction)				
Q2: What is the measurement baseline?				
• **Measurement baselines:** Measurement baselines for technology improvement				
Baseline hypotheses			**Impact on baseline hypotheses**	
-			-	
Interpretation models				
Technology improvement ≥ threshold (measurement baseline or target)				

Fig. 10.9 Abstraction sheet for "Technology improvement"

Figure 10.9 shows the GQM Abstraction Sheet for one of the measurement goals. The purpose of the measurement was to evaluate the attainment of one of the goals defined by the software process improvement group. In particular, the measurement goal was to evaluate the performance of process assessment activities at the contractors.

10.4.4 Costs and Benefits

Costs Although this GQM⁺Strategies application was divided into these four steps, we did not track the effort accordingly. The total effort for this application of the approach amounted to approximately 18 person-days for Fraunhofer IESE and 9 person-days for JAXA (1 person-day corresponds to 8 h).

Benefits   Applying GQM⁺Strategies delivered a measurement program that included multiple internal and external organizations. The application of the approach helped to achieve the two main objectives of this collaboration:

1. For distributed projects with external organizations, GQM⁺Strategies provided reliable project status information and capabilities for the early identification of conflicts.
2. For JAXA's internal software process improvement unit, GQM⁺Strategies provided visibility of its contributions with respect to organizational improvement activities and improved transparency regarding the success of improvement activities.

In consequence, the application of GQM⁺Strategies helped JAXA to clarify the relationships between the activities of different organizational units on different levels of the organization, as well as to explicitly show the contributions of those activities to the attainment of top-level business goals.

Relationships to Other Approaches

11

During several applications of GQM⁺Strategies at different organizations, questions were often raised about the relationship between GQM⁺Strategies and other methods and frameworks. Therefore, in this section, we will discuss the most important methods and frameworks from different domains that are related to GQM⁺Strategies. We will address relationships with approaches to organizational performance measurement as well as to process improvement and reengineering. For this purpose, we will briefly describe these related approaches and illustrate how GQM⁺Strategies could be used as a complement to or as a substitute for these methods or frameworks.

11.1 Organizational Performance Measurement

Approaches from the area of organizational performance measurement, like GQM⁺Strategies, aim to use measurement to improve transparency and coordination between different parts of an organization. In its pure meaning, performance measurement can be defined as the process of quantifying the effectiveness and efficiency of actions (Neely et al. 1995).

What is understood today as organizational performance measurement has its origins in the industrial quality management initiates from the 1970s and 1980s. Until that time, organizations mainly used financial information in management reports, and thus for controlling organizational performance (Nudurupati et al. 2011). Starting in the 1980s, traditional financial measures began to be discussed and criticized in this context as they have an internal and historical perspective only. These discussions resulted in several performance measurement approaches being developed, of which the Balanced Scorecard (BSC) (Kaplan and Norton 1992) is the most prominent one. For this reason, we will discuss the Balanced Scorecard and its development as a representative approach from the performance measurement domain.

V. Basili et al., *Aligning Organizations Through Measurement*, The Fraunhofer IESE Series 169 on Software and Systems Engineering, DOI 10.1007/978-3-319-05047-8_11,
© Springer International Publishing Switzerland 2014

11.1.1 The Balanced Scorecard

The most successful approach in the area of organizational performance measurement is the Balanced Scorecard, which was developed by Kaplan and Norton (1992). Throughout the 1990s, the Balanced Scorecard quickly became very popular and enjoyed widespread use. However, the idea of providing a measurement-based indication of organizational performance that was not based on financial data only was not new at that time. According to Epstein and Manzoni (1998), more than 50 years before the Balanced Scorecard, the concept of the *Tableau de Bord* was developed and used by engineers in France. These dashboards were developed in order to better understand the cause–effect relationships in production processes. Their principles were then transferred to the top management level in order to create better links between engineering and management. The approach allowed defining a set of measures that helped to control the progress of organizational goals and to define corrective actions when needed. Due to its origin in engineering, the Tableau de Bord approach was actually more operation-oriented than the Balanced Scorecard and provided a systematic process for cascading top-level and subunit dashboards by refining goals and actions hierarchically. In practice, the applications of the Tableau de Bord approach often tended to not fully achieve their anticipated benefits. Epstein and Manzoni (1998) state that the major issue was too much emphasis on financial measures, although the approach generally suggested a mix of financial and nonfinancial measures. Additionally, the measures that were defined tended to be internally oriented and often based on already existing measures within a subunit. In part, this led to situations in which data for many measures were collected but the measures lacked goal orientation. This means that data was collected based on internal data availability within organizational units without paying enough attention to the relevance and purpose of the measurements. Consequently, the relevance of the measurements for the overall organization could be relatively low.

The development of the Balanced Scorecard tried to address some of these issues by suggesting a goal-oriented measurement approach aimed at deriving and focusing on the most critical strategic measures and, in addition, balancing financial and nonfinancial measures. The basic concept of the Balanced Scorecard, which was proposed by Kaplan and Norton (1992), suggests the structuring of measurement initiatives according to four perspectives and related questions. The four perspectives are financial, customer, internal business (process), and innovation. These perspectives and associated questions are then used to systematically derive organizational goals that are meaningful with respect to those four perspectives. Additionally, for each goal, measures are specified for the purpose of monitoring goal attainment.

This basic Balanced Scorecard concept has been further developed, based on experience from industrial application, into a strategic planning and controlling approach (Kaplan and Norton 2008). In the first evolution of the approach, Kaplan and Norton (1996) addressed major issues such as introducing a better specified process for selecting measures and assigning selected measures to the four

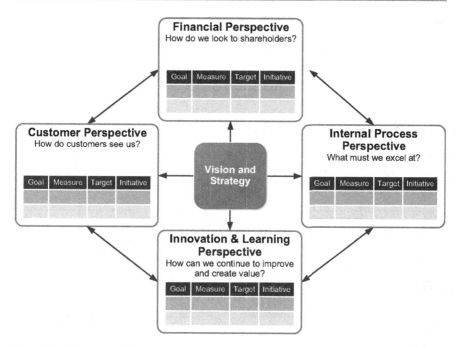

Fig. 11.1 Dimensions of the Balanced Scorecard [according to Kaplan and Norton (1996)]

perspectives. Furthermore, strategy statements based on an organization's vision were integrated into the approach to support more systematic goal specification by deriving goals from these statements. The basic concept was also refined, particularly by distinguishing measures, targets, and initiatives for every goal/objective (see Fig. 11.1).

Another key element that was introduced as part of the development of the approach was the concept of the strategy map (Kaplan and Norton 2004), which specifies the causality between the four perspectives and the goals associated with them (see Fig. 11.2). Explicitly modeling goals and their relationships helps to identify conflicts and strategy maps are therefore a means for improving alignment between goals from the different perspectives.

During the course of this development, the concept of cascading was adopted. Thus, cascades of several Balanced Scorecards can be used for the purpose of operationalizing an organization's vision and strategy throughout the different levels of the organization. This is achieved by considering different organizational units on different abstraction levels of an organization. These units define their own scorecards and the different scorecards are then linked qualitatively. In order to translate goals into action, the authors of the Balanced Scorecard furthermore suggest defining person-specific scorecards that are derived from unit-specific scorecards and contain person-specific measures (Kaplan and Norton 2004).

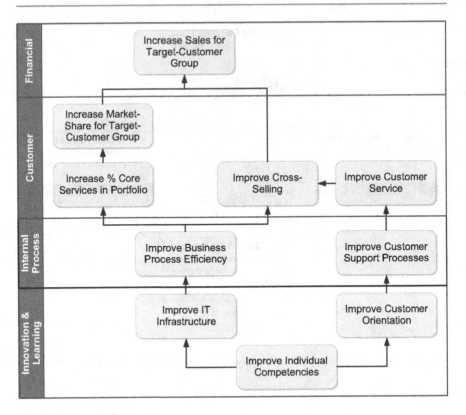

Fig. 11.2 Example Strategy map

11.1.2 BSC and Relationship to GQM⁺Strategies

The overview of the Balanced Scorecard approach shows that its concepts are quite similar to those underlying GQM⁺Strategies. This is the case because the organizational problems addressed by both approaches are similar. Like organizational performance measurement approaches, which were initially developed from industrial quality management initiatives, GQM⁺Strategies was developed in the context of software quality management and process improvement.

Both types of approaches use organizational goals to systematically refine and specify goals and related measures within an organization. The purpose of these approaches is to increase transparency, communication, and coordination, and by doing so to ultimately improve organizational performance through more objective and better aligned decisions and actions.

As GQM⁺Strategies has its foundation in software development, the particular engineering processes for developing software have to be considered in order to compare the different approaches. Software development processes have different characteristics compared to traditional production processes (Rombach and Verlage 1995) and are highly context-specific. Therefore, in order to be able to measure and make objective statements in the domain of software engineering, the context of development activities has to be considered. The Goal-Question-Metric (GQM) (Basili and Weiss 1984) approach was developed with the purpose of addressing this issue and has evolved into a quasi-standard in the area of software development. GQM is a goal-oriented measurement approach that considers the software development context for tailoring and integrating measurement goals with models of the software processes, products, and quality. GQM$^+$Strategies represents an extension of the GQM approach, which allows for modeling and linking organizational goals and strategies on different levels of an organization and combining them with GQM measurement models.

Due to its origin in software development, GQM$^+$Strategies aims at characterizing and explicitly modeling context in more detail. For this purpose, GQM$^+$Strategies distinguishes context factors and assumptions, which can be used to characterize goals and strategies, as well as the relationships between those elements. Context factors refer to factual information describing the organizational and software development environments and are used as rationale for making decisions. Assumptions characterize uncertain aspects of the organizational and software development environments. Additionally, context factors and assumptions can be integrated with interpretation models in order to improve reasoning about the success (or failure) of goals and strategies. Thus, linkages between GQM measurement models and organizational goals become possible.

In the context of software development (projects), several authors stated that such linkage can be difficult to achieve using solely the Balanced Scorecard (Becker and Bostelman 1999; Buglione and Abran 2000). A few solution approaches have been suggested, e.g., integrating GQM with each perspective of the Balanced Scorecard (Becker and Bostelman 1999) or specifying separate GQM models for strategic, process, tactical, and operational issues (Offen and Jeffery 1997). GQM$^+$Strategies aims at addressing the issue of linkage by delivering a method that specifies goals and strategies as well as GQM measurement models together in one approach using a documented specification process.

For these reasons, GQM$^+$Strategies could complement the Balanced Scorecard in specifying goal-oriented measurement systems in the context of software development. GQM$^+$Strategies supports the specification of consistent and traceable goal and strategy hierarchies that link different abstraction levels within an organization. Thus, Balanced Scorecard applications can benefit from using GQM$^+$Strategies to systematically refine goals specified within the different perspectives of a Balanced Scorecard to the level of software development, considering the software development-specific context. Vice versa, GQM$^+$Strategies can benefit from balancing the types of top-level goals according to the perspectives defined in the Balanced Scorecard, particularly for realizing organization-wide measurement systems. An integration of both approaches could be additionally beneficial for specifying causality linkages more precisely. While causality linkages between the different perspectives of a Balanced Scorecard are defined in strategy maps, applying GQM$^+$Strategies could help to refine causality relationships to the operational level. Additionally, context factors and assumptions can be modeled for these relationships, providing explicit rationales. Consequently, depending on the type and scope of a problem, it could be beneficial to consider a combination of the two approaches.

11.2   Business Process Management

Business Process Management (BPM) deals with the systematic identification, design, implementation, documentation, and improvement of business processes (Hammer 2010). Performance measurement is an important aspect of systematic business process management. We will therefore briefly discuss the related approaches of business process reengineering and business process management.

11.2.1   Business Process Reengineering and Management

The notion of Business Process Reengineering was introduced by Hammer (1990) who advocated a view according to which an organization will not achieve significant performance improvement merely by automating their business processes. Modeling current workflows and automating old ways of doing business was therefore not enough. According to Hammer (1990), significant improvements are only possible by fundamentally re-thinking and re-designing business processes, as well as re-implementing them by harnessing the new opportunities for automation that are provided by information technology. This approach is quite radical and typically associated with high risks. The high implementation risk was the major point of criticism identified during practical applications of business process reengineering. Sometimes huge improvements were achieved, but in many cases the anticipated benefits were not realized.

The integration of business process reengineering (Hammer and Champy 1993) with ideas and experiences from statistical process control and quality management leads to the development of a more holistic approach for managing business processes, which also addresses incremental process optimization. This holistic approach, which integrates incremental and radical process improvement, is understood today as BPM (Hammer 2010).

11.2.2   BPM and Relationship to GQM⁺Strategies

Figure 11.3 gives an overview of the activities that are considered in the context of systematic business process management. From the measurement perspective, the two most important activities are "Set Performance Target" and "Measure Process Performance." Both activities are supported by GQM⁺Strategies, and thus it could be beneficial to apply GQM⁺Strategies for target setting and measurement in the context of BPM initiatives.

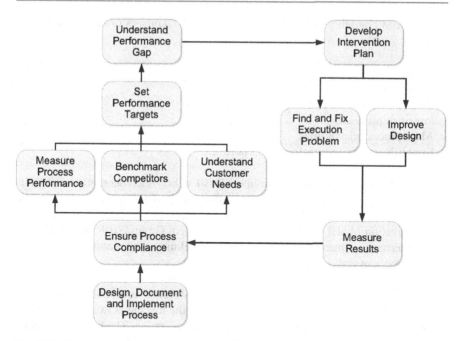

Fig. 11.3 Process management cycle [based on Hammer (2010)]

Applying GQM⁺Strategies would allow systematically deriving goals for a business process improvement initiative from top-level organizational goals. Systematic goal decomposition and refinement have been identified as important means for supporting and realizing improvement in the context of reengineering initiatives (Antón 1994). Using GQM⁺Strategies would allow identifying possible gaps in the linkage between improvement and organizational goals and would create a traceable link between top-level goals and the purpose of the improvement initiative. Additionally, specifying measurement models would help to evaluate the success of such a business process improvement initiative by controlling process performance. Damiani et al. (2008) used GQM⁺Strategies in an example application of business process control in the context of their SAF (Strategic Alignment Framework) approach.

In the sense of creating traceability and value contribution for BPM initiatives, alignment is also considered important in the BPM community (Rosemann and vom Brocke 2010). Burlton (2010) describes a proposed framework for alignment in the context of BPM, which consists of two major building blocks and a total of nine essential activities. The first building block, "Understand the Enterprise," subsumes three activities:

- Validate strategic direction
- Determine stakeholder relationship
- Consolidate strategic criteria

The second building block, "Architect and Align," consists of the following six activities:

- Architect business processes
- Identify measures of performance
- Align process governance
- Prioritize processes
- Align process capabilities
- Establish enterprise transformation portfolio

For each of those activities, Burlton (2010) either references other available approaches or introduces methodological support for performing those activities. In the context of the activity "Validate Strategic Direction," he references the Business Motivation Model (BMM) (Object Management Group 2010) as a means for clearly separating means and ends and for refining and communicating an organization's overall intent.

GQM$^+$Strategies could support this activity as it also distinguishes between ends and means and creates traceable hierarchies of goals (ends) and strategies (means). Thus, it could provide help in identifying gaps in the linkage between lower-level process initiatives and higher-level goals of an organization. The benefit of applying GQM$^+$Strategies would be that it provides a systematic process and support for performing this activity. Additionally, using the measurement models could also help specify measures, during the activity "Identify Measures of Performance," which are directly linked to the previously defined goals.

11.3   Software Process Management

Typically, two major types of software process improvement (SPI) approaches can be distinguished (Basili 1993; Münch et al. 2012): model-based SPI approaches, e.g., ISO/IEC 15504 (also known as SPICE) or CMMI, and continuous SPI approaches, like PDCA or QIP. GQM$^+$Strategies has its origins in Software Quality and Process Management and thus we will discuss both SPI types in the following, as well as their relationships to GQM$^+$Strategies.

11.3.1 Model-Based Software Process Improvement Approaches

Model-based software process improvement (SPI) approaches compare processes in a software organization to a reference model. Typically, a reference model contains requirements for processes defined on the basis of industry best practices (Basili 1993). Consequently, they identify problematic process areas in comparison to best practices specified within the used reference model. Performing such a comparison is called an assessment, and the results of such an assessment are used to derive improvement suggestions. Usually, model-based SPI approaches define capability or maturity levels with different sets of practices. Systematic improvement in an organization is typically guided by improving the organization towards achieving higher capability or maturity levels (Münch et al. 2012).

Model-based approaches are often criticized for being generic in nature as they only assess against the requirements of a reference model and typically do not assess the impact of processes on product characteristics. Therefore, it is difficult to use them for the analytic identification of process problems that can be related to concrete product problems. Furthermore, model-based improvement approaches are not necessarily related explicitly to organizational goals. This is crucial, as it implies that reaching a certain maturity level does not necessarily mean that an organization's goals have been achieved successfully or are even supported better (Conradi and Fuggetta 2002). A closer look at the CMMI, for example, shows that organizational goals are considered sporadically, but not consistently, up to maturity level 3. Two of the practices that relate to goals are, for example, GP 2.10 "Review the activities, status, and results of the process with higher level management and resolve issues" and OPF (Organizational Process Focus) (SP 1.1) "Establish and maintain the description of the process needs and objectives for the organization." Only at high maturity levels (4 and 5) are goals considered explicitly and defined as required. This is defined as follows: OPM (Organizational Performance Management)—"The purpose of OPM is to proactively manage the organization's performance to meet its business objectives"—and OPP (Organizational Process Performance) (SP1.1) "Establish and maintain the organization's quantitative objectives for quality and process performance, which are traceable to business objectives." Additionally, in generic practices: GP 4.1 "Establish and maintain quantitative objectives for the process, which address quality and process performance, based on customer needs and business objectives" and GP 5.1 "Ensure continuous improvement of the process in fulfilling the relevant business objectives of the organization." Although improvement should always be linked to a business purpose and thus to organizational goals, most maturity models explicitly demand a reference to organizational goals only at high maturity levels. Additionally, they typically do not provide support on how to do this. Improving an organization to maturity level 3 typically requires significant effort. When such effort does not correlate with business needs and long-term organizational goals, the improvement initiative will have a high risk of failure or of not delivering the expected benefits.

11.3.2 Model-Based SPI and Relationship with GQM⁺Strategies

Generally, specifying a GQM⁺Strategies grid will help an organization to identify business-related needs for improvement and to create traceable linkage between the improvement initiative and organizational goals.

In the context of model-based improvement initiatives, GQM⁺Strategies can make two further contributions. Using GQM⁺Strategies in organizations at lower maturity levels can help identify the most important process areas that need to be improved. Thus, systematically refining a GQM⁺Strategies grid can support the prioritization of improvement activities by identifying the most beneficial areas according to the current goals of the organization. In particular, if an organization is at a low maturity level, there is typically a multitude of different improvement options, but not all are equally important and beneficial to every organization. Thus, an organization-specific selection, based on an organization's goals, can help to maximize the benefits gained from improvement initiatives.

For organizations that aim for higher levels of maturity (i.e., levels 4 and 5 in CMMI), the benefit of using GQM$^+$Strategies is even more obvious. On those levels, organizations are required to explicitly consider organizational goals to specify improvement, process performance and product quality objectives. But model-based SPI approaches typically do not provide guidance on how to do this. Establishing these explicit linkages between organizational goals and software engineering related goals and activities within an organization is one of the core capabilities of the approach. Thus, GQM$^+$Strategies can provide systematic support in this area and, additionally, provides a way of quantifying the level of achievement of those different aspects.

11.3.3 Continuous Software Process Improvement Approaches

In contrast to model-based approaches, continuous SPI approaches focus on concrete challenges that are important for a specific software organization and drive improvement through closed-loop improvement cycles (Basili 1993). Continuous approaches address a specific problem by analyzing the problem and defining an initial baseline, implementing focused improvement actions, as well as measuring and evaluating the effects of the implemented improvement actions. The analysis of the measurement results is the driver for continuous improvement and can provide concrete insights allowing further improvement. Consequently, the improvement actions performed are often highly effective and efficient as they are focused. Due to the inclusion of measurement, the immediate impact of improvement actions can also be demonstrated (Münch et al. 2012).

Nevertheless, continuous SPI approaches also have pitfalls. Their focused nature and the fact that continuous improvement approaches are often driven by small numbers of internal process experts makes them vulnerable to isolation and lack of commitment (Münch et al. 2012). Using such a focused approach, it typically becomes increasingly difficult to create an overall awareness for quality issues and associated quality initiatives with increasing size of an organization. Therefore, continuous improvement approaches have to be embedded and institutionalized within an organizational improvement framework. Additionally, the benefit of their specific focus should be clearly linked to more general, higher-level organizational goals in order to gain and maintain commitment within the organization. These improvement goals are often not linked directly to organizational goals and thus their contribution might be unclear to higher-level management. This can lead to situations in which the business value of such initiatives is perceived as being low. Of course, this does not mean that the actual value is low for the organization, but rather that the improvement has an indirect influence and thus the value contribution might be difficult to show. Therefore, if the goals of such initiates are not explicitly linked to higher-level organizational goals, they may be questioned and lose commitment among management and stakeholders from engineering departments.

11.3.4 Continuous SPI and Relationship with GQM$^+$Strategies

Again, the problems that have been described here can be addressed by using the core capabilities of GQM$^+$Strategies. Using GQM$^+$Strategies and modeling a grid in the context of a continuous SPI approach will help to advocate the benefits and value contribution of such an improvement initiative. Defining and linking the goals of a focused continuous improvement initiative will thus help to initially gain commitment as well as to maintain commitment over the course of the improvement initiative. As the underlying lifecycle model on which GQM$^+$Strategies is based is the continuous SPI approach QIP (Basili et al. 1994a), GQM$^+$Strategies not only provides the means for linking and aligning improvement goals at the software engineering level of an organization, but also provides the capabilities to specify the measurement models that are needed for evaluating the effectiveness and impact of the improvement actions. Consequently, GQM$^+$Strategies could be used to improve the goal alignment of continuous SPI approaches. Additionally, it can also be used to operationalize corresponding improvement initiatives.

11.4 Summary

In this chapter, we focused on the relationship between GQM$^+$Strategies and other methods and frameworks.

First, we discussed the BSC as a representative of the group of organizational performance measurement approaches. We found the underlying concepts of the BSC to be quite similar to those of GQM$^+$Strategies. This is the case because both approaches address similar organizational problems, although they were developed in different contexts. Both approaches use organizational goals to systematically refine and specify goals and related measures in order to improve transparency, communication, and coordination and thus to improve organizational performance through more objective and better aligned activities. Furthermore, we discussed that GQM$^+$Strategies could complement the Balanced Scorecard, particularly in the context of specifying goal-oriented measurement systems in software organizations.

Next, we addressed BPM and discussed the relevance of measurement in this context. Applying GQM$^+$Strategies in this context would allow for systematically deriving goals for business process improvement initiatives as well as for identifying possible gaps in the linkage between improvement and organizational goals.

In the last section, we discussed model-based and continuous software process improvement (SPI) approaches. With respect to GQM⁺Strategies, we found that for model-based initiatives, specifying a GQM⁺Strategies grid could help to identify specific business-related needs for improvement. It could also help to create traceable linkages between the improvement initiative and organizational goals. For lower-maturity organizations, GQM⁺Strategies could help identify the most important process areas that need to be improved according to the current goals of the organization. Organizations that target higher levels of maturity (i.e., levels 4 and 5 in CMMI) are required to explicitly consider organizational goals for specifying improvement, process performance, and product quality objectives. Here, GQM⁺Strategies can provide systematic support. In the context of a continuous SPI, GQM⁺Strategies can help to advocate the benefits and value contribution of such improvement initiatives. Additionally, as the underlying lifecycle model of GQM⁺Strategies is based on the continuous SPI approach QIP (Basili et al. 1994a), GQM⁺Strategies also provides the means for specifying the measurement models that are needed for evaluating the effectiveness and impact of improvement initiatives.

In summary, we find that GQM⁺Strategies can be a valuable complement for different approaches whenever there is a need for achieving a high level of traceability and alignment between organizational goals as well as for evaluating the success of goal attainment.

Summary and Future Perspectives

12

Measurement provides many benefits to organizations of all types. However, measurement confined to the project level is limited in its ability to provide benefits throughout the organization. Measurement has always been used to help organizations assess and monitor various aspects of their operations and aid executives in strategic decision-making.

While measurement of various kinds is practiced widely in organizations, from top management down to individual projects, a major obstacle for getting the full benefits of measurement is the inability to coordinate and align measurement efforts so that measurement information can be leveraged by different stakeholders in different organizational units to help answer questions and assess their goals. This book introduces GQM$^+$Strategies, an approach designed to remove this obstacle.

We have described how GQM$^+$Strategies is designed to achieve several benefits for the adopting organizations, and we have also, in Chap. 10, shown some examples of organizations in the early phases of adoption who have already achieved benefits.

12.1 Benefits

The first major benefit of applying GQM$^+$Strategies is ***consistent alignment*** of goals and associated measurement plans for different related units of an organization. This allows, for example, data collected from individual projects to be useful in assessing the goals of the entire development unit, and for data collected across projects to be aggregated in a way that can be used by top-level executives to monitor and assess issues of interest to them. A GQM$^+$Strategies grid, through its interlinked interpretation models, provides a blueprint for how data feeds up into higher-level units and how it can be used as part of their measurement plans. The benefits of alignment can be clearly seen in the JAXA case study presented in Chap. 10. Building the GQM$^+$Strategies grid at JAXA not only resulted in the alignment of measurement efforts, but the alignment of goals made it clear how some parts of the organization were contributing to larger business objectives, thus

V. Basili et al., *Aligning Organizations Through Measurement*, The Fraunhofer IESE Series on Software and Systems Engineering, DOI 10.1007/978-3-319-05047-8_12,
© Springer International Publishing Switzerland 2014

justifying expenditures in those areas. Alignment was clearly an important benefit of using GQM⁺Strategies in the IPA/SEC and ECOPETROL case studies as well. Showing the contribution of proposed research or IT projects to higher-level organizational goals was the key to their motivation for using GQM⁺Strategies.

The second major benefit of using GQM⁺Strategies is the ability to have a means for **measurement-based decision-making**. The grid contains not only the goals, strategies, and measurement plans, but also documents the context factors and assumptions that form the rationale for the measurement design. This facilitates the maintenance of the grid over time; as context factors change, or assumptions are confirmed or refuted, the grid can help stakeholders understand what goals and strategies are affected by these changes and make informed improvement decisions. The fact that such context factors and assumptions often remain implicit in organizations leads to a variety of measurement problems that GQM⁺Strategies helps to alleviate. Explicating the assumptions underlying goals and strategies was a particularly crucial aspect of the IPA/SEC and ECOPETROL cases described in Chap. 10. Making these assumptions explicit was a benefit to decision-making and to risk assessment in those cases.

Finally, the third major benefit of GQM⁺Strategies is as an organization-wide means for **transparent communication**. The GQM⁺Strategies grid is a useful tool for organization-wide communication, and the process for building it is a valuable opportunity for stakeholders from different parts of the organization to discuss their goals and strategies and to understand the relationships between them. This not only makes all aspects of measurement explicit, as explained above, but also makes sure that all stakeholders understand how their measurement plan feeds into other goals and strategies in other areas. This benefit was implicit in all the case studies presented in Chap. 10, but was most clear in the ECOPETROL case, where the stakeholders involved were particularly diverse in terms of the business areas they represented and historically had difficulty understanding each other's goals and motivations.

12.2   Future Plans

Work on extending, enhancing, and adapting GQM⁺Strategies is ongoing, supported by a wide network of researchers, consultants, and practitioners worldwide. In this section, we outline some current areas of active research that are likely to produce results and contributions in the near future.

12.2.1 Tool Support

Full use of GQM⁺Strategies on a large scale requires reliable, user-friendly, and comprehensive tool support. Currently, several tools exist for building, editing, querying, and visualizing grids. The GQM⁺Strategies partners are working on an integrated platform that will also allow for such capabilities as specifying alternative goals and strategies, feeding back real measurement data for decision making, and allowing "what if" and gap analyses.

12.2.2 Value-Based Software Engineering

There is an active area of research that investigates the use of value concepts in the management of software development. The perception of software development activities and artifacts from a value-sensitive perspective is featured most prominently in the value-based software engineering (VBSE) framework (Boehm 2003). More recently, it has been used in the area of lean software development (Mandić et al. 2010b).

With respect to GQM$^+$Strategies, there is also ongoing investigation regarding the incorporation of ideas from value-based software engineering into the creation and management of GQM$^+$Strategies grids, as well as the use of the resulting measurement data in making decisions about the value of different activities (Mandić et al. 2010a–c). More specifically, the merger of VBSE and GQM$^+$Strategies allows the user to:

1. Apply the work of value-based software engineering to directly address the return on investment (ROI) of organizational goals and strategies via evaluation of the costs and benefits of the goals and strategies chosen (Mandić et al. 2010c)
2. Calculate a set of earned value metrics that will allow organizations to effectively monitor the implementation of the organizational goals and strategies with respect to costs, schedule, and benefits realization (Mandić et al. 2010a)
3. Identify the risks associated with not achieving various subgoals in a grid by analyzing goal risk exposures and acceptable risk levels for the estimated cost–benefit ratio of goal attainment (Mandić et al. 2010c; Mandić 2012)

12.2.3 Causality Theory

Another area of ongoing research utilizes Causality Theory to deal with the increasing number of dependencies among GQM$^+$Strategies elements (Mandić 2012). Adoption of Causality Theory provides a framework for quantifying dependencies among goals and strategies in the GQM$^+$Strategies grid. In other words, the GQM$^+$Strategies goal hierarchy can be seen as an organizational causal model. This leads to a new understanding of the grid derivation process. As a result, experts who are developing grids can define strategies as causal relations and quantify their beliefs about the causal effects in terms of probabilities. The causal models also provide a theory that can be used to analyze a much wider spectrum of situations that might occur during grid development. For example, it facilitates analysis of how the threat of risky goals impacts the realization of other goals in the grid (Mandić 2012).

12.2.4 Patterns

As in other areas of software engineering—for example, design patterns (Gamma et al. 1994), process patterns (Ambler 1998)—there is potential for the identification, packaging, and reuse of patterns to have a substantial impact on the cost and effectiveness of employing GQM⁺Strategies.

Investigation is ongoing into grids and portions of grids that can be abstracted from theory and practice and packaged for reuse, which is called structural patterns. For example, some of the project goals for a given software project are a direct consequence of the development methodology selected, such as Extreme Programming (XP) or Test-Driven Development (TDD). An example goal for any XP project would be to release working software in predefined increments. Starting with such a goal, we can derive reusable patterns for the associated parts of the GQM⁺Strategies grid that can be instantiated for any XP project. Moreover, such structural patterns allow the capture of lessons learned about what worked and what didn't in that context. Thus, storing context factors in a knowledge base is immensely important as they can help to make a decision regarding alternative methodologies.

Furthermore, the process of building and maintaining a grid is a communication- and analysis-intensive challenge of understanding the organization, its values and vision, as well as the context in which it operates. Another type of pattern that we are investigating are behavioral patterns, which capture the behaviors and actions of GQM⁺Strategies users in defining goals, strategies, context factors, etc., when building a grid. For example, a behavioral pattern could describe a brainstorming method that has been used successfully in eliciting goals and strategies during grid development. These behavioral patterns allow capturing knowledge about the selection of grid-building techniques, about the lessons learned from applying such techniques in a comprehensive and structured way, and about overcoming obstacles encountered in the GQM⁺Strategies process.

Both types of patterns can be organized in pattern catalogs to aid reuse and searching. The patterns can reduce the time required to define and update a grid, and can also enhance the learning process for people new to GQM⁺Strategies. The current research activities focus not only on providing predefined catalogs but also on a method that supports selection of the appropriate pattern for a given situation in a certain context.

12.2.5 Relationships with CMMI

Measurement and improvement efforts in software (and other types of) organizations are often associated with the CMMI (2010). There is great potential, in fact, for GQM⁺Strategies to be used as an aid in an organization's efforts to achieve CMMI certification. Work is being done to build generic GQM⁺Strategies grids that represent the requirements associated with CMMI compliance. An organization could instantiate such a generic grid by customizing the parts that already exist and noting the parts that do not, thus performing a simple "gap analysis" to guide further CMMI compliance efforts. Currently, these research efforts are focusing on CMMI level 4, which is the level most heavily focused on measurement.

Appendix A. GQM⁺Strategies Process Checklist

The following checklist provides guidance for applying GQM⁺Strategies. It aims at easy comprehensibility and lists the logical steps to be performed. More detailed descriptions of the activities in the GQM⁺Strategies process and the GQM⁺Strategies concepts can be found by following the pointers (in parentheses) to the respective sections in the book.

Initialize

- Define purpose (Sect. 3.1)
- Define scope (Sect. 3.2)
- Describe the organizational structure (Sect. 3.2)
- Get management commitment (Sects. 3.1 and 3.2)
- Get personnel resources (Sect. 3.3)
- Plan implementation (Sect. 3.3)
- Motivate and train personnel for GQM⁺Strategies application (Sect. 3.4)

Characterize Environment

- Comprehend and define the environment of the GQM⁺Strategies application (Sect. 4.1)
- Identify risks that might constrain the application of GQM⁺Strategies (Sect. 4.1)
- Identify opportunities that might support the application of GQM⁺Strategies (Sect. 4.1)

Define Goals and Strategies, and Measurement

- Identify existing goals, strategies, and relevant assets (Sects. 5.1 and 5.2)
- Select existing or identify new goals to start with (Sects. 5.3.1 and 5.3.2)
- Provide rationales for the goals (Sects. 5.3.1 and 5.3.2)
- Describe the goals in a structured way by using the organizational goal template (Sect. 5.3.2)
- Identify strategies that contribute to reaching the goals (Sect. 5.3.3)
- Prioritize strategies and select the most promising ones (Sect. 5.3.3)

V. Basili et al., *Aligning Organizations Through Measurement*, The Fraunhofer IESE Series on Software and Systems Engineering, DOI 10.1007/978-3-319-05047-8, © Springer International Publishing Switzerland 2014

- Find and close gaps between goals and strategies (Sect. 5.3.3)
- Define measures for measuring goal attainment (Sect. 5.3.5)
- Define thresholds and potential explanations (i.e., interpretation models) for the success or failure of each goal and related strategies (Sect. 5.3.5)
- Iterate by refining goals and strategies until the scope is covered (Sects. 5.3.1–5.3.5)
- Review and adjust goals and strategies (Sect. 5.4)

Plan Grid Implementation

- Plan strategy deployment with stakeholders (Sect. 6.1)
- Set up measurement, analysis, and reporting procedures (Sect. 6.2)
- Organize training to prepare personnel with respect to strategy implementation (Sect. 6.3)
- Train personnel with respect to measurement, analysis, and reporting (Sect. 6.3)

Execute Plans

- Execute strategies (Sect. 7.1)
- Collect and analyze data (Sect. 7.2)
- Monitor local strategy deployment (Sect. 7.2)
- Adjust strategy implementation, if necessary (Sect. 7.3)
- Adjust measurement, analysis, and reporting procedures, if necessary (Sect. 7.3)

Analyze Outcomes

- Analyze overall strategy deployment and goal attainment (Sects. 8.1 and 8.2)
- Gather feedback from relevant stakeholders (Sect. 8.3)
- Analyze if the environment (i.e., the context) has changed (Sect. 8.3)
- Question the strategies and the assumptions they are based on (Sect. 8.3)
- Make proposals for improvement (Sect. 8.3)

Package Improvements

- Change goals or strategies, if necessary (Sect. 9.1)
- Communicate revised or new goals and strategies (Sect. 9.2)
- Store relevant information and experience from the application of GQM⁺Strategies for future use (Sect. 9.3)

Appendix B. GQM⁺Strategies Evaluation Questionnaire

The goal of this survey is to evaluate the benefits of the GQM⁺Strategies approach for your organization. This input will be used for improving the method in future. All questions are phrased as statements you may agree with or disagree with. There are no right or wrong answers. Your personal opinion is what matters most. All data gathered here will be analyzed anonymously and not be distributed to a third person so that no information about the respondent will be disclosed under any circumstances.

Background Information

A1: What is the name of your company?

A2: What is your current position?

A3: For how many years have you been working in this position?

Training and Expertise in the GQM⁺Strategies Approach

B1: What GQM⁺Strategies training have you already obtained?   How many times?

B1.1: Motivational talk or short (<1 day) presentation

B1.2: One-day method tutorial

B1.3: Two-day method tutorial

B1.4: Training for method trainers and promoters

B1.5: Other training (please specify):

B2: For what purposes have you already used the GQM⁺Strategies approach?   How many times?

B.2.1: I have employed the method in an industrial organization

B.2.2: I have given the motivational talk

B.2.3: I have given the 1-day method tutorial

B.2.4: I have given the 2-day method tutorial

(continued)

V. Basili et al., *Aligning Organizations Through Measurement*, The Fraunhofer IESE Series 189 on Software and Systems Engineering, DOI 10.1007/978-3-319-05047-8,
© Springer International Publishing Switzerland 2014

B2: For what purposes have you already used the GQM⁺Strategies approach? How many times?

B.2.5: I have given the training for method trainers and promoters

B.2.6: I have moderated the 1-day exercise workshop

B.2.7: I have moderated a real-world industrial workshop

B.2.8: Other purpose (please specify):

Assessment of the GQM⁺Strategies Approach

Alignment	Strongly disagree	Disagree	Neither/ nor	Agree	Strongly agree	I don't know
	1	2	3	4	5	–
C1.1: Using GQM⁺Strategies, I'm able to harmonize goals, strategies, and measurement data	❑	❑	❑	❑	❑	❑
C1.2: GQM⁺Strategies supports me in tracking my goals and strategies	❑	❑	❑	❑	❑	❑
C1.3: Using GQM⁺Strategies, I'm able to align my work activities with the goals and strategies of the organization	❑	❑	❑	❑	❑	❑
C1.4: GQM⁺Strategies supports me in aligning goals and strategies across organizational units	❑	❑	❑	❑	❑	❑
C1.5: Using GQM⁺Strategies, gaps between goals, strategies, and measurement data become obvious	❑	❑	❑	❑	❑	❑
C1.6: GQM⁺Strategies supports me in closing gaps between goals, strategies, and measurement data	❑	❑	❑	❑	❑	❑
C1.7: GQM⁺Strategies supports me in identifying nonbeneficial goals, strategies, and measurement data	❑	❑	❑	❑	❑	❑

Transparency	Strongly disagree	Disagree	Neither/ nor	Agree	Strongly agree	I don't know
	1	2	3	4	5	–
C2.1: GQM⁺Strategies supports me in getting a clearer picture of the goals and strategies of my organization	❑	❑	❑	❑	❑	❑
C2.2: Using GQM⁺Strategies, the goals and strategies of my organization become more transparent for me	❑	❑	❑	❑	❑	❑

(continued)

Transparency	Strongly disagree 1	Disagree 2	Neither/ nor 3	Agree 4	Strongly agree 5	I don't know –
C2.3: GQM⁺Strategies supports me in identifying contradictory goals and strategies across different organizational units	❑	❑	❑	❑	❑	❑
C2.4: Using GQM⁺Strategies helps me in understanding the relationships between goals and strategies	❑	❑	❑	❑	❑	❑
C2.5: GQM⁺Strategies supports me in understanding the rationale for defined goals and strategies	❑	❑	❑	❑	❑	❑
C2.6: GQM⁺Strategies supports me in getting a consistent understanding of goals and strategies across different organizational units	❑	❑	❑	❑	❑	❑
C2.7: GQM⁺Strategies supports me in communicating goals and strategies across different organizational units	❑	❑	❑	❑	❑	❑

Measurability	Strongly disagree 1	Disagree 2	Neither/ nor 3	Agree 4	Strongly agree 5	I don't know –
C3.1: GQM⁺Strategies helps me in quantifying my organization's goals and strategies	❑	❑	❑	❑	❑	❑
C3.2: Using GQM⁺Strategies supports me in measuring the success/failure of goals and strategies	❑	❑	❑	❑	❑	❑
C3.3: GQM⁺Strategies supports me in collecting mandatory measurement data	❑	❑	❑	❑	❑	❑
C3.4: GQM⁺Strategies supports me in identifying superfluous measurement data	❑	❑	❑	❑	❑	❑
C3.5: GQM⁺Strategies helps me in optimizing the benefits from collecting measurement data	❑	❑	❑	❑	❑	❑
C3.6: Using GQM⁺Strategies helps me to identify unsuccessful strategies	❑	❑	❑	❑	❑	❑
C3.7: Using GQM⁺Strategies helps me in assessing the attainment of goals	❑	❑	❑	❑	❑	❑

General Comments to the GQM⁺Strategies Approach

E1: What do you like about GQM⁺Strategies in particular?

E2: What don't you like about GQM⁺Strategies at all?

Final Evaluation of the GQM⁺Strategies Approach

F1: What school grade would you give to the GQM⁺Strategies approach?

A	B	C	D	F	I don't know
Excellent	Good	Average	Low	Failed	
❏	❏	❏	❏	❏	❏

Thank you for participating in the survey!

Appendix C. Authors

Victor Basili

Victor Basili is Professor Emeritus of Computer Science at the University of Maryland. He holds a PhD in Computer Science from the University of Texas, Austin and is the recipient of two honorary degrees from the University of Sannio, Italy (2004) and the University of Kaiserslautern, Germany (2005). He served as founding director of the Fraunhofer Center for Experimental Software Engineering and the Software Engineering Laboratory at NASA/GSFC. He has worked on measuring, evaluating, and improving the software development process and product using methods that include Iterative Enhancement (IE), the Goal–Question–Metric Approach (GQM), the Quality Improvement Paradigm (QIP), and the Experience Factory (EF). He has developed, tailored, evaluated, and evolved these techniques for several organizations. He has been the recipient of grants from government agencies and companies including NSF, NASA, AFOSR, ONR, AFOSR, AFRL, DARPA, IBM, Hughes, NEC, Amdahl, Coopers and Lybrand, Ricoh, Mutsuhito Panasonic, Daimler Benz, Bellcore, and Fujitsu. Dr. Basili is the recipient of several awards, including the NASA Group Achievement Award (1996), ACM SIGSOFT Outstanding Research Award (2000), IEEE Computer Society Harlan Mills Award (2003), and the Fraunhofer Medal (2007). He has authored over 250 journals and refereed conference papers and is Co-Editor-in-Chief of the Journal of Empirical Software Engineering. He is an IEEE and ACM Fellow.

Jens Heidrich

Dr. Jens Heidrich is head of the Process Management division at the Fraunhofer Institute for Experimental Software Engineering IESE in Kaiserslautern, Germany and a lecturer at the University of Kaiserslautern, Germany. His research interests are in the area of measurement-based improvement of processes in general, specifically in the field of cost and effort estimation of development projects, assessment of software product quality, and agile development practices. Prior to his current position, he was the head of the Processes and Measurement department at IESE where he was responsible for research and technology transfer projects. He graduated

V. Basili et al., *Aligning Organizations Through Measurement*, The Fraunhofer IESE Series on Software and Systems Engineering, DOI 10.1007/978-3-319-05047-8,
© Springer International Publishing Switzerland 2014

from the University of Kaiserslautern, Germany, with a Diploma degree in Computer Science (summa cum laude) and received his doctoral degree (Dr. rer. nat.) from the same university (summa cum laude).

He has been teaching and training in both university and industry environments since 2001 and is a member of the program committees of different national and international conferences, such as the International Conference on Product Focused Software Development and Process Improvement (PROFES) and the EUROMICRO Conference on Software Engineering and Advanced Applications (SEAA). He is a member of the German Informatics Society (Gesellschaft für Informatik e.V.) and part of the managing committee of the section "Software Measurement."

Martin Kowalczyk

Martin Kowalczyk is a researcher at Technische Universität Darmstadt, Germany, at the Department of Information Systems. His current research focuses on Business Intelligence and Analytics in the context of organizational decision-making processes.

Prior to his current position, Martin was a researcher and consultant at the Fraunhofer Institute for Experimental Software Engineering IESE, where he was a member of the Processes Management division. His research activities focused on subjects concerning software development processes and goal-oriented measurement approaches. In the context of industrial projects, he provided consultancy services to several international organizations from the aerospace, finance, and services domains on topics from the area of software process improvement and measurement. He has led process improvement initiatives and has established measurement programs for his customers.

Martin graduated from the University of Karlsruhe, Germany, with a Diploma degree in Industrial Engineering. He is coauthor of one book and several international peer-reviewed publications on topics related to software process management, software-business alignment, and measurement.

Jürgen Münch

Jürgen Münch is a full professor in the Department of Computer Science at the University of Helsinki, Finland, and head of its Software Systems Research Group. His research centers on software measurement and quantitative analysis, process and quality engineering, global software development, cloud-based software engineering, and empirical software engineering. Münch has been a principal investigator in numerous research and industrial development projects. Prior to his current position, Münch was a division head at the Fraunhofer Institute for Experimental Software Engineering IESE in Kaiserslautern, Germany, where he was responsible for research and technology transfer in the area of software process and quality engineering. He was also an executive board member of the temporary research institute SFB 501 at the University of Kaiserslautern, Germany. Münch has been awarded the Distinguished Professor Award FiDiPro (endowed with €1,900,000) of Tekes, the IFIP TC2 Manfred Paul Award for Excellence in Software Theory and Practice, several best paper awards, and the Technology Innovation Award sponsored by the Rhineland-Palatinate Lotto Foundation. He has been the chair of several renowned software engineering conferences such as the International Conference on Software and Systems Process (ICSSP), and the ACM/IEEE Symposium on Empirical Software Engineering and Measurement (ESEM). He is Vice-Chairman of the German Association for Software Metrics and Cost Estimation (DASMA).

Dieter Rombach

Prof. Dr. H. Dieter Rombach studied mathematics and computer science at the University of Karlsruhe, Germany, and obtained his Ph.D. in Computer Science from the University of Kaiserslautern, Germany in 1984. Since 1992, he has held the Software Engineering Chair in the Department of Computer Science at the University of Kaiserslautern. In addition, he is the founding and executive director of the Fraunhofer Institute for Experimental Software Engineering IESE in Kaiserslautern, Germany. He is the author of more than 200 scientific publications. In 1990, he received the "Presidential Young Investigator Award" of the National Science Foundation (NSF) in the USA. He has been awarded the Service Medal of the State of Rhineland-Palatinate (2000); the Distinguished Postdoctoral Award of the College for Computer, Mathematical, and Physical Sciences of the University of Maryland (2003); the Federal Cross of Merit on Ribbon of the Federal Republic of Germany (2009); an honorary doctorate degree by the University of Oulu, Finland (2009); and the Fraunhofer Medal (2013). Since 2009, he has been the chairman of the IEEE Awards Committees for the Software Process Achievement Award (SPA) and for the Harlan Mills Award. Furthermore, he is coeditor of several international journals (e.g., McCluwer Journal for Empirical Software Engineering) and acts as a program committee member and chair of several software engineering conferences. He is a member of the Gesellschaft für Informatik (GI) and a Fellow of both the ACM (since 2010) and the IEEE Computer Society (since 2003).

Carolyn Seaman

Dr. Seaman is an Associate Professor of Information Systems at the University of Maryland Baltimore County (UMBC). Her research generally falls under the umbrella of empirical studies of software engineering, with particular emphases on maintenance, organizational structure, communication, measurement, COTS-based development, and qualitative research methods. Dr. Seaman is also a Research Fellow at the Fraunhofer Center for Experimental Software Engineering,

Maryland, where she participates in research on experience management in software engineering organizations and software metrics. Her current research focuses on the effective and efficient management of Technical Debt in software systems under maintenance. She holds a PhD in Computer Science from the University of Maryland, College Park, an MS in Information and Computer Science from Georgia Tech, and a BA in Computer Science and Mathematics from the College of Wooster (Ohio). She has worked in the software industry as a software engineer and consultant and has conducted most of her research in industrial and governmental settings (e.g., IBM Canada Ltd., NASA, Xerox).

Adam Trendowicz

Adam Trendowicz is a senior consultant at the Fraunhofer Institute for Experimental Software Engineering IESE in Kaiserslautern, Germany, where he leads the Measurement and Prediction team. He received his PhD in Computer Science from the University of Kaiserslautern, Germany. Dr. Trendowicz has led multiple measurement-based software improvement activities in software companies of different sizes and from various domains (e.g., in Germany, France, Japan, and India). He has been involved in functional software size estimation (Function Points Analysis) and productivity benchmarking in organizations from both industry and the public sector. Dr. Trendowicz has trained and coached IT/software strategic alignment with measurement in both industrial and academic contexts. Last but not least, he has led the development of measurement-based project governance initiatives in the context of software development organizations. Dr. Trendowicz has authored the book "Software Cost Estimation, Benchmarking, and Risk Assessment. The Software Decision-Makers' Guide to Predictable Software Development." Moreover, he has coauthored more than 20 international journals and conference publications. Dr. Trendowicz's other software engineering interests include: (1) project management, (2) software product quality modeling and evaluation, and (3) technology validation by means of empirical methods.

Bibliography

Accenture (2004) Managing IT investments in the high-performance business. Strategic information technology effectiveness (SITE). Report, Accenture LLP

Ambler SW (1998) Process patterns: building large-scale systems using object technology. Cambridge University Press, Cambridge, UK

Antón AI, McCracken WM, Potts C (1994) Goal decomposition and scenario analysis in business process reengineering. In: Wijers G, Brinkkemper S, Wasserman T (eds) Advanced information systems engineering. Springer, Berlin, pp 94–104

Basili VR (1981) Data collection, validation, and analysis. In: Tutorial on models and metrics for software management and engineering, IEEE Catalog no. EHO-167-7, pp 310–313

Basili V (1985) Quantitative evaluation of software methodology, keynote address. In: Proceedings of the first Pan Pacific computer conference, vol 1, pp 379–398

Basili VR (1989) Software development: a paradigm for the future. In: Presentation at the thirteenth international computer software and applications conference, Los Alamitos, CA

Basili VR (1993) The experience factory and its relationship to other improvement paradigms. In: Proceedings of the fourth European software engineering conference (ESEC), Garmisch-Partenkirchen, Germany. The Proceedings appeared as Lecture Notes in Computer Science 717

Basili VR, Caldiera G (1995) Improve software quality by reusing knowledge and experience. Sloan Manag Rev 37(1):55–64

Basili V, Green S (1994) Software process evolution at the SEL. IEEE Software 11(4):58–66

Basili VR, Rombach HD (1988) The TAME project: towards improvement-oriented software environments. IEEE Trans Software Eng 14(6):758–773

Basili VR, Weiss DM (1984) A methodology for collecting valid software engineering data. IEEE Trans Software Eng SE-10(6):728–738

Basili VR, Caldiera G, Rombach HD (1994a) The experience factory. In: Marciniak JJ (ed) Encyclopedia of software engineering, vol 1, 2nd edn. Wiley, New York, pp 469–476

Basili VR, Caldiera G, Rombach HD (1994b) Goal question metric paradigm. In: Marciniak JJ (ed) Encyclopedia of software engineering, vol 1, 2nd edn. Wiley, New York, pp 528–532

Basili V, Zelkowitz M, McGarry F, Page J, Waligora S, Pajerski R (1995) Special report: SEL's software process-improvement program. IEEE Software 12(6):83–87

Basili VR, Green S, Laitenberger O, Shull F, Sørumgård S, Zelkowitz MV (1996) The empirical investigation of perspective-based reading. Empir Software Eng 13(12):1278–1296

Basili VR, Lindvall M, Regardie M, Seaman C, Heidrich J, Münch J, Rombach HD, Trendowicz A (2010) Linking software development and business strategy through measurement. IEEE Comput 43(4):57–65

Beck K, Andres C (2004) Extreme programming explained: embrace change. Addison-Wesley, Boston, MA

Becker SA, Bostelman ML (1999) Aligning strategic and project measurement systems. IEEE Software 16(3):46–51

Boehm B (2003) Value-based software engineering. ACM SIGSOFT Software Eng Notes 2(28):3–15

Briand LC, Differding CM, Rombach HD (1996) Practical guidelines for measurement-based process improvement. Software Process Improv Pract 2(4):253–280

Brindgeland DM, Zahavi R (2008) Business modeling: a practical guide to realizing business value. Morgan Kaufmann, Boston, MA

Budd CI, Budd CS (2009) A practical guide to earned value project management, 2nd edn. Management Concepts, Vienna, VA

Buglione L, Abran A (2000) Balanced scorecards and GQM: what are the differences? In: Proceedings to the third European software measurement conference, pp 18–20

Burlton R (2010) Delivering business strategy through process management. In: vom Brocke J, Rosemann M (eds) Handbook on business process management 2. Springer, Berlin, pp 5–37

Chillarege R, Bhandari IS, Chaar JK, Halliday MJ, Moebus DS, Ray BK, Wong M-Y (1992) Orthogonal defect classification – a concept for in-process measurements. IEEE Trans Software Eng 18(11):943–956

Ciolkowski M, Laitenberger O, Rombach D, Shull F, Perry D (2002) Software inspections, reviews and walkthroughs. In: Proceedings of the 24rd international conference on software engineering, May 2002, pp 641–642

CMMI Product Team (2010) CMMI for development, version 1.3. Technical report CMU/SEI-2010-TR-033, Software Engineering Institute, Carnegie Mellon University, Pittsburgh, PA

Conradi R, Fuggetta A (2002) Improving software process improvement. IEEE Software 19(4):92–99

Damiani E, Mulazzani F, Russo B, Succi G (2008) SAF: strategic alignment framework for monitoring organizations. In: Proceedings to the eleventh international conference on business information systems, Innsbruck, Austria. Springer

Deming WE (1986) Out of the crisis. Massachusetts Institute of Technology, Center for Advance Education Services, Cambridge, MA

Eckerson WW (2005) Performance dashboards: measuring, monitoring, and managing your business. Wiley, Hoboken, NJ

Epstein M, Manzoni J-F (1998) Implementing corporate strategy: from Tableaux de Bord to balanced scorecards. Eur Manag J 16(2):190–203

Fagan M (1976) Design and code inspections to reduce errors in program development. IBM Syst J 15(3):182–211

Gamma E, Helm R, Johnson R, Vlissides J (1994) Design patterns: Elements of Reusable Object-Oriented Software. Addison-Wesley, Boston, MA

Gartner (2010) Gartner executive programs CIO survey. Press release, Gartner, Inc.

Gartner (2011) Forecast alert: IT spending, worldwide, 2008–2014, 4Q10 update. Press release, Gartner, Inc.

Gresse C, Hoisl B, Wüst J (1995) A process model for planning GQM-based measurement. Technical report STTI-95-04-E, Software Technology Transfer Initiative, University of Kaiserslautern

Hammer M (1990) Reengineering work: don't automate, obliterate. Harv Bus Rev 68(4):104–112

Hammer M (2010) What is business process management? In: vom Brocke J, Rosemann M (eds) Handbook on business process management, vol 1. Springer, Heidelberg

Hammer M, Champy JA (1993) Reengineering the corporation: a manifesto for business revolution. Harper, New York

Humphrey A (2005) SWOT analysis for management consulting. SRI Newsletter: History Corner, SRI International, pp 7–8

ISO (2009) ISO/IEC 20926 – IFPUG functional size measurement method 2009, 2nd edn. International Standardization Organization, Geneva

Kaplan RS, Norton DP (1992) The balanced scorecard: measures that drive performance. Harv Bus Rev 70(1):71–79

Kaplan RS, Norton DP (1996) Balanced scorecard: translating strategy into action. Harvard Business School Press, Boston, MA

Kaplan RS, Norton DP (2004) Strategy maps: converting intangible assets into tangible outcomes. Harvard Business School Press, Boston, MA

Kaplan RS, Norton DP (2008) Execution premium: linking strategy to operations for competitive advantage. Harvard Business School Press, Boston, MA

Kerth NL (2001) Project retrospectives: a handbook for team reviews. Dorset House, New York

Laitenberger O (2002) A survey of software inspection technologies. In: Chang SK (ed) Handbook on software engineering and knowledge engineering. World Scientific, Singapore, pp 517–556

Mandić V (2012) Measurement-based value alignment and reasoning about organizational goals and strategies: studied with ICT industry. Doctoral dissertation, University of Oulu, Finland

Mandić V, Basili V, Oivo M, Harjumaa L, Markkula J (2010a) Utilizing GQM$^+$Strategies for an organization-wide earned value analysis. In: Proceedings of the 36th EUROMICRO conference on software engineering and advanced applications, 1–3 Sept 2010, pp 255–258

Mandić V, Oivo M, Rodríguez P, Kuvaja P, Kaikkonen H, Turhan B (2010b) What is flowing in lean software development? In: Proceedings of the first international conference on lean enterprise software and systems, Helsinki, Finland, October 2010

Mandić V, Basili V, Harjumaa L, Oivo M, Markkula J (2010c) Utilizing GQM+Strategies for business value analysis: an approach for evaluating business goals. In: Proceedings of the fourth international symposium on empirical software engineering and measurement, Bolzano-Bozen, Italy, pp 1–10

Münch J, Heidrich J (2004) Software project control centers: concepts and approaches. J Syst Software 70(1):3–19

Münch J, Armbrust O, Kowalczyk M, Soto M (2012) Software process definition and management, Fraunhofer IESE series on software and systems engineering. Springer, New York

Neely A, Gregory M, Platts K (1995) Performance measurement system design: a literature review and research agenda. Int J Oper Prod Manag 15(4):80–116

Nudurupati SS, Bititci US, Kumar V, Chan FTS (2011) State of the art literature review on performance measurement. Comput Ind Eng 60(2):279–290

Offen RJ, Jeffery R (1997) Establishing software measurement programs. IEEE Software 14(2):45–53

OGC (Office of Government Commerce) (2009) Managing successful projects with PRINCE2 2009 edition manual. The Stationery Office, UK

OMG (Object Management Group) (2010) The business motivation model (BMM) V. 1.1. Object Management Group

PMI (2013) A guide to the project management body of knowledge (PMBOK guide), 5th edn. Project Management Institute, Newtown Square, PA

Porter ME (1996) What is strategy? Harv Bus Rev 74(6):61–78

Porter ME (2008) The five competitive forces that shape strategy. Harv Bus Rev 86(1):78–93

Rombach HD, Verlage M (1995) Directions in software process research. In: Zelkowitz MV (ed) Advances in computers, vol 41. Academic, Boston, MA

Rosemann M, vom Brocke J (2010) The six core elements of business process management. In: vom Brocke J, Rosemann M (eds) Handbook on business process management, vol 1. Springer, Heidelberg

Sarcia SA (2010) Is GQM+Strategies really applicable as is to non-software development domains? In: Proceedings of the 2010 ACM-IEEE international symposium on empirical software engineering and measurement, Bolzano-Bozen, Italy, pp 1–4

Schwaber K (2004) Agile project management with scrum. Microsoft Press, Redmond, WA

Selby RW (2005) Measurement-driven dashboards enable leading indicators for requirements and design of large-scale systems. In: Proceedings of the 11th international software metrics symposium, Como, Italy, 19–22 September, pp 1530–1435

Shewhart WA (1939) Statistical method from the viewpoint of quality control. The Graduate School of the Department of Agriculture, Washington, DC. Reprinted by Dover Publications in the Dover Books on Mathematics series in 1986

Trendowicz A, Heidrich J, Shintani K (2011) Aligning software projects with business objectives. In: Proceedings of the joint conference of the 21th international workshop on software measurement (IWSM) and the 6th international conference on software process and product measurement (Mensura), Nara, Japan, 3–4 Nov 2011, vol I. IEEE Computer Society Press, pp 142–150

van Solingen R, Berghout E (1999) Goal/question/metric method. McGraw-Hill, New York

The Fraunhofer Institute for Experimental Software Engineering (IESE)

Fraunhofer IESE in Kaiserslautern is one of the worldwide leading research institutes in the area of software and systems engineering. A major portion of the products offered by its customers is defined by software. These products range from automotive and transportation systems via automation and plant engineering, information systems, healthcare and medical systems to software systems for the public sector. The institute's software and systems engineering approaches are scalable, which makes Fraunhofer IESE a competent technology partner for organizations of any size—from small companies to major corporations.

Under the leadership of Prof. Dieter Rombach and Prof. Peter Liggesmeyer, the contributions of Fraunhofer IESE have been a major boost to the emerging IT hub Kaiserslautern for more than 15 years. In the Fraunhofer Information and Communication Technology Group, the institute is cooperating with other Fraunhofer institutes to develop trendsetting key technologies for the future.

Fraunhofer IESE is one of the 60 institutes of the Fraunhofer-Gesellschaft. Together they have a major impact on shaping applied research in Europe and contribute to Germany's competitiveness in international markets.

V. Basili et al., *Aligning Organizations Through Measurement*, The Fraunhofer IESE Series
on Software and Systems Engineering, DOI 10.1007/978-3-319-05047-8,
© Springer International Publishing Switzerland 2014

Index

V. Basili et al., *Aligning Organizations Through Measurement*, The Fraunhofer IESE Series 203
on Software and Systems Engineering, DOI 10.1007/978-3-319-05047-8,
© Springer International Publishing Switzerland 2014

Printed in the United States
By Bookmasters